TOTAL NUTRITION
for Breast-Feeding Mothers

Other Books by Betty Kamen, Ph.D., and Si Kamen

THE KAMEN PLAN FOR TOTAL NUTRITION DURING PREGNANCY

KIDS ARE WHAT THEY EAT:
WHAT EVERY PARENT NEEDS TO KNOW ABOUT NUTRITION

IN PURSUIT OF YOUTH:
EVERYDAY NUTRITION FOR EVERYONE OVER 35

OSTEOPOROSIS:
WHAT IT IS, HOW TO PREVENT IT, HOW TO STOP IT

TOTAL NUTRITION DURING PREGNANCY:
HOW TO BE SURE YOU AND YOUR BABY ARE EATING
THE RIGHT STUFF

NUTRITION FOR NURSES

TOTAL NUTRITION

for Breast-Feeding Mothers

Betty Kamen, Ph.D., and Si Kamen

Little, Brown and Company   Boston · Toronto

FIRST EDITION

Library of Congress Cataloging-in-Publication Data

Kamen, Betty.
   Total nutrition for breast-feeding mothers.

   Includes index.
   1. Breast feeding.   2. Mothers—Nutrition.
3. Infants (Newborn)—Nutrition.   I. Kamen, Si.
II. Title.
RJ216.K34   1986   613.2   86-2933
   ISBN 0-316-48254-4

All of the facts in this book have been very carefully researched, and have been drawn from the most prestigious medical journals. However, in no way are any of the suggestions meant to take the place of advice given by your physician.

RRD-VA

Designed by Jeanne F. Abboud

*Published simultaneously in Canada
by Little, Brown & Company (Canada) Limited*

PRINTED IN THE UNITED STATES OF AMERICA

DEDICATED TO

our daughter
KATHI KAMEN GOLDMARK

who offered her son
the special opportunity she missed and
in role reversal
taught us the nuances of breast-feeding

The child was made for the breast and the breast was made for the child, and nothing else, in this line, was made for either; therefore, when the child is fed otherwise than at the breast, it is fed by [that which] is, by comparison, infinitely inferior in value and properness to the generic food which the Author of Nature supplied for it, and so constructed its organs and parts as to fit them to receive it and to be developed by it.

I hold it to be a sacred duty for all those persons whose circumstances admit of it, to provide the new-born child with the milk of a human nurse, and not to expose it to the hazards — I should say the dangerous risks — of distressing illness . . . that threaten the great majority of those children that are brought up on the spoon.

— Charles D. Meigs, M.D., 1849

Contents

FOREWORD

by Lester A. Luz, M.D., San Francisco

Twenty-five years have elapsed since the medical profession reawakened an interest in breast-feeding as opposed to the formula routine, which evolved in the first two decades of the present century. By the mid-forties only a small minority of mothers in urban areas was encouraged to breast-feed, whereas presently in cities such as San Francisco, Los Angeles, and San Diego, as many as 98 percent of new mothers breast-feed for at least the first six weeks.

In San Francisco by the mid-forties, largely because of the encouragement of Dr. John Miller and the La Leche League, 45 percent of newborns were being breast-fed. By the mid-seventies the proportion had increased in my own practice to 75 percent. Presently, more than 99 percent of my new mothers breast-feed for six weeks to two and one-half years.

Initially the general pediatric concern was that breast milk was not wholly adequate. It was common practice to introduce solid foods into the diet as early as three weeks of age, and vitamins were administered from the onset. By three months of age the nursing infant was receiving cereal, fruits, vegetables, and, in some cases, meat. By the mid-seventies, however, investigators had learned so much about breast milk that it was frequently referred to as "the miracle substance of the seventies." This recognition (derived from the knowledge of the nutritional and immunological advantages of breast milk plus the admission by most investigators that it is a complete food) has encouraged increasingly delayed administration of solids. Now, many physicians do not encourage the introduction of supplemental substances until after three, six, or nine months. A few even suggest waiting twelve months.

Controversy still exists among pediatricians relative to the necessity for iron and vitamin D as a supplement, but in the twenty-five years of my own experience, I have encountered no need for either as long as the infant is exposed to daylight regularly and has not been the subject of numerous infections. I may add that in my experience with infants and toddlers in Peru, all of whom were breast-fed, I saw no vitamin D deficiency, although after they were denied breast-feeding following the birth of a new sibling, every other vitamin deficiency became evident.

There are, as might be expected, antibodies against communicable diseases such as varicella (chicken pox), pertussis (whooping cough), poliomyelitis, and tetanus in breast milk, although insufficient to wholly prevent infection. More important, within two hours of an infant's acquiring an infection, antigens will be found in the infant's mouth and will gain access to the mother's breast. She will then produce specific antibodies to that infection, together with increased lymphocytes and ferratin. (Lymphocytes are cells that participate in immunity, and ferratin is an iron-binding protein that competes in the infant's intestinal tract for iron and therefore destroys bacteria.)

The nutritional and immunological aspects of breast-feeding have been clearly defined by numerous investigators. Attention is now being directed toward maternal nutrition and its effects on the nursing infant. Betty and Si Kamen are addressing the very obvious effect of good maternal nutrition and its potential for maximizing the good health and development, present and future, of the nursing infant.

All substances that are absorbed by the gastrointestinal tract will to some degree find their way into breast milk. It becomes increasingly necessary to understand and cope with the quality of food a mother ingests, whether it is incorporated into our food chain or is part of our social intercourse.

The authors, with the thoroughness that distinguished their previous publications, have researched the subject as completely as is presently possible and, as in the past, offer a clearer understanding of the more recent approaches to infant nutrition, development, and good health as they relate to maternal nutrition.

It is remarkable that it has taken us so long to attempt to understand, control, and appreciate a phenomenon that has a history of so many millennia.

Acknowledgments

OUR IDEAS WERE SHAPED AND SHARPENED

by the medical professionals

who know this subject from a *clinical* point of view:
Lester A. Luz, M.D., and Martin Milner, N.D.,
and Lewis A. Barness, M.D., Ruth A. Lawrence, M.D.,
Derrick B. Jelliffe, M.D., Joan Feateau, R.N.,
Lynn Fraley, R.N., Dr.P.H.

by the breast-feeding professionals

who know this subject from a *personal* point of view:
Kathi Kamen Goldmark and Andrea Rosenblum
and Nancy Dyer, Catherine Hayden, Alice Cutler,
Angela Milner, Angie Jones, Amanda Metcalf-Welch, Sandra Bryson,
Marion Sakow, Julia Romero,
Lorraine Killian

by the reading consultants

who refined judgment, sobered language,
and challenged concepts:
Joanne Catz, Perle Kinney, Kathi Kamen Goldmark

ACKNOWLEDGMENTS

by the publishing professionals

who made it all happen:
Evan Marshall, Beth Rashbaum,
Christina H. Coffin, Peggy L. Anderson

by the research professionals

who delve and dig:
Julie Kahl and Kathie Renick

Prologue

IN WHICH WE EXPLAIN

Why breast-feeding was discarded along with spats, the bustle, hula hoops, and jitterbugging

Why there has been a resurgence of breast-feeding

Why the termination of breast-feeding occurs too early

Why it shouldn't

How your decision to breast-feed is helping to change the history of your time

*Nature does not lack experience. A well-filled
breast with a good nipple is the ideal
producer and supplier of a perfect product,
based on a million and more years of
evolution.*

— SIMON S. LEVIN, M.D.

As parents-to-be, we questioned our obstetrician about breast-feeding. His shocking response was, "You are not a cow." The year was 1948.

Most cultural changes take place slowly, but the middle of the twentieth century witnessed a revolution in infant feeding. For the first time in human history, natural feeding was discouraged. A prehistoric ritual that had remained intact through millennia tumbled like a house of cards. With precipitous haste, bottled feeding became the order of the day.

Doctors were convinced that this change clearly demonstrated the measure of the distance the world had traveled. In an age of industrialization, technology, and processed food, breast-feeding was considered old-fashioned. *You are not a cow* implied animal behavior beneath human dignity in modern times.

If you are in your thirties, it is likely that you were nurtured on formula. If you are in your teens or twenties, chances are you *and* your mother were not breast-fed. Perhaps your mother or grandmother, like many of our friends, feels cheated — even angry. Of all the billions of infants born, a small percentage were not breast-fed because the doctors of the present chose to discard the natural ways of the past.

But happily, a breast-feeding renaissance occurred in the 1970s. Nature reasserted its influence. Motivating factors that helped to set things back on track were the knowledge that breast-feeding:

· provides protection against infection
· facilitates mother-infant bonding
· may at times be more convenient than bottle-feeding
· is emotionally satisfying
· offers better nutrition than cow's milk formula
· is a natural way to feed infants

The return to breast-feeding, however, has been somewhat slower than its temporary demise. People have been slower to return to the practice than they were to abandon it in the first place. As recently as 1984, breast-feeding was included in a list of "unconventional" foods in an article published in a prestigious medical journal. In this article, called "Food Faddism in Pediatrics," the doctor wrote: "Among the several prevalent types of food faddism are some that are not harmful or can be beneficial, *such as breast feeding* [emphasis added]. . . . Those wishing to feed their children unconventional diets should have such diets carefully evaluated to avoid deficiencies of essential nutrients."[1]

"Breast is best, but it's not really of actual importance," has dominated as the major advice given new mothers. Among the reasons are the promotional efforts of the premade formula industry (which is competing for the space in your child's stomach) and the risk of inducing guilt feelings in those who think they are unable to breast-feed.[2]

And so we have a problem: our society now lacks the attitudes and knowledge necessary for long-term breast-feeding success.[3] Only 19 percent of mothers interviewed in one research project were breast-feeding after the first month of their baby's life (and only 12 percent of those women were exclusively breast-feeding), whereas 68 percent breast-fed initially.[4] An analysis in another study indicated a similar failure rate: 50 percent of mothers who started to breast-feed stopped when their baby was only six weeks old.[5] The expectations of the breast-feeding experience are positive. The realities are not. Researchers note:

· There is a marked absence of breast-feeding role models among young women. (How often do you see a mother breast-feeding on TV?)

- A high percentage of people feel breast-feeding is unacceptable in social situations.[6]
- Being unmarried and living with parents or other relatives proves to be an impediment.[7]
- Counseling while pregnant, though important, may not be the optimal way to motivate women to breast-feed. (Friends who have successfully nursed are more influential than advice given in the doctor's office.[8])
- Most mothers introduce solid foods before the baby is old enough, influencing the early termination of breast-feeding.[9]
- It is not uncommon for babies to be bottle-fed in hospitals soon after birth, and there is a significant association between bottle-feeding before the first breast-feeding session and early breast-feeding failure.[10]
- More babies are breast-fed in higher family income groups than at lower socioeconomic levels.[11] (Increased reading leads to awareness of breast-feeding benefits; middle-class women are better able to find and use resources, and to adapt advice applicable to their own situation.)
- A large number of women stop breast-feeding when they return to work.
- Women who are disturbed by issues of modesty and sexuality are not as successful at breast-feeding as women who aren't.
- Many mothers complain of inadequate milk production.

In summary, despite the general increase in breast-feeding in the last decade, the practice is of short duration, often abandoned before infants are two or three months old. It is unlikely that those who fail to breast-feed do so because of a true physiological incapacity to produce enough milk. In societies where breast-feeding is the cultural norm, all mothers continue beyond six months. Are these mothers biologically different from our mothers? We believe that women are influenced by several environmental factors (including nutrition), discussed in detail in subsequent chapters.

In traditional societies, an experienced mother is given the task of helping new mothers, offering accurate and timely support and advice. Because of the anti-breast-feeding trends of the 1940s, 1950s, and 1960s (and to a degree even today), experienced nursing mothers are rare. The American baby's maternal grandmother has been shown to exert the greatest influence on the decision to be a breast-feeding mother.[12] The mobility of Americans has contributed to widening the gap between an age that slipped out — taking long-term natural feeding with it — and the new age that hastened in. You may have to visit your *grandmother* — if she's still around — for help. And chances are (if she is alive and well) she lives far away. But this book can be that grandmother!

The aim of this book is to enhance successful breast-feeding and reduce the rapid falloff rate. The weaning process is not complete until about two to three years of age in most societies that have yet to be caught up in industrialization. Regardless of the outworn shape of the past, your baby remains biologically unchanged. Lactation is an extremely ancient physiological function. (*Lactation* is another word for breast-feeding.) The need for human milk (not formula or the milk of another animal) was imprinted in your baby's genes a million or more years ago. Breast-feeding almost got away through the high-tech meshes of time, but we learned at zero hour that to change nature is to break the laws that govern *optimal* survival.

We're all wanting new ways, but not at the sacrifice of life quality and the health of the next generation. And the next after that, because nutrition crosses generation lines.

You have the option of returning a rightful human heritage to your child — a heritage that has belonged to all cultures and to all mammals for the length and breadth of recorded days.

TOTAL NUTRITION
for Breast-Feeding Mothers

CHAPTER
∞ 1 ∞

Breast Milk:
The Mystery of Its Mastery

IN WHICH WE DISCUSS

Why breast milk offers optimum life quality and is the only food known for certain that was meant for human consumption

How breast milk confers unique immune protection

Why it is believed that breast milk increases intelligence

How early ingestion of cow's milk may lead to health problems

How breast milk differs from formula

A breast-feeding mother has a special relationship with her baby. At the same time, breast-feeding is a source of security and love for the infant. And there's an added benefit: breast milk is closer to providing nutritional perfection than anything else in existence.

*A pair of substantial mammary glands have
the advantage over the two hemispheres of
the most learned professor's brain in the art
of compounding a nutritive fluid for infants.*

— OLIVER WENDELL HOLMES

The doctor who assisted at my mother's birth in 1902 arrived at Grandma's New York City apartment in a horse and buggy. More than a half century later, my mother reflected on his mode of transportation as she sat watching the astronauts emerge from their spaceship and walk on the moon. Despite the fact that we have witnessed such an explosion of high technology, the concept of Joyce Kilmer's famous poem ("only God can make a tree") is as valid today as it was when my mother was born. The sophisticated scientists of the 1980s may be able to identify all the components of an orange or duplicate each of its elements with exact chemical precision. They can even mimic orange flavor, orange smell, or orange texture. Try as they may, however, the chemists cannot combine the ingredients to produce a real orange. Breast milk is to infant formula as the orange is to its separate constituents — space age notwithstanding.

The drug companies, despite their "breast is best" caveats on each container of formula, say, "Children can and do thrive without breast milk." In *FDA Consumer*, our government writes, "Next to mother's milk, there's infant formula."[1] Formula may be acceptable. The question arises as to what is optimal. Let's examine the facts.

THE IMPORTANCE OF BREAST MILK

BREAST milk has the unique capacity to change. The first milk that
flows for a few days after a baby's delivery (called *colostrum*) is
distinct from that which is produced days later. This in turn varies
from milk formed months later, which is different from milk generated after the baby has celebrated a birthday or two. Even the
hour of day and the mother's emotions have an effect on the milk's
composition, to say nothing of diversity during a single feeding, and
aberrations from woman to woman.[2] *Breast milk supplies nutrients
in a specific pattern. The pattern is dependent on many variables,
including a built-in timetable: the nutritive composition of breast
milk evolves to match the baby's needs at each particular stage of
growth and development.*

We are beginning to understand why these changes take place. As
the chemist continues struggling to identify the integral parts of the
orange, the cellular content of human milk is also under intensive
investigation.

IMMUNOLOGY

Think of the baby being thrust into this world from its sterile, pro-
tected enclosure. The new baby, germfree in the mother's uterus,
steps into a complex microbial environment. Within hours a small
population of bacteria is present in its digestive cavities. In days the
colonies have grown into dominant communities.[3] In spite of a
unique capacity to handle the invaders, at least 10 percent of babies
are seriously infected during delivery or in the first few months of
life.

Recent discoveries reveal a preponderance of "soldier" cells in
human milk. These cells are called *antibodies*. An antibody is a molecule which, like an antiaircraft missile, is designed to destroy. Its
target is a toxic substance in the body. The more antibodies a person
has, the more immunity. The particular antibodies in human milk
defend the gastrointestinal system. Human milk produced in the
early months of a baby's life contains fifty times the amount of antibodies given to treat patients who are totally lacking in this kind of
protection.[4] Colostrum, the especially potent milk produced immediately after delivery, boasts even more antibodies. Because colostrum is so fully charged with safeguards, it is referred to as
"antiseptic paint." Specifically, we know the following:

· Nature restricts the volume of feeding in the first two days of a baby's life. The small amount of milk secreted is striking. Uninformed mothers think they are at fault — that they are not producing enough milk. But colostrum is different from milk that is produced later on. It contains many more cells, lots more protein, and, as stated, a heavy endowment of important immunologically active substances. Colostrum is the food geared by nature to the infant's just-born capacity.[5] It should be comforting to mothers to know that a healthy baby at birth has stores of nutrients adequate to last about seven days before it requires additional feedings.[6]

· Immune cells found in breast milk prevent infection by hindering bacterial multiplication. The concentration of this type of immune cell is three hundred times that found in cow's milk.[7]

· An iron-building substance has been identified in human milk. This product also helps to inhibit infections.

· Antibodies against many different microorganisms, including polio and influenza viral agents, have been measured in breast milk.[8]

· Runny nose, hacking coughs, and middle-of-the-night screams from earache pain are mitigated if not eliminated when a baby is breast-fed.[9]

· An antibiotic activity of human milk that destroys parasites is not found in any other known substance, not even in the milk of other mammals.[10]

· At birth, the protective system of the gut is like a fortress with guns not yet in place. If a newborn doesn't develop a good gastrointestinal defense, the consequences may be: susceptibility to infection; food sensitivities in later life that would not otherwise occur; a high risk of allergy to cow's milk; and the potential development of life-threatening diseases. An assault can be initiated by cow's milk *at any time in life,* and the attack is more vicious if there is a family history of allergies.[11]

In summary, substances in colostrum confer significant disease resistance to the breast-fed infant without stressing the newness and immaturity of the baby's metabolism. Breast milk offers a unique immunity advantageous to the gastrointestinal tract and an impediment to many diseases. Fewer allergic reactions are another benefit.[12]

The guardian-angel quality of breast milk is not entirely under-

stood. But it has worked through millennia, and we do know it is a
safe and effective buffer against illness.[13]

NUTRITION

Roger Williams, world-renowned biochemist, brings home the fact
that we live in an imperfect world. We all know that an ideal day is
an uncommon occurrence. How often are the wind, temperature,
barometric pressure, degree of sunshine, and humidity exactly
right? Williams states that just as such a perfect day is infrequent, so
is nutritional excellence rarely attainable. The nutritional process
operates at various levels of adequacy or inadequacy in every cell in
your body, but never with complete perfection. You, however, have
an opportunity to feed your child nutritional excellence. *Breast milk
is closer to providing nutritional perfection than anything else in
existence.*

As the human milk detective work continues, discoveries are star-
tling. Now we know why breast-fed babies are less likely to suffer
from rickets than bottle-fed babies. (In the last decade a previously
unrecognized form of vitamin D was found in human milk that is
not present in cow's milk.) Now we know why iron absorption
from human milk is higher than it is from cow's milk. (Vitamin C
and lactose, contained in human milk, are handmaids for iron absorption.[14]) And now we understand the unique vitamin B_{12}–bind-
ing compound existing in human milk.[15] (This prevents bacterial
growth.)

At least seventy enzymes have been identified in human milk, and
some of them are control-point catalysts for major pathways.[16] In
more simple terms, they make the right things happen at the right
time: they help to maintain the essence of living tissue — arrange-
ment and context. When the enzymes are absent or disturbed, disease processes are set in motion.

The longer a baby is breast-fed, the less risk it has of developing
celiac disease (faulty absorption of food caused by sensitivity to
gluten, a protein substance found largely in wheat).[17] Celiac is more
common than is generally recognized. Contrary to popular belief,
the disease is not outgrown. Once a celiac, always a celiac — a fact
not understood because symptoms of the disease change after childhood. Although it is still far too prevalent, the good news is that celiac disease is on the downswing. And it's the increased
breast-feeding that's the underlying cause for the reduction.

Male infants require more zinc than females. There is an extraordinary concentration of zinc in the prostate gland. Testicular atro-
phy occurs with zinc deficiency.[18] Not to worry: despite the
significantly lower zinc content of breast milk compared to bottled
milk, the zinc in breast milk is more *bioavailable* — that is, more
readily assimilated. So boys (and girls) get all the zinc they need
when breast-fed.[19]

Obesity occurs less often among breast-fed infants than among
bottle-fed infants.[20] One reason may be that breast-fed babies regulate their own intake. Sometimes a mother mistakes a formula-fed
baby's thirst for hunger — thirst caused by the formula's "heavier"
load on the immature kidneys. (It's a good thing breast milk containers aren't transparent, so that mothers can't keep tabs on how
much milk is being consumed.)

The duration of breast-feeding was compared with cholesterol
levels in more than one hundred seventeen-year-old women. The
longer the young women had been breast-fed as infants, the lower
their current cholesterol readings.[21]

We could add an almost endless list of breast-feeding benefits: it
prevents anemia;[22] markedly reduces the risk of sudden infant death
syndrome;[23] checks improper thyroid function; forms virus-de-
stroying interferon;[24] impedes infectious diarrhea;[25] creates far less
malocclusion (improper alignment of upper and lower teeth);[26] results in fewer cavities;[27] encourages a more normal insulin response;[28] maintains normal vitamin E levels (which are commonly
depressed in formula-fed babies);[29] and reduces the risk of degen-
erative diseases like breast cancer,[30] multiple sclerosis,[31] and atherosclerosis[32] in later life. It also increases magnesium levels;[33]
protects against colitis, tuberculosis, and infant meningitis;[34] increases body activity during the first two weeks of life;[35] and even
affects the reproductive functioning of the baby as an adult.[36]

How many unknowns are yet to be unlocked? The hunt has only
scraped the surface. There are those who say that the scientists
could have known about breast milk's superiority a long time ago.
They had only to consult with Great-grandma. She learned about
its grandeur from her grandma.

BRAIN AND BEHAVIOR CONNECTION

"The breast-fed child is always more intelligent than the bottle-fed
child. The longer the breastfeeding, the more intelligent the child is

because of the constant interaction with the mother." These are the words of the eminent educator Joseph Chilton Pearce.[37]

The relationship between childhood intelligence, parent-child interaction, and nutrition, especially as it pertains to breast-feeding, has been the subject of many studies. Here are some of the research results:

· Tests of about one thousand children showed a tendency to higher scores among those who were breast-fed than those who were bottle-fed.[38]
· Mathematical attainment tests completed by two thousand fifteen-year-olds showed that those who had been entirely bottle-fed scored significantly lower than those who had been entirely breast-fed.[39]
· Demand breast-feeding is related to earlier development and to increased security.[40] (Demand feeding occurs when the baby is nursed at the child's will rather than on an imposed schedule.)
· Children who are fed cow's milk grow faster and larger, but they have smaller heads than those who are breast-fed. The assumption is that breast-fed babies have better brain development.[41]
· Breast-feeding is associated with a higher level of intelligence, and this is thought to be the result of early skin-to-skin contact. Studies have shown that the breast-fed boy in particular reads and speaks better than his bottle-fed equivalent.[42]
· When test animals are deprived of proper nutrition, the number of cells in their brains is permanently fixed at a lower level. When they are supernourished, they manufacture an above-normal number of brain cells. Not only the timing but the duration of malnutrition is critically important.[43]
· Comparisons with animals show that the more intelligent and skillful groups within a species are nursed longer.[44]

COW'S MILK: HEALTHFUL OR HAZARDOUS?

IN 1985 the prestigious journal of the American Academy of Pediatrics printed a dramatic warning written by Frank Oski, M.D. Dr. Oski said:

Whole [cow's] milk should not be fed to infants during the first year of life because of its association with [hidden] gastrointestinal bleeding, iron deficiency anemia, and cow's milk allergy. The consumption of whole milk after the first year of life should be discouraged because of its potential role in a variety of disorders including atherosclerosis, recurrent abdominal pain of childhood, cataracts, milk-borne infections, and juvenile delinquency.[45]

Here is evidence to support this position:

· If cow's milk is fed as the primary source of nutrition during the first year of life, it cannot meet an infant's iron requirements. Cow's milk decreases the absorption of iron from other foods.[46] The longer cow's milk feeding is delayed, the less chance of developing iron deficiency.
· Recurrent diarrhea, repeated vomiting, persistent colic, eczema, frequent runny nose, recurrent bronchitis, spitting, bloody stools, weight loss, malabsorption, colitis, and asthma are regarded as common manifestations of cow's milk allergy.[47] The incidence of cow's milk allergy has been increasing.
· As early as the sixth day of life, *all* infants fed cow's milk have been found to have circulating toxins (poisons) related to the milk.[48]
· It is widely recognized that babies absorb human milk fat more efficiently than they absorb cow's milk fat.[49] (The importance of proper fat absorption for brain growth is discussed in Chapter 4.)
· At least 20 percent of children up to age three years have some indication of an adverse antibody reaction to food. We have already cited the link between bottle-feeding and subsequent intestinal allergies. The risk is greater when one parent is allergic, and still greater when both of them are.[50, 51]
· Protein in cow's milk may injure the mucous membrane of the baby's intestine, causing persistent, hidden bleeding.[52] The bleeding contributes to the development of iron deficiency.
· There's no mix and match when it comes to milk. Milk is *species specific*, the specifics relating to the animal's growth requirements. For example, the less protein there is in a particular species' milk, the longer the life span of that animal.[53] The faster an animal grows, the higher the protein. The protein content of milk can vary from 1 to 20 percent. The milk of a rat contains 12 percent protein; that of a reindeer, 11.5 percent; and in human milk it is less than 1 percent. Cow's milk contains 3.3 percent protein.[54] The

cow's health priority is muscle mass and bone, and the animal has a tiny, unsophisticated brain. The nutritional needs of the human baby, who generally doubles its birth weight in five months, are obviously different from those of a calf, whose birth weight doubles in about six weeks.[55]

· The use of growth as a nutritional yardstick can be misleading. Bottle-fed infants double their weight earlier, probably because of the high protein content of cow's milk. But *more* is not always *better*. Growth has a quality to it, and sheer increase in size does not necessarily measure that quality.

In his impassioned plea to discontinue the use of cow's milk, Dr. Oski eloquently concludes:

> Why give it at all — [in infancy] or ever? In the face of uncertainty about many of the potential dangers of whole [cow's] milk, it would seem prudent to recommend that whole milk not be started until the answers are available. Isn't it time for these uncontrolled experiments in human nutrition to come to an end?[56]

We share Dr. Oski's view that cow's milk should be avoided until more is known. Small quantities (four ounces daily) may be given without adverse consequences at age four or five — when a child's digestive system is more developed. In its current pasteurized, homogenized form, cow's milk is not a highly nutritious food. Other researchers have referred to the use of cow's milk for infants, even modified into formula, as one of the world's largest uncontrolled biological experiments. And the human baby is the guinea pig.[57] The widespread trial of cow's milk for feeding infants has only been in vogue for about fifty years, or 5/100,000 of humankind's existence. It started with the use of domestic cow's milk, followed by processed cow's milk, followed by a changing succession of cow's milk–based formulas.[58] The fact is that almost any mammal's milk would be easier to modify than cow's milk. One researcher explains: "Pig's milk is actually nearest to human milk. Camel milk and mare's milk have a better balance for humans. Sheep's milk is okay and so is goat's. Reindeer milk would be a bit fat, dog's milk a bit thin. Now, otter's could be just right. Perhaps we should look into it."[59]

If otter's milk were a moneymaking enterprise, maybe we would have it. But the dairy industry appears to be interested in what's widely available and cost-effective. Or, in all fairness, the dairy industry may have been misguided (like everyone else) into thinking that cow's milk is far more nutritional than it actually is.

ARTIFICIAL FEEDING

HUMAN milk is a non-profit-making commodity. The infant formula industry has attempted to provide safe and convenient substitutes for breast milk. Energetic efforts have been made to promote such products. The manufacturers have been more successful in achieving the latter than the former. (No one spends hundreds of thousands of dollars a year advertising breast milk.)

When a baby is fed formula, it is the sole source of the infant's nutrition. Therefore, quality control is essential. In the seventeenth and eighteenth centuries, artificial feeding in America was accompanied by such a high mortality rate that breast-feeding was necessary for the survival of the race.[60] Hygiene, pasteurization, and refrigeration have changed the statistics. But real nourishment involves more than being "safe" and "convenient."

There are hundreds of infant formulas worldwide, and those in our country all have more protein than needed.

Infant botulism (food poisoning) causing sudden death indistinguishable from typical crib death occurs only in infants who have been formula-fed.[61] Infants exclusively breast-fed have significantly fewer symptoms of disease than those who are fed artificially or are partially breast-fed.[62]

The bioavailability of many nutrients is reduced in formula, as it is in any processed food. An example involves the important nutrient folate (folic acid). Giving babies 78 micrograms of folate in a formula is not as effective as giving them the 55 micrograms that occur naturally in an equivalent amount of breast milk.[63] Folate plays an important role in growth, in cell division, in nucleic acid production, and in a baby's developing nervous system. If formula-developed red blood cells could talk, they would look up and cry: they, too, require folate for optimal health. Breast milk is more than the sum of its parts; formula is far less.

In the 1950s a few cases of vitamin A deficiency were reported in infants receiving a formula made from defatted soy flour.[64] In 1966 acute bleeding into the skin and intestinal tract was described in infants fed formulas based on casein or meat while receiving sulfa

drugs or antibiotics, frequently prescribed for diarrhea.[65] A few
years later, skin lesions appeared in infants fed milk-based formulas
with low levels of linoleic acid.[66] Acidosis and failure to thrive were
the result of a formula recommended in 1972.[67] A very serious formula error occurred in 1980, when babies sustained permanent
damage — mental and physical — from a chloride-deficient preparation. In April 1985 the Food and Drug Administration announced
the voluntary recall of a formula said to be deficient in nutrients
needed for healthy development.[68] As recently as September 1985,
the Division of Nephrology, Bone and Mineral Metabolism at the
University of Kentucky, along with the Department of Pediatrics at
the University of Miami, announced the identification of high concentrations of aluminum in proprietary infant formulas (including
Similac PM 60/40), which had not been considered as a source of
aluminum in the past. The researchers note that there is clearly a
link between aluminum ingestion and central nervous system toxicity.[69]

Many mothers leave the hospital with their baby and a bonus:
free formula samples. It has been shown that "sample" mothers are
less likely to be breast-feeding at one month, and more likely to have
introduced solid foods by two months.[70]

We urge you to go to your local supermarket to examine the ingredients of the assorted infant formulas available. (Take a magni-
fying glass. The print is small.) Here is the information given on the
label of one popular brand:

Infant Formula:
For your baby's important first year. Concentrated liquid. Ingredients: water, nonfat milk, lactose, soy oil, coconut oil,
mono- and diglycerides, soy lecithin, vitamins (ascorbic acid,
alpha-tocopheryl acetate, niacinamide, calcium pantothenate,
vitamin A palmitate, thiamine chloride hydrochloride, pyridoxine hydrochloride, riboflavin, folic acid, phylloquinone, vitamin D_3, cyanocobalamin), carrageenan, minerals (ferrous
sulfate, cupric sulfate, manganese sulfate) and taurine.
Good until June 1986. [We purchased the can in March 1985.]
Instructions: Wash and rinse equipment thoroughly. Prepared
formula not used immediately and opened can (covered)
should be stored in refrigerator and used within 48 hours. Discard unused formula remaining in bottle after feeding. Store
unopened cans at room temperature.

Terminal Feeding Method: To a bottle or pitcher, add enough concentrated liquid to make one half of the total formula needed. Add an equal amount of water and stir. Pour formula into bottle(s). Invert nipple(s), put disc(s) in place, and loosely attach screw ring(s). Sterilize for about 25 minutes in a sterilizer. After cooling, tighten ring(s).
Preparing One Feeding: Boil bottle, nipple, and ring before use. Boil water for 5 minutes and cool. Add equal amounts of concentrated liquid and previously boiled water to the bottle. Put nipple and ring on bottle, shake well, test temperature, and feed.

In the 1940s, when breast-feeding was not popular, a friend read instructions like these while she was pregnant. "I decided to breast-feed," she said, "because I tend to be careless and I knew I would never get the instructions right."

The labeling is accurate, but it is too limited in scope to define quality. The destination of food is the stomach, not a test tube. Complex biological processes that have little to do with isolated nutrients take place in your body. Bricks can be a beautiful structure or a pile of rubble.

Few people, including health professionals, are aware that even minimal processing can be a mainspring for a drop in nutritional quality. Heating foods causes destruction of essential nutrients, breakdown of important tissue structures, and formation of undesirable substances that may be toxic. The label on the package of formula does not reveal the information that boiling water concentrates some of the contaminants in that water. Nor does it explain that protein quality and percentages of nutrients decline with exposure to heat. Changes in your water supply can alter the formula.

Formula is designed to be stored for months at room temperature. It contains various thickening, emulsifying, and stabilizing agents such as carrageenan or mono- and diglycerides — permitted as additives to provide uniformity. These additives are at best non-nutritive and at worst harmful. Formula may be adequate, but it cannot be optimal.

Is it any wonder that there is a vast difference in the health status of breast-fed and formula-fed infants? Our views are mirrored in the statements of Dr. Ross Hume Hall, professor of human nutrition and biochemistry at McMaster University in Canada, who comments on attempts of food technologists to outengineer nature:

· No one knows enough about nourishment to redesign what
  nature evolved.
· Eating is a total phenomenon. You don't eat myristicin or
  goitrogens. You eat carrots and broccoli. You cannot remove
  these from their biological context.
· Corporations exert enormous influence over regulatory con-
  trols.
· The FDA is concerned with whether food poisons you today
  or tomorrow — not 20 years down the road.
· If you eat a candy bar, you don't expect much in the way of
  nourishment, but if you consume bread [or feed your baby a
  prescribed formula], there is implicit trust that you [and
  your baby] will be nourished. [Such trust may be mis-
  placed.]
· Infant formulas by necessity are bottles of ignorance.[71]

Researchers have shown that the beneficial effects of breast milk
may last a lifetime.[72] Alternative foods and methods are modern
phenomena, no more than sixty or seventy years old. If survival
benefit counts, remember that breast-feeding has been around for
millions of years.

Perhaps at this point you are saying, "My neighbor's kid wasn't
breast-fed, and she's doing fine." Or, "I wasn't breast-fed, and I'm
okay." People can and do survive with average (and even poor)
health. Unless we examine, analyze, and properly interpret tissues
down to the cells, we cannot see the sacrifice to life quality, or the
disease process that doesn't emerge for years to come, or the stress
necessary to "do fine" and "be okay." There are always limitations
to achieving excellence — in health or anything else. The least you
can do for your baby at life's starting line is offer the best takeoff.
Can you think of a better gift to give your child?

COMPENDIUM

Breast milk is best because it

Changes composition to match baby's growth and development
Confers immunity
Helps develop intestinal membrane to prevent absorption of toxins

Offers more bioavailability of nutrients
Prevents anemia through better iron absorption
Results in fewer illnesses (for baby as infant and in later life)
Reduces potential for allergies
Produces more brain cells, higher intelligence, and better memory
Contains enzymes necessary for important biological processes
Contains growth factor necessary for optimal development
Prevents overfeeding, food sensitivity, infant obesity, and celiac
   disease
Provides nutrients still unknown to science
Cannot boast a profit motive
Is the most economical infant food
Is totally sanitary and temperature-controlled
Is the *perfect food* for babies

Cow's milk is not *best because it*

May cause many allergic manifestations, including diarrhea, ec-
   zema, and runny nose
Results in poor nutrient absorption
Contains too much protein for human development
Has immune factors specific for cows, not humans
May induce anemia because of poor iron absorption
Is linked to disease in later life
May cause inefficient fat absorption, promoting obesity
Produces larger body and smaller head
Is pasteurized and therefore nutrient-deficient
Is the perfect food only for a calf

Formula is not *best because it*

Is heated, sterilized, pasteurized, and contains stabilizers to give it
   shelf life
Has the potential for error in formulation
Has the potential for error in home preparation
Reduces bioavailability of nutrients
Contains no immune factors
Has more protein than necessary for humans
Is associated with crib death
Has altered protein quality caused by processing

CHAPTER

∽ 2 ∽

Breast-Feeding: The Expectations

IN WHICH WE GUIDE YOU

through success and failure as expressed by two women who share their visions of the breast-feeding experience and answer questions about:

> *nutrition*
> *breast self-examination*
> *nipple preparation*
> *milk-producing hormones*
> *relaxation*
> *effects of breast-feeding on the figure*
> *effects of breast-feeding on sex life*
> *influence of age*

A mother's attitudes toward breast-feeding are shaped by complex personal, cultural, social, and family factors, and are usually fixed by early pregnancy or before. These factors are more influential than classes, reading, or professional advice during pregnancy.

*During my pregnancy, I envisioned an
enthusiastic baby at birth, eager to suck at
my breast — from which milk would flow
freely.*

ALICE CUTLER

Most pregnant women seek all the help they can get to prepare for the experience of giving birth and then rearing their newborn. They usually attend an assortment of classes — Lamaze, Bradley, natural birth, alternative birth, prenatal, postnatal, exercise, Red Cross, and/or child-care. In addition to reviewing articles about pregnancy in newspapers, magazines, and books, they interrogate their obstetrician and pediatrician, and consult at length with Aunt Rosie, Grandma, and the neighbor next door.

Without benefit of classes or expert opinion, most animal mothers know exactly what to do when their new babies locate their breasts just after birth. For humans, breast-feeding does not take root automatically. Even after the lessons. And the inquiries. We, along with other primates, do not have totally adequate innate responses for the breast-feeding process. We can't rely on instinct alone.

Higher mammals depend on learned behavior — based on observation and example — plus instinct. The first two chimpanzees born in a zoo to a nonwild mother were reported in 1920 to have died of starvation due to ignorance of the nursing procedure.[1] In 1974 a nonwild female gorilla in a California game park was successfully assisted to nurse by the use of films of lactating gorillas shown to her during her pregnancy.[2] The gorillas stemmed the tide better than many American women, who are often ill prepared to breast-feed efficiently or without difficulty.

In traditional societies women learn the art of natural feeding by cultural osmosis. They do very little to get ready for the event. But they are psychologically rehearsed because it's the norm for that society. American women do not share this warm shelter of habit. In our country, the experience is new and unknown, a shift from the familiar. Many women have never seen a baby feeding at the breast.

For this reason, the last months of pregnancy, the events surrounding birth, and the first few days after delivery are of critical importance. These circumstances correlate with successful initiation and continuation of breast-feeding.

TWO MOTHERS: LOOKING FOR ADVICE

WE interviewed two women about their breast-feeding experiences. One succeeded at nursing, the other failed. To encourage honest responses and because of the personal nature of the questions, the women remain anonymous. Their accounts reflect actual incidents and feelings. Laura is thirty-eight. She gave birth to three boys in five years. Wendy's only child was born on the day of her thirty-fifth birthday. Each of these women had given birth within the previous twenty months when they were interviewed. Wendy, who succeeded at breast-feeding, was still nursing her son at the time of the interview. Laura never breast-fed exclusively, and stopped completely before each of her children reached two or three months of age. Their responses to our questions follow.

Did you seek advice on breast-feeding before the birth of your first child?

LAURA: I joined La Leche League to learn about breast-feeding, and discussed the subject with my doctor. He said he was all for it. I got plenty of encouragement, yet not enough. Either I needed more personalized help, or I wasn't very good at breast-feeding. I thought the cloud would go away with each baby. It never did.

WENDY: My obstetrician explained with honesty that physicians do not receive formal education on breast-feeding — that his nurses are better able to teach, having personally enjoyed the ecstasies and

endured the agonies. I arranged appointments with the nurse practi-
tioner, who counsels pregnant patients on nutrition and nursing.

The frankness of my doctor, coupled with advice from care-givers
who had experienced breast-feeding, made me feel confident that I
would be on easy terms with natural feeding.

*Did any of the health professionals discuss the relationship between
successful breast-feeding and nutrition?*

LAURA: Only to say, "Eat balanced meals," which for me turned
out to be juggling wholesome foods in one hand and junk foods in
the other. I ate whole grains, lots of deep ocean fish, and fresh vegetables. But I also consumed the wrong foods. I turned from sparrow
to vulture, gaining fifty pounds during each pregnancy, eating anything that wasn't nailed down. My willpower was down to zero as I
planned my next snack before the one in my mouth was devoured.

WENDY: The nutritionist at the doctor's office recommended both
a diet and a supplement regimen. Her suggestions were: (1) eat
foods as close to natural as possible (an apple, not apple juice or ap-
plesauce); (2) vary the selections daily (yellow, green, red vegetables; leaves, roots, stems); (3) include raw portions as well as lightly
cooked dishes; (4) omit processed foods (nothing — or very little — canned, frozen, or packaged); (5) include supplements specifically designed for pregnancy and breast-feeding.

I heard these rules before, but for the first time in my life I re-
sponded with intense alertness and commitment.

Were you given advice on breast self-examination?

LAURA: I assumed that was my doctor's role. I did question the
relationship between the size of breasts and ability to produce milk,
and learned there was none. Big or small, no matter — the milk
should flow as it has for millions of years before I came along.

Additional notes: A primitive tribe in India considers small, flat
breasts to be the most effective for nursing, and large, pendulous
breasts the most cumbersome.[3] Milk is not stored in the breast but
produced as needed, just as your eyes manufacture tears in response
to emotion.

WENDY: When my doctor examined my breasts, he explained
what he was doing and why. He described that he was checking for
breast texture — the more elasticity they have, the less prone they

are to engorgement after delivery. Engorgement is just what it sounds like — congestion of the breasts, which can be painful and can interfere with the baby's ability to suck. If my breasts were inelastic, he would insist on more massaging and closer attention to preventing engorgement.

The doctor also clarified the difference between the areola and the nipple, and how he was checking to see that there were no malformations.

Additional notes: The nipple contains the milk openings. The areola (the brown area surrounding the nipple) has supporting muscle and glands that secrete a lubricating substance that protects the nipples during nursing. It may also function as a scent organ to guide the nursing baby's reflex.

Were you told to prepare your breasts in any way?

LAURA: My doctor gave me a list of books to read. I had many questions and would have preferred an open discussion with him. I interpreted his typed reference sheet as a put-off. He made me feel that I was imposing on his time when I asked questions.

WENDY: I was told to read as much as I could, but I was also encouraged to ask questions. My doctor taught me how to strengthen my nipples during the last six weeks of pregnancy. I started rubbing my nipples with a rough washcloth about thirty times each day, and I pulled on my nipples. The nipple-pulling was done by supporting my breast gently with my fingers while grasping the nipple with my thumb and index finger. Then I drew the nipple out to the point of discomfort and released it. The daily shower was my time and place for these exercises.

Another recommendation was for my husband to simulate the sucking act.

The doctor also suggested that I sunbathe my breasts if I could — to help toughen them. During each visit, I was questioned about my nipple-preparation progress. The caring and sharing attitude encouraged me to comply.

I was warned not to hand express any milk the last few weeks before delivery. [By the fourth month of pregnancy, the placenta begins to release hormones to stimulate the secretion of colostrum.] This manipulation could stimulate the uterus to contract and cause premature labor. It may even lead to mastitis [inflammation of the breasts].[4]

I did not wear a bra for as long as I was comfortable, in order to allow my nipples to rub against clothing, which helps to toughen them. Women who don't wear bras are less likely to have cracked nipples for this reason. If breasts are heavy enough to require support, nursing bras with the flaps down may serve the purpose. The breasts of many women become too heavy, however, even for the "flaps-down" maneuver.

Additional notes: Women who have small or flat nipples can check for protractility — that is, to see how the nipple "draws," or thrusts out. This is done by compressing the areola between the forefinger and the thumb just behind the base of the nipple. If the nipple can be manually made to protrude, flatness or inversion will correct itself when the baby starts to breast-feed. Daily exercise, consisting of pulling out the nipples, releases the adhesions anchoring the nipple to the underlying tissue. It is easier for the baby to nurse when nipples are extended. During pregnancy, nipples increase in size and protract more, helping to reduce breast-feeding problems.[5]

How much personal experience did you have watching friends or relatives breast-feed?

LAURA: Absolutely none. Except for one woman in a restaurant once, which embarrassed me. At the time, I never thought I would breast-feed. The idea was almost repugnant, and appeared to be so primitive.

WENDY: I had seen a cousin nurse her baby on only one occasion — and that was fifteen years prior to my own pregnancy. I never forgot the beauty of the intimacy of mother and baby — both mutually dependent. But because my personal experience was severely limited, I sought out nursing mothers a few months before my baby was born. These women were delighted at my interest and very willing to share experiences. Again, I noted an amazed sense of peace and harmony. I was also impressed with the instant availability of the human milk meal: an old-fashioned food with a nineteen-eighties' buzzword descriptor: convenience.

It was surprising to me that breast-fed babies don't have to be burped as often as bottle-fed infants. They swallow much less air. My new friends (the nursing mothers) explained that an attempt at burping is advisable between breast changes, but it doesn't always happen.

Additional notes: Burping the baby appears to be a Western cultural activity not practiced in more traditional societies. If, however, the baby has fussed a lot prior to feeding, a burp is more likely because of air swallowed in the crying process.

Did you understand how the breast makes milk? Or the roles of the special hormones secreted in breast-feeding?

LAURA: I am a biology teacher and have often explained the process. The mechanisms involved in the actual production of milk are very complex. The amount of milk produced, however, depends on how much the baby consumes. The emptying of the breast activates the release of prolactin, a hormone that stimulates and sustains the formation of milk by encouraging the glands to manufacture more. Oxytocin, a hormone that is also stimulated by sucking *and by emotions,* releases milk from the sacs where it is stored and sends it into the ducts in the breast. The process is called the *let-down* or *milk-ejection reflex.* So the baby's lunch awaits only the release of these hormones. But release is not always that simple.

Prolactin responds to breast stimulation (the best activator) and also to sleep, sexual intercourse, exercise, and estrogen levels. Many drugs suppress its production and release. Oxytocin is secreted just before nursing and during sucking. It is a conditioned response, like Pavlov's dog and the bell: it can be liberated when you hear your baby crying or when you get ready to feed. And the discharge has nothing to do with milk volume. But just as oxytocin is released on signal, it can be switched off by anxiety, cold, or pain. A nursing mother should be free of stress prior to nursing as well as during the process.

Intellectually, everything was clear.

WENDY: I tend to skip physiology chapters in books. An overall appreciation for the elegance of human milk was enough for me. My curiosity was satisfied with the knowledge that milk flows through a dozen or more lavishly supplied ducts to little storage areas inside the nipple. The baby's sucking draws out the waiting milk, and then the "warehouse" fills up again.

I was more interested in fertility information. I had intentions of continuing my career, and I didn't want a second pregnancy — yet. Prolactin is believed to cause infertility by delaying ovulation. Even though breast-feeding probably prevents more pregnancies worldwide than all the modern forms of contraception put together,[6] it is not reliable. Other forms of contraception are definitely advisable.

Additional notes: Prolactin concentrations remain elevated for a longer time when babies are permitted to feed on demand.[7] This is another reason to avoid strict schedules. Nature doesn't seem to want us to outwit the baby's designs.

GETTING READY

Were you taught relaxation techniques?

LAURA: No, but when any of my friends have babies now, I buy tapes of music to present as gifts. These tapes are specially prepared for the purpose of relaxation during breast-feeding. The more relaxed you are, the greater your chance of breast-feeding success. Certain types of music provide a very nurturing, soothing environment, something I wish I'd known a few years ago.

WENDY: I started practicing several quick-acting techniques, which are referred to as "one-minute vacations":

· I am falling right through the chair or bed. My entire being loosens.
· I am a rag doll with all the stuffing slowly oozing out. This is especially good visualization for breast-feeding, because flowing milk is the name of the game.
· I pull my shoulders up to my head and then let them drop. Next, I breathe in deeply, slowly — letting the air fill my abdomen. Then I breathe out, slowly.
· I am on a spaceship, taking off. I feel increasing gravity, and my body tenses. But suddenly I break through the gravity field and I'm weightless. Every part of me feels limp. I am floating. My mind is alert, but my body is effortless. Calm envelops me.[8]
· I remember an unforgettable moment on Petite St. Vincent, an island in the Caribbean. I feel the warm trade winds. From my vantage point on a small mountain, I can see forever. White fluffy clouds. Colorful spinnakers on boats gliding over blue and purple waters. Other islands. Soft rhythmical music in the background. A tropical fruit drink in my hand. I feel mellow and tranquil.

· I am the snowman I used to build on the front lawn when I was a kid. The sun is shining, and I am melting away. Butter. Putty. Yielding. That's me.

These simple exercises can be done anyplace, anytime. They make me feel "baggy" or unglued. Relaxation exercises not only relieve stress but affect hormonal systems, and what better time to have hormones in the best working order?

What were your specific questions about breast-feeding before your baby was born?

LAURA: I was concerned about the effect of breast-feeding on my figure. I learned that the shape of women's breasts is influenced more by lack of exercise and poor diet.

I also wondered if a woman's age has anything to do with her ability to produce enough milk, or even to breast-feed successfully. I was assured that the important factors are attitude and nutrition.[9]

Additional notes: The effect of lactation on the shape of breasts is minimal. As for weight, women add about nine pounds of fat during pregnancy. These caloric stores are for the breast-feeding process, and they're depleted as milk is produced. Many women report a slimming effect as they continue to nurse.

Assimilation, elimination, circulation, and other metabolic pathways are less efficient when we are older. For this reason older women must be even more concerned about what they are eating. The bottom line is not age but the presence of an ample supply of the complete range of nutrients.

WENDY: I wanted to know how soon after birth the milk begins to flow, or how I could determine if my baby was getting enough milk. How would I know how often to feed? The answers:

As soon as the placenta has separated, lactation begins. Placing the baby on the breast after delivery has the added advantage of causing the uterus to contract in order to get back to normal after all that stretching.

As for nursing frequency, babies fed on demand show a wide variation. The average, however, is four feedings during the first twenty-four hours, and five during the second twenty-four hours.[10] But those are the first days. As the baby makes increasing demands on life, I could expect to nurse fifteen or more times a day. The baby's stomach empties its supply of breast milk in about one and a half hours, so frequent feedings are not unusual. In the first three months as many as fifty percent of babies may feed every one and a half to two hours[11] or even more frequently.

I had another important question. If my baby sleeps with me when necessary, as recommended by La Leche League, there is bound to be interference with sex. The only advice here was the philosophical view that although at present you seem to be forever separated from the past and the future, the early months go by quickly. Love and understanding is what it's all about.

Additional notes: The lower the protein content of an animal's milk, the more frequent the feedings. Human milk, of course, has relatively low protein (now believed to be less than 1 percent). The milk of a mouse is also low in protein. Mice nurse almost 80 percent of the time, whereas the rabbit (with 10 percent protein) feeds once a day.

A baby has its own regulators that control the pattern of intake, and although the volume of milk consumed doesn't change during the first month, the feeding time usually decreases.[12]

Most of the milk is taken within the first four minutes of a feeding, with 50 percent consumed in the first two minutes.[13] The second half of a ten-minute feed is lower in nutrients.[14] The fat content of the milk increases toward the end of a feeding, presumably to satisfy the baby and terminate the feeding.

Women who are positive in their attitude toward breast-feeding have three times the success rate of those who have negative attitudes.[15] Many women, like Laura, say they would have preferred to breast-feed longer if they had been given more encouragement and support both before and after delivery.[16]

Preparation for breast-feeding is like a baseball team's going into spring training. The team would not appear on opening day without months of conditioning. You, too, can hit a home run or pitch a perfect game: bring your blue-ribbon baby into the world with breast-feeding "spring training."

But for those women who are about to give birth or who are already breast-feeding, remember that many women have successfully breast-fed without preparation. It's a confidence trick, so just relax. Although it's easier when you're fully prepared, you're very likely to succeed unprepared *if you want to.*

COMPENDIUM

Breast-feeding for humans and higher mammals depends on

Learned behavior
Instinct

Choose a doctor who

Encourages breast-feeding
Gives advice on breast preparation during pregnancy
Answers your questions personally and shows interest
Discusses your nutrition requirements (or has a staff nutritionist)
Recommends a regimen of safe food supplements
Recommends a variety of helpful reading material
Suggests local support groups, such as La Leche League
Is willing to do it *your* way

Nutrition for lactation includes

Foods as close to natural as possible
Varied selections
Raw and lightly cooked foods
No (or limited) processed foods
Supplements

Examine your breasts

Know that size makes no difference
Check for

   texture and elasticity
   nipple inversion
   flat nipples

Prepare your nipples during pregnancy by

Massaging with rough cloth thirty strokes daily
Pulling and stretching nipples thirty times daily
Exposing breasts to sun if possible (don't overdo)
Discarding bra or wearing nursing bra with flaps down

Do not hand express milk toward end of pregnancy

Understand lactation physiology by learning about

Let-down reflex (releases milk from glands)
Nipple-erection reflex (facilitates the sucking process)
Prolactin (secreted to maintain milk production)
Oxytocin (causes milk release from mammary gland)
Areola (the brown area surrounding nipple)

Learn relaxation techniques, and practice

Feeling like a rag doll or melting snow
"Falling" through the chair or bed
Visualizing beach or ocean scenes
Breathing in and out slowly
Listening to relaxation music

Know that lactation

Does not change breast size (after termination)
Often has a slimming effect
Is not influenced by age
Is influenced by nutrition
Begins as soon as placenta has separated
Helps uterus to contract

Your baby will probably feed

Four times in first twenty-four hours
Five times in second twenty-four hours
Fifteen or more times daily after that if on demand

The rate of milk consumption is

Fifty percent of meal in first two minutes
Most of balance in next two minutes

Milk contains high fat content toward end of feeding to satisfy baby

Arrange your support system and bolster confidence by

Attending classes
Reading useful books
Joining La Leche League
Visiting women who are nursing

CHAPTER

～ 3 ～

Breast-Feeding: The Reality

IN WHICH WE CONTINUE

the comments of two breast-feeding women who discuss their first nursing experiences, including

> *hospitals — options and nurses*
> *engorgement*
> *treatment for breasts*
> *sore and normal nipples*
> *support systems*
> *La Leche League*
> *supplemental formula and water*
> *baby's bowel movements*
> *more on sex*
> *their best hints for success*

"For now sits Expectation in the air," said Shakespeare in *Henry V*. Preparation, as suggested in this chapter, can help the reality of your experience match your expectation.

My baby — just after birth — was not in-
terested in feeding. I didn't seem to have
much milk. I felt rejected and discouraged.

— ALICE CUTLER

Congratulations! It's a boy. Another one for Laura, a first for Wendy. Laura hoped that this time around she'd be more successful. Wendy, having done all she could in preparation, suddenly wondered if she had done enough.

THE FIRST DAYS AFTER DELIVERY

How soon after the birth of your baby did you start nursing?

LAURA: My first baby was brought to me six hours after delivery. Forget breast-feeding. I was nervous just picking him up. He was so delicate. I never had any experience with babies, and I was terrified. The second time around, I gave birth on a stretcher before arriving at the door of the delivery room. This baby was given to me simply because there wasn't another pair of hands available.

Initial feeding attempts in the hospital didn't appear to work. I never seemed to have enough milk. Either my babies surrendered to sleep, or just fussed. Each child had been bottle-fed and given sugar water before my first efforts.

WENDY: I saw my baby a few minutes after birth. First, he was warmly bathed, and given the Apgar test [a system of scoring an infant's physical condition one minute after birth].

Breast-feeding success was very important to me. I have been impressed with Joseph Chilton Pearce's words: "If you bond a mother with an infant, you can't *keep* her from responding to her own instinctual processes — the natural genetic encoding." Mothers with early contact are known to nurse fifty percent longer,[1,2] so I selected a doctor and hospital that supported immediate bonding. I also wanted to take advantage of the intense sucking reflex of the first twenty or thirty minutes after birth,[3] and all the assets that go with it: instant immunity for the baby, less engorgement for me, even less blood loss after delivery.

This moment had been in my thoughts for many months. I planned a cascade of interactions, anticipating the high excitement of my child's first forty-five minutes. I wanted to stimulate all his senses — sight, sound, smell, taste, touch. Even eye-to-eye contact. In my dreams I often thought of women experiencing after-birth bonding for more generations than we can count. It fascinated me to think that women might have had the same thoughts down through the ages.

When my son was born, the reality was even more intense than the images in my mind's eye. It is one rare moment in life never to be forgotten.

The delivery table was narrow — I couldn't place the baby on my side — and the hospital gown was an impediment because it prevented me from getting to my breasts easily. One would think there would be special gowns and wider tables for the purpose. (Perhaps I'll have my next child at home. Or ask the nurses to prop a pillow at my back for support on the narrow table.) I felt slightly clumsy, and my son didn't seem to be responding to my attempts at feeding. But I remembered that the first milk that flows — the colostrum — is not very plentiful. The nurses told me not to worry if I wasn't an immediate breast-feeding success. Most women, they said, have similar experiences. I wanted to believe that, so I did. Belief is rooted in emotion, isn't it?

Additional notes: The chance of failure is cut almost in half when babies are put to the breast within four hours of birth, and in those who are demand fed.[4,5] (Demand feeding means feeding at the baby's request rather than on a schedule.) The ideal time for the first feeding is immediately after birth.

Existing routines in many maternity wards, such as weighing the baby before and after breast-feeding, can inhibit the establishment of lactation and increase the number of early failures. The greatest effect observed is that of skin-to-skin and sucking contact during the first hour after delivery, which increases the average duration of breast-feeding by two and a half months![6] When there are rules and regulations (looking at the clock), supplementary bottles are more likely to be used, weaning begins by the third month, engorgement is not uncommon, and the let-down reflex is inhibited, causing milk supply to vary from scheduled feeding to scheduled feeding.

Was your husband with you during labor and delivery?

LAURA: Yes, and he was very helpful throughout.

WENDY: Yes, and I had prearranged to have his favorite meal brought to him immediately after delivery. I knew that so much attention would be directed toward me and the baby. I didn't want him to feel left out. I got the flowers; he got the sushi platter.

The hospital arranged for a special "togetherness" time. After delivery, the three of us — my husband, my brand-new son, and I (plus flowers and sushi) — were given a small room for a few hours. We were supposed to remain undisturbed, but we (and the nurses) allowed the excited grandparents to break the rules and join us after a while. The grandparents took turns holding the baby briefly, viewing their prize with much satisfied vanity. One set of grandparents said, "He looks just like Wendy," as the other set was beaming, "He looks just like Joe."

Did you have any drugs during delivery?

LAURA: Only with my first baby. I requested an analgesic. All I wanted was a mild painkiller. Instead, I was misunderstood and given an anesthetic. I was completely out. That's why I didn't see my first baby for six hours.

WENDY: I had a mild muscle relaxer. My baby appeared to be very sleepy at first, and I was told later that this was because of the drug, moderate as it was.

Additional notes: Drugs given in labor lead to altered interaction between mother and infant in the first ten days, such as different sucking patterns and more difficult feeding interactions.[7] It is important for mothers to understand this — not to create guilt if drugs are necessary during the birthing process, but because it is helpful to recognize the reason for difficulties in initial feeding efforts.

Did the hospital offer a choice of feeding or rooming-in facilities?

LAURA: Yes, and I chose the four-hour schedule. I was afraid I'd be too tired with rooming-in arrangements. I also elected to have the nursery give the baby one feeding at night so that I could rest. Perhaps it was selfish on my part, but I didn't want to return home ready to drop. The scheduled meals, the sugar water given to each baby, and the bottle offerings were not conducive to my breast-feeding self-reliance.

Additional notes: Breast-fed babies who are given added water in the first few days of life lose more weight and are less likely to start gaining than those who are entirely breast-fed.[8]

WENDY: I had several options. I had hoped to enter the alternative birthing center [ABC] when and if it was determined that I would not have any labor or delivery difficulties. [The ABC is a hospital room that has the appearance of a cozy bedroom, and is free of sophisticated hospital equipment. More importantly, mother, father, and baby remain in this room for twenty-four hours following delivery.]

But a minor complication developed, and my doctor asked me if I would be disappointed if I didn't enter the ABC. Although he wanted me to participate in the decision, I was in no condition to make any judgments at that particular time.

I did have other privileges. I requested that no dextrose be fed to my baby, and a sign was posted on his bassinet stating this preference. [Dextrose is a form of sugar dissolved in water and given to babies to keep them quiet.] I chose demand feeding. The hospital was too crowded for rooming-in arrangements. Whenever my baby cried or fussed, he was brought to me.

Additional notes: Demand feeding, along with assuring greater success in nursing, supports the natural course of growth. Girls fed on demand are significantly lighter and show thinner skinfolds than girls fed at fixed intervals. Boys show a similar tendency in weight but the opposite tendency in skinfolds.[9]

Were the hospital nurses helpful?

LAURA: When I presented my problems to one nurse, she said, "I'll see what I can do," and she did nothing. My baby didn't seem hungry for at least a couple of days. He just sort of laid there. I wondered: if he didn't eat, when would he stop looking as though his face had curdled under his skin — that brand-new baby look? My concern mounted.

I was afraid to pick him up, thinking I might hurt him. I never had any experience with babies. The first time I changed his clothes, I thought I would break his arm if I bent it, so I cut his shirt away with a pair of scissors. You can imagine the state I was in!

WENDY: What I appreciated most was that the nurses did not treat my baby as though he was "theirs." Because he wasn't receiving any bottles of formula or water, I was the one my baby needed the most, however inadequate my beginning efforts might have been.

But I have one friend who was more helpful than the nurses. When I thought I was losing milk because my breasts became smaller after a few days of nursing, she explained that this was a natural phenomenon. She also described growth spurts, which occur when a baby is four to eight days old, again between two and six weeks, and then every other month or so. These are times I could anticipate more hunger — my baby would require more feedings.

None of my attempts at nursing in the hospital were comfortable. I had to shift around and find what I thought were unconventional positions to avoid the pain of my healing episiotomy. (I had a big baby. The doctor thought the cut would facilitate delivery.) Now I know that there are no rules about positions as long as mother and baby are comfortable. Lying sideways, sitting with your feet up — anything that works is okay.

My baby would lie with his mouth on my nipple even when he wasn't sucking. This didn't feel natural to me, but the nurses explained that many babies do this.

How were you told to care for your breasts once you started nursing?

LAURA: Glands in the breast secrete a sebaceous material that cleanses and lubricates the areola and nipple, and this protective substance can be removed with soap. So rinse but don't soap your breasts. The baby's mouth must make contact with at least a portion of the areola when nursing.

WENDY: The use of A and D ointment [available at any drugstore under several brand names] or lanolin around the nipple, but not over the ducts and areola, can also be helpful if applied twice a day. An excellent gift for a new mother is an aloe vera plant that is more than three years old. Younger plants aren't as effective. The gel from its broad leaf is a fantastic anesthetic and soothing ointment.[10] And it's no problem if the baby's mouth comes in contact with the gel. [A diluted tincture of marigold herb or St.-John's-wort (each diluted 1 part in 9) is an additional soothing agent.]

What were you told to do in the event of engorgement, which is so common during the first two weeks?

LAURA: I was told, "It's common, live with it; it will go away." And so I suffered. Engorgement made my breasts hard, swollen, and tender, and my nipples inelastic. Early on, this is caused by congestion — fluid collected in tissues and extra blood in vessels. Later, accumulation of milk is the culprit.

Additional notes: One method of relieving engorgement: while nursing, manually express the other breast. Don't overdo it. Continued pumping defeats the purpose by stimulating milk production, so knowing when to stop is the key. *Stop at the point where relief is first felt.* The best prevention is an enthusiastic infant who starts feeding immediately after birth and nurses frequently at short intervals.

When milk accumulation is the problem, nursing replacements — such as skipped feedings, pacifiers, other foods, or supplementary bottle feedings — can be responsible for the engorgement. See if there is a connection. The good news is that engorgement is no problem after a first child.

WENDY: I expressed small amounts of milk by gentle manual manipulation to relieve the pressure of engorgement. This makes the nipple softer and more pliable, so the baby can grasp the nipple more easily. I did it this way: using two hands, I brought my thumbs toward the areola, compressing the areola between my thumbs and other fingers. With the areola grasped, I applied pressure toward my chest and then released the pressure, stimulating the milking action. After putting my baby on my breast, I compressed the areola between two fingers to make it easier for him to grasp. This method works only when the areolae are engorged. Sometimes blood vessels are engorged, and then pumping won't help. But it's a temporary condition, and lying flat on my back proved helpful, as did cold packs. [Cold packs slow the let-down re-flex. Don't use this technique before nursing.]

Alternating hot and cold water in the shower is another helpful hint. Sometimes I used a heating pad set on low, which I applied to my breasts to help release milk. Again, my little relaxation exercises came in handy.

Did you ever suffer from sore nipples?

LAURA: Yes. I kept rubbing breast cream on (they gave me the cream in the hospital), but it didn't help. I had the feeling that my baby was sniffing the cream and rejecting it, the way my dog sniffs at something and then turns away. When the irritation was too painful, I would give the pained breast a break for forty-eight hours and not use that side.

At one point I was given breast protectors in the hospital. They're like rubber nipples placed on top of your own nipple. I think my baby had to work twice as hard to suck.

Redheaded, fair-skinned women like me are more prone to de-velop cracked, sore nipples.

WENDY: My sore-nipple stage was brief but uncomfortable. It was the one time I wished I had more than two breasts.

To lessen discomfort, I started each feeding on the breast that was less sore. By the time the baby got to the second breast, he was not sucking quite as vigorously. Although the baby sets the pace, short, frequent feedings are best the first few days. Limiting the amount of sucking only delays soreness. When nipples are sore, feedings should never be spaced beyond two hours.

When one nipple was painfully sore, I used the other breast ex-clusively for a few feedings. To avoid engorgement, I expressed milk by hand from the unused breast.

Additional notes: About 5 percent of women stop breast-feeding because of sore nipples or engorgement,[11] but many more have some degree of difficulty, mainly because of improper preparation.

A recommended pattern is to feed for five minutes on each breast, increasing the time by a minute each day until the baby is nursing fifteen or twenty minutes on each side. Babies on demand feeding are not as ravenous as those that have to wait for their meals. The on-schedule babies are usually hungrier and suck harder.

To prevent the baby from hurting you by pulling at your nipples at the end of a feeding, gently release the suction by placing your finger into the corner of his mouth.

Another nipple-toughening trick is exposure to warm, dry air. Put your hair blower to work for this one. Or use an electric lamp with a sixty-watt bulb for twenty minutes a few times a day.

.Healing is reported to be rapid, and the success rate excellent when a small amount of mother's milk is expressed and applied gently to the nipple and areola and allowed to dry.[12] This is a salve that doesn't have to be removed before breast-feeding! It seems like such an obvious solution, since breast milk contains so many anti-infective agents. Fresh breast milk is used in some cultures as eye-drops for treating conjunctivitis.[13]

Were you given instructions for normal nipple care?

LAURA: I was told to keep my nipples dry by exposing them for about twenty minutes between feedings, and to change absorbent pads frequently. Loose cotton blouses are ideal.

WENDY: I avoided plastic coverings (they prevent air circulation) and oils (we want *tough*, not *soft*). If leaks caused my clothes to stick, I used water to wet my clothing. This helps to peel off rather than pull off a sticky garment, preventing tissue damage.

BREAST-FEEDING AT HOME

Did you find that things improved after you were home?

LAURA: I was glad to leave the unhospitable hospital, and I started to feel a bit more comfortable about the feeding once I was home. But each of my babies was cranky and screamed a lot — the kind of crying that you know won't agree to an appeal or an out-of-court settlement.

Additional notes: A nutrition detective would have no difficulty solving some of Laura's problems. Several of her comments indicate that her children are cow's milk–sensitive. Many women who have similar difficulties omit milk and milk products (cheese, ice cream, baked goods made with casein, and so on) from their own diets, and find that their babies no longer behave like charged wires. (Milk sensitivity is discussed in greater detail in Chapter 7.)

WENDY: Getting home from the hospital with a new baby is like the day after the fair. The hoopla is over, and I must take on more responsibility. I called my friend with all the answers. She has a born hand with children, a healing presence, and experience at breast-feeding. Doesn't everyone know someone like that? She and my mother helped to establish a sense of order that I knew would make things work. They, and my husband, were also instrumental in preventing my fatigue by doing the shopping, cooking, and housework.

If my baby fell asleep on the first breast, I would wait a little, wake him, and then move him to the second breast. Since moving about was not yet easy, my husband or mother would move the baby for me. I tried to allow five minutes on each side, knowing that frequent small feedings provide good stimulation to the breast without stressing me. The best way to stimulate the milk supply is to have the baby suck. The amount of milk produced relates directly to the length of time the baby sucks. It's a simple matter of supply and demand.

Additional notes: According to one researcher, "The common denominator for success in breast-feeding is the assurance of some degree of help from some specific person for a definite period of time after childbirth. The remarkable calm that can be experienced in the presence of a confident caring person is incredibly relaxing."[14] Exhaustion can be a powerful deterrent to successful breast-feeding.

Soreness from an episiotomy adds stress. (It may also lessen sexual desire.)

The baby's smile may not sweep away fatigue or lessen the complications of a changed life-style, but all family members will have fallen under the infant's charm. Patience. This trying but delicious and special time shall pass. Maybe even too quickly.

Did you understand and experience the let-down reflex?

LAURA: Understand, yes; experience, no. The let-down reflex occurs when the increased fluid pressure in the breast is relieved by sucking. In earlier feedings, the let-down reflex may not occur for as long as three minutes after nursing begins. Later on, it's supposed to happen within thirty seconds. Either I did not know when it was happening or it never happened. I'm still confused about that.

The baby's mouth stimulates the nipple to become erect. I did experience the nipple-erection reflex, as this is called, and enjoyed the sensation.

WENDY: This is one bit of information I learned from books and not in any class or doctor's office. I experienced the let-down reflex a day or two after my milk came in. It feels like a tingling, warm sen-sation inside the breast.

When my baby was very young, the sound of another infant cry-ing would be enough to stimulate the let-down.

I work part-time. Once, when I expected my mother to bring my son to me for feeding, the baby had fallen asleep. My mother de-cided not to disturb him, and she didn't come. But anticipation of the baby's arrival caused leakage. I was uncomfortable all day. Now that he's older, it takes sucking to stimulate the reflex action.

Do you think your diet had anything to do with your milk supply or your baby's behavior?

LAURA: I really don't know. I was certainly eating for two, but I didn't produce enough milk. Once, my baby bit me and I got black and blue. I think he bit me because he was frustrated from lack of milk. My babies' imperative needs were in sharp contrast to text-book predictions. The reality was not the vision.

I never felt that my babies were getting enough. I was especially frustrated because I knew that the potential milk yield for most women is higher than the amount they actually produce. Mothers of twins manufacture almost twice as much milk as women feeding single babies.[15] Even comatose women have been known to feed, as well as adoptive parents.[16] Why couldn't I?

Additional notes: To discourage biting, terminate the nursing for that feeding. If biting becomes a habit, you'll be in pain when your baby's teeth come in.

When the let-down reflex is not well established, the baby will be hungry and unhappy, having received only a small amount of low-fat milk. (The filling fat component of the milk is present toward the end of the feeding.) Laura assumed she did not have enough milk. More likely, her milk remained out of reach of the baby be-cause of the inhibited let-down action.

Variations among individual babies should also be considered. How easy it would be if infants were as alike as dolls cut from folded paper. The daily volume of milk consumed at any given age can be more than twice as much for some babies as for others. A seemingly inadequate amount of milk produced by a mother may be perfectly satisfactory if her baby happens to be more metabolically efficient.[17] Recognizing the let-down reflex is not significant, either. Not all women perceive this sensation.

Hunger spurts are another phenomenon to be recognized. Some babies are especially hungry at the end of the first week, and again at around six weeks of age, as Wendy's friend had indicated. Increased frequency of sucking in response to this hunger stimulates milk production to catch up with demand. This is normal and does not mean that milk is insufficient, or that the baby is not happy.[18] It may be more than coincidental that many women give up breast-feeding after six weeks!

WENDY: I think I had an adequate diet. I was always hungry, so I ate a lot. I had enough milk, but I also had a hungry baby. My pediatrician explained that there are two kinds of babies: barracudas and gourmets. I had a barracuda. My son was a big guy (almost nine pounds at birth) with an appetite to match. During the early weeks, he wanted to nurse constantly. The doctor advised me to space feedings two hours apart. That didn't work — I was getting an insistent message of hunger long before two hours elapsed.

Back to my usual resource for help: my friend with all the answers. She said (in less polite terms), "Your doctor doesn't have to listen to your baby cry, and he's not as new at this as you are. Feed your baby whenever he wants to be fed. Forget two hours." That's exactly what I did. I surrendered to circumstances. When my baby slept, I slept. When he wanted to feed, I fed him. I stopped looking at the clock. If that's what my son needed to get started in this world, that's what I would give him. Looking back, those early days were exhausting but worth the effort. My son is almost two, and still nursing happily.

Additional notes: The human infant has been called a "constant feeder." Ethologists (those who study the characteristics of animals) claim that the human infant is designed to nurse between forty-five and sixty times daily. This conclusion is based on the protein and fat content of the milk, which determines the schedule of sucking for each species.[19] As the baby grows, the number of feedings decreases.

Did you ever call La Leche League for help?

LAURA: It would have been nice to have someone from the league helping me. I think I was too depressed about the whole experience, too tired to call. Quitting was easier.

There was another factor. I took the complete La Leche League course. One woman told me that her child was in kindergarten, and that she was still breast-feeding. Because of my lack of experience, I thought she was overdoing it. I was having trouble enough with the concept of a small baby sucking from my breast. La Leche League is an international organization. The women who follow its tenets in our society are above average economically and are well educated. But the league encourages feeding behavior more characteristic of women in developing countries: they say that weaning should occur in response to the baby's needs, whatever its age. Anyway, that's how I felt about it at the time. I now recognize all the advantages of La Leche League's teachings. For me, it was "too little, too late."

Of course, I did enjoy the closeness and cuddling that goes along with breast-feeding. I really had regrets each time I gave it up. I guess I had mixed feelings.

WENDY: I called La Leche League when I thought I was getting a nipple infection. The kindest woman told me what signs to look for. I called the league instead of my doctor because of an experience described by my cousin. She developed breast abscesses, and her doctor told her to stop feeding at once. Instead, she called La Leche League, and a wonderful woman spent days with her, encouraging her to continue to breast-feed all the way in spite of any discomfort. In a week the sores disappeared, and she was feeding successfully. If she had listened to her doctor, she and her child would have missed the breast-feeding experience. I wasn't taking any chances. I didn't want anyone telling me to stop nursing.

Did you use supplementary formula or bottles of water?

LAURA: I don't think my babies would have survived without formula. I felt forced to supplement. And I used sugar water. I rationalized: after all, they had given this to my children in the hospital. And I knew that the excess salt and "heavier" quality of formula requires additional water.[20]

WENDY: My son wasn't too interested in water. It was one less problem to deal with. When he was a little older, he had no difficulty switching from breast to expressed milk in a bottle, and back again. The best nipples to use are the Nuk brand nipples. They are shaped most like human nipples.

Additional notes: Water requirements of infants even in a hot, humid climate can be provided entirely by the water in human milk.[21] Many babies reject the breast after bottle exposure because the sucking action required for the rubber nipple is so different. Fluids flow more quickly and easily out of rubber nipples and don't require much active sucking effort.

Were you prepared for the strange bowel movements of the breast-fed baby?

LAURA: No! I thought my baby was sick. Apparently I had forgotten what I once knew about meconium, the first blackish green stools. And when my son passed small, soft, or liquid stools, I thought he had diarrhea. My doctor assured me that this was normal.

WENDY: More or less. You really have to see it to know it. I was surprised at the mildly sweet smell, and the fact that movements could follow every meal, or be as infrequent as one to three times a week. The change in smell and consistency was anything but subtle once my son started to eat other foods at eight and a half months.

When did you stop breast-feeding?

LAURA: I stopped when each child was three months old. By that time they were practically on full-time formula anyway. I introduced baby foods at four or five months. I knew I should have been making the food myself, but it was so much easier to buy supermarket stuff. My doctor said it was okay to use the commercial foods. I knew about nutrition for adults, but I was afraid I'd mess things up if I attempted to prepare foods myself for my fragile little babies. My sense of confidence in prepared baby foods, however, was not well founded.

As it is, my sons' health has been far from perfect. Allergies, respiratory ailments, and occasional fevers were part and parcel of the first twelve months. And they still catch every germ that blows through town. My assumption has been that this is average for little kids.

By the way, none of my sons could handle milk formulas. They had to go on soy-based mixtures.

WENDY: My son is twenty months old, and I am still nursing several times a day. I introduced solid food at eight and a half months.

He got through his first year of life without the slightest ill-health incident.

How supportive was your husband throughout the breast-feeding months?

LAURA: My husband is a very child-oriented person, and I felt that I was failing him as well as my babies by not succeeding at breast-feeding. He participates a great deal in the care of our sons, and I think he secretly wished that he could nurse them as well as change their diapers.

WENDY: I received all the support in the world from my husband and my parents and his parents. But my husband was more comfortable being alone with the baby when our son was no longer an infant — when he was about a year old.

Did any problems arise because of lack of information — difficulties that could have been eliminated or decreased if you had been better prepared?

LAURA: I remember being concerned about my newborn baby not being able to breathe when I fed him. By the time I got to Number Three, I learned to make a V with my fingers — with the index finger above the nipple and the middle finger below the nipple when helping to place the nipple in the baby's mouth. This increases nipple control and allows the baby's nasal passage to be free.

I was not prepared for the milk leak that took place during sex, especially during orgasm. Nor was I prepared for the decrease in my general desire to have sex. Women should know that this is normal. Nursing can cause a slowdown in the production of hormones that are responsible for sexual desire. On the other hand, some women have an increased desire. In any case, I had my fill of touching and cuddling through the nursing process all day — especially with my second and third babies: I was hugging the siblings as well as the infant. My meter ran out at night. I really needed a break from physical contact.

WENDY: I wish I had known that it was normal for a baby to develop a definite preference for one breast. Apparently, there are marked variations in size, function, and consistency of the two breasts. When my son showed his preference for one, I was concerned. I knew how important it was for me to have him feed on both breasts.

If you had it to do again, is there anything you would do differently?

LAURA: I would try rooming-in, feeding by instinct rather than schedule, and no anesthesia, if possible. I would not give supplementary bottle feedings. All of my past decisions related to me, not my babies. I regret that now. This is hard-won knowledge. Perhaps changing my diet would have given me more energy.

WENDY: I would spend a little more time in advance on relaxation techniques and breast preparation. I might even read the science sections in the breast-feeding books — maybe.

What's the best hint you can give to a pregnant friend concerning breast-feeding?

LAURA: Select a doctor who will spend time discussing the nuances of breast-feeding (or one who has a nurse who will do it), prepare your nipples ahead of time, and find a nutrition-oriented pediatrician — one who can say, "Most of my babies are breast-fed."

Since the initial experience can be so traumatic, every new mother should fully understand that the first milk that flows is small in quantity — that frequent early sucking leads to a quicker and more vigorous flow of mature milk. Frequency is more important than duration at this stage.

Don't expect the milk to look like the stuff you pour from containers. Colostrum has a bright lemony yellow and thick appearance. The milk that follows is thin and bluish. It can also vary in color from day to day. Again — I thought something was wrong with me. [A kangaroo's milk is pink!]

WENDY: At the start of several feedings, I drank dark beer. This is against my deeply ingrained nutrition principles, but it was worth the compromise. Wine and beer have been recognized for centuries as important tonics for lactation, mainly because they are relaxants. It's too bad these products are now riddled with additives. They're not recommended beverages for women who are breast-feeding. But the beer helped me to learn how a good breast-feeding session is supposed to feel when everything is working right. And that's all I needed — just a few tries.

I would emphasize that these early days of motherhood have little to do with the reality of the rest of your life. Your world has shifted, but it's a temporary alteration. All too soon your baby will be feeding himself, and you may be wishing for this time again when you had such a totally captive audience.

Additional notes: A very important bit of advice is to drink two and a half quarts of water a day. Although your water intake has no physiological effect on the volume of milk secreted, your own body tissues will become dehydrated in deference to the milk. Prolactin, the hormone that stimulates milk production, has an antidiuretic, water-sparing effect to keep the water content of the milk high. If the mother doesn't drink enough, *she* will be drained of water. The milk itself will not be tapped.[22]

New mothers should know that within six months the total time per feeding (including naps, diaper changes, and so on) will be reduced from one hour for the newborn to about ten minutes, but some babies have slower or more intermittent sucking patterns and will always require more than ten minutes to feed.

Laura's discomfort with the concept of breast-feeding could have been part of the reason for her failure. It has been shown that one of the most common causes for giving up breast-feeding is embarrassment.[23] The success of breast-feeding is intertwined with attitude.

Confidence is the single most important determinant. If the mother thinks she will succeed, she will.

COMPENDIUM

Arrange your support system by

Having someone bring quality food to you while in hospital
Planning for friend or relative to stay with you for one week following delivery
Arranging for special treat for baby's father following delivery

The hospital you choose should

Have an alternative birthing center (ABC) that

looks like room at home
allows father to remain for twenty-four hours or more

Allow visitors during labor

Allow time and place for father's visit following delivery if not in
   ABC
Have around-the-clock rooming-in arrangements for baby
Allow for demand feeding of baby
Encourage nursing immediately after delivery
Send mother, baby, and father to recovery room together
Encourage early discharge of healthy mothers and infants

The hospital you choose should not

Offer babies glucose water
Give any bottle feedings without consent
Allow formula-supplement samples as "gifts"

Nurses should

Support initial breast-feeding trials
Understand that baby is *yours*, not *theirs*
Offer knowledgeable advice before patients' discharge

Care for your breasts by

Rinsing with warm water
Not using soap
Not using oils or ointments unless prescribed

Alleviate nipple soreness by

Keeping nursing sessions short
Applying soothing agents

   breast milk; allow to dry
   A and D ointment
   lanolin
   natural remedies: aloe vera gel, marigold herb, St.-John's-wort

Exposing to air for twenty minutes after each feeding
Applying warm dry air with

   hair blower
   sixty-watt bulb
   sunshine

Starting each feeding on less-sore breast
Releasing suction with finger at end of each feeding
Calling support group for help

Continued feeding on inflamed breast

Is safe
Helps resolve infection better than abstaining

Relieve engorgement by

Not delaying feeding
Nursing frequently
Releasing milk to relieve pressure
Applying cold packs (but not before nursing)
Alternating hot and cold water in shower
Using heating pad set on low
Practicing relaxation techniques

Causes of engorgement may be

Use of pacifier
Use of bottled water or supplementary formula
Scheduled rather than demand feeding
Skipped feedings

For first feedings

Nurse five minutes each breast, increasing a minute a day, up to fif-
    teen to twenty minutes
Wake baby if asleep during nursing
Learn to break suction with fingers when ending session
Alternate breasts each starting time
Call La Leche League if you have problems

Expect

To ask a lot of questions
To be tired
Milk to look different

    colostrum is bright lemony yellow
    later milk is thin and bluish

Baby's stools to look different

    first stools (meconium) are blackish
    breast milk stools are mustard yellow, soft, more frequent

Frequent feedings, even at night
To succeed
To enjoy the experience

Don't expect

Milk to flow freely the first few days
Your baby to require water if totally breast-fed
Baby to burp as much as bottle-fed babies
Baby to sleep through the night
Your usual sexual responses
To be totally infertile during breast-feeding
Much time away from your baby for a while
Not to melt when you see baby's first smile

Demand to be catered to for a while

CHAPTER

〜 4 〜

Breast Milk and the Primal Diet

IN WHICH WE DISCUSS

foods that offer optimal nourishment and those that don't and what it all has to do with human milk

When our children were teenagers, we were grateful that no medical researcher came up with a miracle cure for tiny pimples: the lack of such a remedy kept our children away from junk foods. The medical literature, however, states that a miracle does exist for a lactating woman — her children survive even if her diet is nutrient-deficient. But *surviving* is very different from *thriving*. Meanwhile, such misleading information prevents many women from selecting foods with more care.

The purpose of this chapter is to present an overview of the concept of primal food, whole, real, unprocessed food, the kind that helps to produce quality breast milk.

There is one bonus (among many) of learning about such foods: *you will complete the breast-feeding experience with both you and your baby in the best of health.*

*Lactation will not produce a drain on the
mother if the amount of energy utilized and
the requirement of any given nutrient is re-
placed in the diet.*

— RUTH A. LAWRENCE, M.D.

A s recently as fifty years ago — and for centuries before
that — Chinese women knew the ancient art of testing for
milk quality. A small amount of milk was dribbled on a
table. The drop formed had to be round and raised, and it should
not be possible to blow it into smaller drops.

The benchmark for the character of your milk may not be the
table test. But its quality will be reflected in the health of both you
and your child.

The milk-producing "factory" inside your mammary glands
functions like most factories. Some of the components necessary for
the milk's production are readily available, similar to the utilities of
any big company. Other supplies (raw materials) are totally dependent on the efficiency of the purchasing department.

A factory may use more energy, thereby creating more product.
In a similar manner, the milk you manufacture is mainly a function
of the amount of sucking at the breast, provided you have the necessary raw materials.

Not every employee in a given factory works up to his or her full
capacity. This is to be expected. Your breasts don't work up to 100
percent efficiency either. There is an energy loss to milk production.

So you see that to produce your finished product, you require supplies (both those on hand and those to be "purchased"), plus energy to convert the supplies to milk, plus a little extra because that's the way it is.

Sometimes a factory requires more material than the business can afford and has to operate at a loss. The factory may borrow money and continue to operate. The nutrient-deficient lactating woman is partially subsidized by her own stores of nutrients, and that debt must eventually be paid. It is not unusual for a woman to achieve a satisfactory lactation performance at the expense of her own health.

It is true that all over the world women produce enough milk on inadequate diets. But gone are the days when we thought the baby was a totally privileged parasite, receiving whatever it needed through breast milk, at the sacrifice of its mother, the host. This paradigm does not consider the nutrients in human milk that are contingent on the mother's day-to-day intake, or the adequacy of those that are stored in her body.

Although breast-feeding is remarkably efficient and persistent even under conditions of extreme deprivation, our goal is excellence: the top-notch health and intellectual development that is the realization of a baby's genetic potential. The point cannot be overemphasized. Regardless of your diet, *breast is best.* But this chapter leads the way to *better* than best. *Optimal nutrition* is the level and duration of intake that promotes the highest attainment of health and intelligence. We think you should be at least as particular about the quality of the breast milk you produce as you probably are about many other things in your life.

We recognize that you may find it difficult to comply with the life-style changes involved in achieving optimal nutrition. At the same time, we want you to be aware of the options, and to point out why they are significant. The choice, of course, is yours. Today, women are nursing with milk of a quality that is often under par, and for shorter periods than ever before. That's the statistic we hope you will change by following our suggestions. The prescription is twofold: (1) a minimum of one year of breast-feeding (longer is better), while delaying the addition of other foods for the baby for at least eight or nine months; (2) consumption of primal foods to insure optimal nutrition for mother and baby.

If you're not convinced that breast milk quality in America could be less than perfect, look at the daily nutrient intake of "healthy" infants at the end of six months of being exclusively breast-fed. These averages (taken from "sixth-month" milk) are compared with estimated daily recommended allowances.[1] The amounts of calories, calcium, iron, vitamin A, thiamin, and niacin found in breast milk are significantly lower than those recommended in the allowance charts.

	Sixth-Month Milk	*Recommended Allowance*
Energy	664 calories	720 calories
Calcium	310 milligrams	540 milligrams
Iron	4.7 milligrams	15 milligrams
Vitamin A	1,650 IU	2,000 IU
Thiamin	0.15 milligrams	0.4 milligrams
Riboflavin	0.4 milligrams	0.5 milligrams
Niacin	1.61 milligrams	6 milligrams
Ascorbic acid	40 milligrams	35 milligrams

The chart reveals that after six months of breast-feeding, your body may not be producing milk that meets quality-control standards. The miracle is beginning to wear thin. But it need not. Hippocrates said, "While calling on the gods, a man should himself lend a hand." So let's lend a hand and keep the miracle going. *That's your option.*

We will discuss the broad food categories of protein, fat, and carbohydrates; we will also address calcium requirements, vegetarianism, the effects of dieting, and a few other significant factors that relate very specifically to the quality of your breast milk and to your health. Understanding these general principles of nutrition will help you to make better food choices.

PROTEIN AND YOUR BREAST MILK: QUALITY AND QUANTITY

SUPPOSE you have a bowl of alphabet soup and you need to pick out letters to assemble the complete alphabet. You will be able to create one set of letters if you have each of the twenty-six characters. You could produce several sets if you have enough additional letters to go around. But if you are missing *one* letter, you are prevented from making even one complete set. So it is with protein. When you eat protein, your body takes that protein apart, separating the amino acids (the individual components of all protein). Then your body reassembles the amino acids into the unique pattern and sequence of human protein. It can only do this when it has the right amount of each amino acid that it needs to accomplish this function. Just as with the alphabet soup, if you are in short supply of one amino acid, the other amino acids are useless.

So the protein content of foods must be judged not only for quantity, but also for quality. Quality protein foods contain ratios of amino acids as close as possible to the ratio required for the human reassembly job. All foods contain all amino acids, but protein that lacks quality usually lacks the necessary *quantity* of one or more amino acids necessary for the manufacture of human protein.

How does this affect human milk, especially since the quantity of protein in human milk remains constant? (In fact, the protein percentage of milk even from poorly nourished mothers is high.[2]) Although protein quantity remains the same, however, the baby gains more weight when the mother's diet includes *quality* protein.[3] Again — quality protein contains an amino acid profile most similar to that of human protein.

We are just beginning to understand why it is that quality protein in your diet improves the overall health of your baby, even though the quantity of protein in your milk remains fixed. One reason is that lysine and methionine, two essential amino acids, play a key role in the optimal growth of infants. *The amount of these amino acids in your milk is dependent on your intake.* You will only get a sufficient quantity of these amino acids from quality protein.

PROTEIN COMPLEMENTARITY

The amino acids required can come from one food or several foods — your body doesn't really care where they come from, as long as they are all present and accounted for at the same time. Animal protein contains better ratios of amino acids, but the strict vegetarian can increase protein value by using several techniques, among them: (1) consuming legumes — peas, beans, and lentils — in which the concentration of protein is high; (2) combining foods so that the weaknesses of one food (the limiting amino acids) are strengthened by the support of another; cereals with legumes, for example, as rice with beans, provide a mixture of protein that is more complete, a phenomenon known as *complementarity;* (3) adding small amounts of animal protein to vegetable or grain dishes to boost protein quality.

The best complementarity trick we know is that of adding Protein-Aide sesame seeds to grain dishes, soups, and salads. (We don't usually mention brand names, but Protein-Aide sesame seeds are mechanically hulled and chemical-free. Unhulled seeds contain high amounts of calcium-binding oxalic acid, and chemically hulled seeds retain residues of caustic substances used in the hulling process.)

Sesame seeds provide two very important amino acids. One is methionine, mentioned above, which is in short supply in most vegetable foods. The other is tryptophan, which is known as the tranquilizing nutrient. (Because turkey is high in tryptophan, it has been theorized that this is the reason everyone is ready for a nap after Thanksgiving dinner.)

PROTEIN AND FOOD PROCESSING

Food processing alters not only protein quantity but the structural makeup of proteins as well.[4] Researchers at the department of food science and technology at Oregon State University report that proteins are so delicate that mild treatment which does not change ordinary chemicals will affect protein.[5] A raw egg has better protein quality than a cooked egg, and a lightly steamed egg has better protein quality than a hard-boiled egg, just as rare meat has superior protein when compared to meat that is well done.

FAT AND YOUR BREAST MILK: BRAIN POWER

HERE'S exciting news: you can actually contribute to the development of your child's brain while breast-feeding! If that sounds extreme, hear this: the control panel is the *fat* in your diet. Fat in human milk has not received the attention it deserves.

CONTRIBUTING TO INTELLIGENCE

Just as with protein, the percentage of fat in your milk remains constant regardless of your diet. If you are not eating enough fat, you scoop up fat from your body stores to maintain the quota in the milk. When you give up too much of your own supply, you are depleted of energy. You become exhausted. But your baby gets the quantity he or she needs. Nature goes to all that trouble for good reason. *Fatty acids are necessary in your milk to promote optimal brain growth.*[6] But certain kinds of fat are more important than others.

There are two major categories of fat, both designated as fatty acids: storage and structural. Storage fat is visible, as in "on my hips." Structural fats are key constituents of cellular membranes, certain enzymes, and myelin (the important substance surrounding nerve fibers). The brain contains a high amount of structural fat. In fact, the brain contains more structural fat than protein.[7]

The ratio of the many different kinds of fat in your milk is called the *fatty acid profile.* If you are getting enough fat in your diet, your milk's fatty acid profile matches the design of the fat you are consuming. If you're not eating enough fat to supply the milk, the fatty acid profile, or ratio, duplicates that of your body stores.[8] The fat in your milk is dependent on your diet — on the quantity and types of fat you are eating or have eaten. *Your child's brain development is directly related to the amount of polyunsaturated, or structural, fat in your milk.*

SOURCES OF "BRAIN" FAT

Modern high-fat beef has a high percentage of the wrong kind of fat.[9] So does the processed fat found, for example, in pie crust, ice cream, and even innocent-looking little crackers, which may contain altered molecular fatty acid structures that do not fit the natural body systems. In addition to being the wrong kind of fat, these fat molecules, because they increase blood fat levels, cause a less efficient transport of oxygen. At the same time, they require twice the amount of oxygen for their breakdown. Processed fats have also been indicted in breast milk jaundice, discussed in Chapter 7.[10]

Your daily quota of brain-promoting essential fatty acids is available in the same supermarket that sells the wrong variety. All you need is a sizable portion of white fish such as cod, snapper, or sole, or about three ounces of a high-fat fish such as salmon or mackerel. These intakes, particularly three ounces of fish per day, are not unrealistic or unachievable.[11]

The average American diet contains an almost undetectable amount of two particular essential polyunsaturated fats. One is eicosapentaenoic acid, referred to as EPA, found in substantial quantities in the kinds of fish noted.[12] And these fish include the other vital fatty acid, docosahexaenoic acid, referred to as DHA, which also constitutes a major proportion of the brain.

Remember: the amount of the different kinds of fat, and the quality of that fat in your milk, are entirely dependent on what you consume, and this influences your baby's brain development. Before Grandma surrendered her intuitive grasp of healthful foods to supermarket convenience, she knew the source of brain-promoting fat. Didn't she call fish "brain food"?

CARBOHYDRATES AND YOUR BREAST MILK: GOOD GUYS AND BAD GUYS

THERE are two kinds of carbohydrates. One variety represents the essence of primal food: vegetables and whole grains — a carrot, a zucchini, green peas, brown rice, and so on. The other division is processed — candy, macaroni, boxed cold cereals, jellies, and any other "tampered" carbohydrate made from milled flour and/or refined sugar.

Foods in the first group, known as complex carbohydrates, are terrific. But even here, there are caveats.

BEWARE THE PROCESSED PRIMAL FOOD

A vegetable is not a vegetable is not a vegetable. Not any longer. In today's world, we need to know the pedigree of a vegetable before we can evaluate its quality. Has it escaped the perils of food processing? Certainly not if it's been canned, and probably not if it's been frozen. Freezing damages texture, color, and flavor, so additives are necessary to restore the vegetable to a more "natural" appearance. Frozen peas, for example, are usually bathed in a chemical (EDTA) before packaging. This process strips the peas of important minerals that ordinarily cause "paling" if the vegetable is not consumed fairly soon. Nutrients are lost in processing, and deterioration continues during storage.

Every time food passes through a freeze-thaw cycle, nutrition is overthrown. *Any* kind of processing causes a drop in quality — a decrease in vitamins and minerals, breakdown of tissue structures, and often the formation of undesirable substances.

THE SUPREMACY OF FRESH VEGETABLES

Although nutrients are discussed individually in detail in Chapter 5 (see the Lactation Nutrient Reference Chart on pages 109–125), a few key vitamins and minerals found in fresh vegetables are mentioned here as a guide to better food selection.

Vitamin A. Vitamin A aids in growth and repair of body tissues, protects mucous membranes, and reduces susceptibility to infections. It is also valuable for good eyesight.

Breast milk provides vitamin A only under optimal conditions. Like B vitamins, vitamin A in your milk is affected by what you eat. Most lactating women consume marginal amounts of vitamin A.[13,14] The supply is generally higher in the spring and summer months, when dark-green leafy and yellow vegetables are more plentiful. These contain the vitamin A precursor, carotene. (Other good sources of vitamin A or its precursor include cantaloupe, liver, eggs, and yogurt.)

Vitamin K. Too many babies are born with vitamin K deficiencies. Vitamin K is essential for proper blood coagulation. Your diet can be a rich source of vitamin K with dark leafy greens. Alfalfa sprouts, cauliflower, and cabbage also contain vitamin K.

Iron. Leafy greens have a range of important nutrients, iron among them. Iron in human milk doesn't appear to be affected by the content of the mother's diet. But women who have higher hemoglobin levels are more likely to have successful and extended breastfeeding histories.[15] Iron during infancy must be considered in relation to all biological sources. (In addition to leafy greens, iron is also found in whole grains, eggs, liver, shellfish, and legumes.)

Folic acid. Folic acid (folate) is another nutrient found in leafy greens. It's necessary for the synthesis of nucleic acids (RNA and DNA), which take part in cell replication and in the control of cellular function. Here, too, is found a significant correlation between levels in the mother's milk and in the baby.[16] Iron and folic acid deficiencies are common among lactating women.[17] Leafy greens, anyone? (Folate is also found in liver, whole grains, and lentils. Is it beginning to sound like a broken record?)

THE VALUE OF WHOLE GRAINS

Whole grains contain fiber, B vitamins, and a range of important minerals.[18] Milled grains (white flour, white rice, and so on) contain little if any of these nutrients. Adding whole grains — such as millet, brown rice, and buckwheat — to menus provides diversity.

B vitamins. The B vitamins in your milk are related to your intake. The amount of thiamin (vitamin B_1), for example, will be reflected by whether you have eaten one-minute, quick-cooking, nutrient-depleted white rice, or the primal version, brown rice. Thiamin affects nerve function and general metabolism.

Riboflavin (vitamin B_2) is essential for cellular growth; niacin is involved in respiratory mechanisms; vitamin B_6 is necessary for the metabolism of nerve tissue; folic acid helps to produce red blood cells; and vitamin B_{12} is involved in the production of nucleic acids — these are but a few processes controlled by the B-complex nutrients.

Zinc and other minerals. A large proportion of minerals, including 78 percent of zinc, goes down the food-processing drain when white flour is the end product. Studies with test animals demonstrate that zinc-deficient diets during lactation cause a marked reduction of zinc content in the milk.[19] And even a moderate zinc deficiency during lactation takes its toll: the consequence is significantly greater dental cavities for the baby, affecting both the enamel and dentin of the teeth.[20] Ninety-eight percent of Americans have at least some form of dental disease.

The minerals in your milk are well absorbed, so your baby will get the full benefit of whatever minerals are on hand. But it may not be enough for excellence. These nutrients are also of crucial importance to *your* health, which ultimately affects your baby,[21] and to other nutrients that do affect your baby directly. Nutrients act in concert. Like acrobats on a trapeze at the circus, they tumble together, the success of the "act" and the safety of the "performers" dependent on each other. Zinc, for example, is essential for effective digestion, absorption, and metabolic utilization of a wide range of other nutrients, including vitamin A.[22] Despite limited evidence of the connection between the mother's zinc and breast milk zinc, a recent study shows that the majority of breast-fed babies receive no more than 70 percent of the recommended intake of this nutrient.[23]

The importance of trace minerals in human nutrition has only become apparent during the past decade. As with the macrominerals (sodium and potassium, calcium and magnesium), it's the *ratio* of the trace minerals that is significant. For example, the ratio of zinc to copper is more significant than the quantity of each mineral alone. Other trace minerals are selenium, fluorine, aluminum, and titanium. Consuming whole grains assures an ample supply and a good ratio of most minerals.

THE PROBLEMS OF REFINED SUGAR

The high-sugar load of sweet desserts is a nutritional disaster. Refinement of sugarcane or sugar beet — or, more recently, corn — removes the sugar from its natural context of co-nutrients (especially B vitamins), making the substance a nonfood. When refined sugar arrives in your digestive tract without these accompanying nutrients, it must borrow from Peter to pay Paul. The debt is made good by your body's cache of nutrients, if available. Again: *B vitamins in human milk are dependent on the mother's daily intake.* Nature did not anticipate foods of high technology. In this case, both you and the baby suffer. But your baby suffers more, because the earlier the malnutrition, the more permanent the effects.

A FEW SPECIAL CONSIDERATIONS

CALCIUM-AWARENESS is everyone's concern these days, but it should receive particular attention if you are breast-feeding. In addition, the kind of liquids consumed, cholesterol foods, dieting, and vegetarianism are other areas that deserve special consideration.

CALCIUM AND OLD WIVES' TALES

We all know that calcium is important for bone growth. Calcium is also essential for normal clotting of blood, normal functioning of nerve tissue, and for heart health.

"You will lose a tooth for every baby." This maxim is still making the rounds, with justification. Well, maybe not a whole tooth.

When there isn't enough calcium to go around, your body knows where to find a plentiful supply: your bones.[24] Contrary to popular belief, the most readily mobilized calcium is found in portions of bone and not in teeth. When calcium requirements increase during lactation, the message is, "Do not pass go. Go directly to Mother's bone."[25] One study indicates that the average lactating woman jeopardizes about 2 percent of her skeletal calcium over one hundred days of nursing.[26] Another report projects a loss of 7 to 8 percent in six months.[27]

Calcium in human milk remains constant, despite a mother's insufficient intake. Even under conditions of a mother's extremely low consumption, the calcium content of her milk does not change; it appears to be entirely independent of the quantity in her diet. So if it's not in your food, the serving will come from your bones. In this instance we don't worry about the baby; you are the concern.

Once you understand calcium *absorption*, you can shepherd yourself safely past calcium losses.

Among the factors influencing calcium absorption are foods ingested in the same meal. Foods that enhance the absorption of calcium are fatty fish, eggs, butter, and liver. Foods that diminish the absorption of calcium are milk, sodas, and unleavened wheat bread (because of the phytates present when the dough doesn't undergo a full rising).[28] These two menus offer identical calcium content:

	Menu A	*Menu B*
Breakfast	scrambled eggs	cornflakes and milk
Lunch	salmon salad	hamburger and cola
Dinner	liver and onions	beef stew with pita pouch
Between-meal snacks	herb teas and rice cakes	soft drinks

Despite offerings of equal amounts of calcium, the amounts utilized by the body are as divergent as chalk from cheese. Among the differences: menu A contains high-fat foods, encouraging calcium absorption; menu B contains high-phosphorus foods, having the opposite effect. Excellent sources of calcium are whole-milk yogurt, eggs, leafy greens, nuts, seeds, and tofu.

The absorption of calcium and fat are interrelated.[29] Small amounts of fat improve calcium absorption. (Whole milk contains only about 3 percent fat, but reducing this amount makes a difference.) Excessive amounts of fat, however, interfere with calcium absorption.

Other factors that influence calcium absorption follow. Favorable factors include:

· excellent general nutrition status — diets high in complex carbohydrates encourage calcium absorption
· synergistic nutrients — magnesium, copper, zinc, manganese, silicon, molybdenum, and vanadium are calcium allies

- physical activity — just enough, but not too much, is highly beneficial
- vitamin D — walking on the sunny side of the street is one of the best calcium-helpers
- selecting the right genes — no one understands why, but inherited tendencies help

Unfavorable factors are:

- foods high in phosphorus — this includes almost all processed or canned meats (hot dogs, ham, bacon); processed cheeses; baked products that use phosphate baking powder (commonly used); cola drinks and other soft drinks; instant soups and puddings; toppings and seasonings; bread; cereal; meat; potatoes; phosphate food additives
- emotions — when the stress effect devours vital nutrients, it's your calcium that's zapped
- age — we can tell by looking at your bones how old you are
- immobilization — see what TV soaps and sitcoms and video rentals have done to us (at least you have to go to the store for the rentals)
- salt — there is a direct correlation between salt intake and calcium excretion

In summary, it's not the *amount* of calcium that is significant, but your ability to absorb the calcium that you are ingesting and then to utilize it properly.

In the time period during which the number of women in this country doubled, the incidence of osteoporosis quadrupled. Osteoporosis is a debilitating bone disorder caused by bone porosity, affecting more women than men. In just a few years, osteoporosis, once unheard of by most women, has become a common concern. You do not have to be included in the statistics that correlate lactation and osteoporosis in later life. On an *optimal diet*, breast-feeding does not steal your calcium.

As a nursing mother, you have one advantage. Calcium excretion is decreased in lactation. You have greater retention and absorption than at any other time in your life except during pregnancy. But judging from statistics, apparently nature's help is not quite enough. You have to do the rest yourself.

BEVERAGES AND YOUR BREAST MILK

Nursing mothers have an increased thirst, which usually means a need for added fluid intake. When fluids are restricted, mothers experience a decrease in urine output, but not in milk. Here again, nature protects the baby, not you. Many women know they must replenish fluids but use fruit juices, milk, and/or diet sodas as vehicles for accomplishing this goal.

Fruit juices. Fruit juices are not whole, natural, or primal, and therefore not health-promoting. They are too high in simple carbohydrates (sugar) and are often highly processed. Many are pasteurized, condensed, and/or reconstituted. Apple juice is ingested and assimilated more than ten times faster than an equal quantity of apples. Apple juice causes a rebound fall in blood sugar levels that does not occur after consuming the natural fruit. There is a higher level of insulin in your blood after consuming juice than there is after chewing apples, which is responsible for the blood sugar drop. These disturbances foster unfavorable "overnutrition."[30] An apple is intended to be consumed while still retaining the fibrous architecture of the whole fruit. An apple is a primal food.

Soft drinks. Phosphorus is a calcium antagonist. The worst offender is the type added to sodas to maintain the fizz and bubble, which is an inorganic form — absorbed by the body with efficiency.[31] The impact of phosphorus on calcium metabolism, which is already at risk during lactation, commands attention. Seltzer, club soda, and ginger ale present other problems — too much sodium, the addition of buffering agents to counteract acidity, the use of saccharin, and so on. In the United States, we drink soft drinks almost as much as we do water.

Skim milk. The removal of the small percentage of fat from milk makes it an unbalanced food because this causes the protein and carbohydrate content to increase. In addition, fat is necessary for proper assimilation of calcium. Skim milk is not a primal food. Nor are the 1 percent or 2 percent varieties.

To cut the "skinnyness" of real skim milk, emulsifiers such as tapioca are often used. Without an emulsifier, fat-free milk would be unpalatable. (Tapioca, derived from the root of the cassava plant, is highly processed. Cassava is primal, tapioca is not.)

Some physicians recommend low-fat or skim-milk products because of concern for contaminants that are absorbed by fat molecules. If a food is rejected as unhealthful for any reason, does it become better when that same food is offered in a more processed, unnatural form? We don't think so, especially with the knowledge that significant proportions of nutrients are found in the fat fractions of milk.

Problems with milk in general center on its high allergenicity. Many people don't even know that they are sensitive to milk or have milk intolerance. Manifestations of the sensitivity can throw the less knowledgeable doctor off track. Almost everyone who eliminates milk and milk products from the diet usually reaches a surprising level of well-being.

In addition, the large amount of phosphate that occurs naturally in milk can lead to low calcium levels, in spite of milk's high calcium content.[32] *You don't have to drink milk to produce milk.* Most lactating women of the world do not drink milk. And neither do cows. (See Chapter 9.)

CHOLESTEROL AND YOUR BREAST MILK

The cholesterol levels in human milk are very high. Nature doesn't leave anything to chance. Cholesterol is so important that, like you, your baby can manufacture this vital substance. Abundant and easily available supplies are believed to facilitate the development of the central nervous system and enzyme pathways.[33] High cholesterol levels in infancy appear to result in lower levels in the adult.[34] It's not so much that high cholesterol given in infancy is protective later on, but rather that formula-fed infants grow up with disturbed cholesterol mechanisms.[35]

We should use breast milk as a model. It is, after all, the most primal of all foods — the only food we know for certain was meant for human consumption. The lesson is: don't be concerned about eating natural or primal foods containing cholesterol (foods like eggs or shellfish). Processed foods, stress, and lack of exercise are major contributors to raised cholesterol levels — not the ingestion of primal foods, even those high in cholesterol.

DIETING WHILE LACTATING

Most women are eager to shift the sand back to normal in their hourglass figures as soon after birth as possible. But it's not a good idea to restrict calories for the purpose of dieting because this could lead to an immediate reduction in milk supply.[36] *What* you are eating is more significant than *how much* you are eating. A breast-feeding woman can be overcaloried and undernourished. The buzz phrase that describes this phenomenon is *affluent malnutrition.*

A daily increase of about 500 calories during the first three months of breast-feeding (and even more beyond this time) is recommended.[37] In all, you require about 940 additional calories to support the lactation process. The other 440 come from the nine-pound store of extra fat tissue laid down in pregnancy. Our advice, however, is to put your calorie computer away. These figures do not consider variations in activity or individual differences in metabolism. Counting calories is not practical and rarely works in real life.

Women who don't breast-feed have a difficult time losing the lactation fat reserves, and for them the battle of the bulge usually continues forevermore.

A major note of caution concerns the possible release of environmental contaminants that have been stored in fat tissue. As explained earlier, when you are not ingesting enough fat, the lactation process draws on your body stores. As the stored fat tissue is mobilized to support your lactation, there is an acute release of substances, including environmental contaminants.[38]

THE VEGETARIAN LACTATER

The importance of an exemplary diet for non–meat eaters cannot be overemphasized. Twinkies, potato chips, Tofutti, saltines, sugar-laden peanut butter, and corn curls are vegetarian foods, but they are hardly conducive to the production of quality breast milk (or good health for anyone, for that matter).

We recommend eggs, fish, and organic chicken and liver for the ovo-vegetarians, the "almost" vegetarians. A healthful vegetarian diet excludes processed foods, red meat, milk, cheese, or any other milk-based foods, with the exception of fermented dairy products (yogurt, acidophilus, buttermilk, and so on). Requirements for virtually all nutrients increase during lactation, but those for iron are often the most difficult to meet. That's one reason we recommend eggs, fish, and liver.[39] The strict vegetarian excluding these foods must pay close attention to the complementarity suggestions outlined above and should be especially careful not to indulge in processed foods. The high temperatures that go hand in hand with the technology of food manipulation usually lower amino acid content, thereby reducing the ability to create human protein. (Remember: although the quantity of protein in human milk remains fixed, the quality can be altered.)

The vegetarian lactater who is concerned about vitamin B_{12} — found mostly in animal foods — can relax *if* she is eating primal foods. Vegetarians consuming healthful diets usually have more than adequate B_{12} levels. People who suffer from anemia in this country are almost always meat eaters or vegetarians on junk food diets.

SOUP'S ON: GOOD, BETTER, BEST

PUT on your best bib and tucker: we're going to join Laura and Wendy for the transient pleasures (but more lasting effects) of the dinner table. Using the general facts stated above, you can easily judge which of the two menus is more likely to produce quality breast milk.

LAURA'S MENU

Dinner
porterhouse steak
baked potato topped with sour
    cream and margarine
frozen peas
artificially sweetened soft drink

WENDY'S MENU

Dinner
brown rice, mixed with stir-fried
    vegetables, scrambled eggs, tem-
    peh, and Protein-Aide sesame
    seeds
tossed salad, with Bibb lettuce,
    parsley, watercress, grated car-
    rot, assorted sprouts, sprouted
    sunflower seeds, red peppers,
    cauliflower, cabbage, avocado;
    seasoned with garlic and kelp

Supplements
lactation formula, GLA, carrot-
    grown acidophilus, brewer's
    yeast, desiccated liver, cod-liver
    oil, algae supplement (all dis-
    cussed in Chapter 5)

Dessert
apple pie
vanilla ice cream

Evening snack
skim milk
cheese
crackers

Dessert
herb tea
whole apple

Evening snack
baked sweet potato, served cold
rice cakes

A tremendous amount of energy is expended during the breast-feeding process. Many women simply do not eat enough to compensate for this energy release, and that's one reason they are often so tired. Laura and Wendy, however, are getting their calories. So much for quantity. Let's discuss quality.

ANALYZING LAURA'S MENU

Porterhouse steak, sour cream, margarine, cheese. Laura's dinner includes lots of fat. There's fat in the steak, the sour cream, the margarine, the ice cream, the cheese — even in the crackers. But —

Is Laura getting brain-promoting fat, or just any old fat? (Or is she just getting fat?) According to the experts, Laura is not getting high-test fuel. The steak and the dinner embellishments contain saturated (storage) fat, *not* the type of fat necessary for optimal brain development.[40]

Meat does contribute moderate amounts of many B vitamins, a bit of iron and zinc, and generous quantities of niacin and phosphorus. But these nutrients can also be obtained from complex carbohydrates, and without the excess fat and high protein.

There are disadvantages in consuming too much protein, which creates a need for additional calcium and magnesium. Toxic effects of excessive protein have also been noted.[41]

The aphorism "good things come in small packages" applies to protein. Protein should be supplied in small, quality-laden doses. Additional problems with meat consumption are discussed in Chapter 6. Red meat may enhance a poor diet, but remember our goal: *excellence.* Fish is a superior choice. (And it's not as fattening.)

Peas, potatoes. Potatoes and peas contribute fiber. But —
Most people, like Laura, are unaware that processing techniques

weaken if not annihilate vital life forces of food. How could you know? Not necessarily from the label, and hardly from appearance. Frozen peas have the facade of wholesome vegetables, the aroma and taste of being freshly prepared, and the advertising campaign behind them telling you that "frozen at peak" is better than fresh. As explained earlier in this chapter, that just isn't so.

Baked potato with butter and raw peas (served in the pods — what could be easier?) or lightly steamed fresh peas rate as better choices for primal foods.

Diet soda, skim milk.   Laura knows that she should have liquids. But —

Her choice of beverages, like many of her other food choices, is also the result of lack of knowledge. She drinks skim milk to avoid the 2 or 3 percent of fat contained in whole milk, but she eats cheese, which is 80 percent fat. The lowered fat content in the milk interferes with calcium absorption, as does the excessive fat in the cheese.

Diet soda presents two problems: (1) the jury is still out on artificial sweeteners, and (2) its high phosphate content is a calcium antagonist.

The question usually posed at this point is: what should I drink? If plain water is too mundane for you, treat yourself to flavored bottled mineral water or spruce up some water yourself with a twist of lemon or lime. And give the herb teas a chance. Try various combinations until you find a few you like. Go for diversity to avoid high concentrations of any single herb.

Ice cream, apple pie.   The sweet reward programmed in Laura's psyche since childhood manifested itself with renewed vigor when she became a lactating mother. She went after desserts as never before. She rationalized: apple pie contains fruit; crust is made from flour; ice cream is composed of milk. Why, if this dessert could boast a bit of meat, it would honor the four-food-group concept. But —

In addition to being a nutrient thief, sugar races through your body, exerting stress on blood sugar mechanisms. Continued consumption of high doses of refined sugar may also lead to higher blood levels of undesirable fat. Refined sugar renders a food inadequate in general, and nutrient-deficient in particular. And one good food doesn't rescue a bad one. Lactation is a time of high energy need. Negative food factors do not help the process.

Crackers.   Crackers are tasty, easy to eat, and have a long shelf life. But —
Crackers contain white flour and sugar, a pair of nutritional ghosts, having form but no substance. The fiber and many vitamins and minerals originally contained in flour have been processed away. Fiber protects colon function, glucose tolerance, blood pressure, and heart actions. Crackers, like apple juice, cannot sustain optimal health.
None of these highly processed foods were available in quantity — if at all — at the turn of the century; nor did nature prepare us for them genetically.

Laura's other meals.   Laura confessed to having little variety in her meals. She routinely eats boxed cold cereal for breakfast. Lunch alternates between fruit yogurt and cottage cheese. She typifies Americans who are locked into sameness in diet. Laura needs ideas and recommendations for widening her choices. Her diet lacks fiber, vitamin A, zinc, and a host of other nutrients.
Parents invariably deplore anything that challenges their children's security. Laura, like so many others, is unaware of the nutritional threat. But she does regret her lack of breast-feeding success. The chance to breast-feed these children will never come again. Laura would have made major changes in her diet if she had known about the correlation between what she was eating and her failure to breast-feed.

ANALYZING WENDY'S MENU

Brown rice.   Wendy's Oriental brown rice dish is her *spécialité de la maison*. It's delicious, inexpensive, and versatile. While the rice is cooking (it takes a half hour), she does other things. Unlike white rice, brown rice is high in both fiber and nutrients, including molybdenum. This trace mineral is involved in carbohydrate metabolism, essential during lactation. Life itself would not be possible without molybdenum, which is only found in significant quantities in whole grains.

Stir-fried vegetables.   The vegetables added to the brown rice are almost raw (they could also be lightly steamed). The selection varies, depending on what's in season and what's in the vegetable bin that day. Fresh vegetables in general are of high nutrient value and the most unadulterated of primal foods. You can indulge in an excess of any other food category and get into trouble, but you can't overdose on vegetables if you take advantage of the many different kinds available. This is one case where more is better. The very bulk of vegetables limits the quantity you can consume. Small amounts of a large variety of vegetables supplies carotene, B vitamins, calcium and other minerals, plus fiber.

Scrambled eggs.   We noted earlier that the addition of animal protein improves protein quality. The small amount of scrambled eggs (one egg per two persons) adds a touch of "meatiness" and improved protein value to the preparation. With the exception of breast milk, eggs contain the amino acid profile most like that of human protein. Egg protein is also highly digestible, which means it is absorbed efficiently.

To obtain the greatest nutrient benefit from eggs, they should be produced by free-running chickens, capable of becoming fertilized if given the opportunity, and prepared so that the yolk is still runny: soft-boiled, poached, or sunny-side up. Scramble lightly only when embellishing grain dishes.

Adding scrambled eggs to the rice dish employs the ancient Asian custom of improving overall amino acid composition with the use of small quantities of animal protein.

Tempeh, sprouted sunflower seeds.   Strict vegetarians who are on healthful diets have more than adequate B_{12} blood levels, despite the apparent paucity of B_{12} in their foods.

Low levels of vitamin B_{12} have been recognized in the milk of poor vegetarian women in third world countries. It may also be an affliction of those with affluent malnutrition. Even though vitamin B_{12} is found mostly in animal foods, deficiency does exist among people who consume meat. But those who eat peanuts, sunflower seeds, and sprouts appear to have adequate levels of B_{12}. The nutrient may be manufactured in the gut when the diet includes these foods. Eating seeds, especially when sprouted, apparently promotes B_{12} synthesis.[42]

For the skeptical who take no chances, tempeh has more vitamin B_{12} than any other plant food. Tempeh is a popular Indonesian fermented (cultured) food consisting of tender-cooked soybeans, bound together in compact, three-quarter-inch-thick white cakes or patties. It is sold fresh, refrigerated, or frozen in natural food stores, Oriental food shops, and many produce markets. Sliced, then stir-fried or steamed, tempeh is nutty and meaty, and lends flavor and chewy texture — plus vitamin B_{12} — to any salad, grain, or vegetable dish.

Sprouted sunflower seeds, in addition to providing Wendy with vitamin B_{12} insurance, are an excellent source of the *right* kind of fatty acids, plus calcium.

Protein-Aide sesame seeds. This is Wendy's answer to protein complementarity because sesame seeds contain amino acids that are in short supply in most other plant foods.

Bibb lettuce, parsley, watercress. These are the *leafy greens* that offer more nutrient value than most foods, including vitamin K. Until the baby begins to manufacture its own supply, vitamin K is obtained by the baby from its liver as well as from your milk.

Assorted sprouts. Sprouts are Wendy's method of "beating the establishment." They are cheap and organic, have an extensive range of nutrients, and are literally growing until minutes before consumption. (When you grow sprouts, the farm is on your kitchen counter.)

Red peppers, cauliflower, cabbage, avocado. Red peppers contain lots of vitamin C, and cauliflower and cabbage are now known as anticancer vegetables. Avocados contain a range of fantastic nutrients, including quality protein and those wonderful brain-promoting fats. Since every processing step — including cooking — is nutrient depleting, a mixture of many raw vegetables is a must. The more extensive the medley, the better the salad. Wendy varies her salads with the use of grated raw carrots, diced zucchini, tofu, raw asparagus, steamed and cooled tempeh, and so on.

Kelp, garlic. The iodine content of human milk is greatly influenced by the mother's dietary intake.[43] Iodine is needed for thyroid gland competence. Goiter is the result of iodine deficiency. The best source of iodine is any sea vegetable. But how many Americans consume sea plants? Among the varieties of seaweed that comprise 10 percent of the Japanese diet, kelp is considered superior. This sea plant is a far better vehicle for obtaining iodine than iodized salt, America's source for this valuable nutrient. (See Chapter 6.)

Garlic offers flavor plus important antibiotic characteristics.

Supplements. Wendy adds nutritional supplements "just to be sure." The biocides in our environment, the additives, colorings, preservatives, and flavor enhancers in our food supply system, and the hundreds of toxic waste dumps that are seeping contents into our waters have an effect on human health. Supplements, if selected with care, may help to replace nutrients depleted from foods, and to compensate for the body's nutrient losses — expended in the need to detoxify so many contaminants. Wendy's supplement regimen is explained in detail in Chapter 5.

Herb tea, apple, baked sweet potato, rice cakes. Wendy does not feel deprived of snack foods. Limited fruit, hypoallergenic rice cakes, and sweet potatoes prepared during dinner hour become the favored treats.

Wendy's other meals. People have expressed surprise that Wendy never consumed milk or its derivative foods during her pregnancy and lactation. Wendy's pediatrician confirms that she doesn't have to drink milk to make milk.[44] Reasons for eliminating milk from the diet of breast-feeding women are explored in detail in Chapter 7. Wendy's total diet is heavily endowed with the Top Ten — the ultimate in primal foods, described below.

BLUE-RIBBON FOODS: THE TOP TEN

Any healthful food usually offers parallel benefits: a food of particular value from the standpoint of one nutrient usually has other vital nutrients too. The fact that similar categories of foods are recommended frequently is graphically demonstrated in the Lactation Nutrient Reference Chart at the end of Chapter 5. The Top Ten are, in order of frequency:

· fresh vegetables, including leafy greens
· whole grains
· liver and other organ meats
· fertile eggs
· deep ocean fish or fish with high fat content (cod, salmon,

halibut, snapper, mackerel)
· nuts and seeds (especially sprouted)
· legumes (peas, beans, and lentils, especially sprouted)
· brewer's yeast
· fruit
· fermented dairy products (yogurt, acidophilus, etc.)

Note that fruits, although recommended, are not a high-priority food. The simple sugars they contain can disturb blood chemistry for the many people who have blood sugar imbalances and for anyone consuming fruit in excess.

And here's a bonus: the foods on Wendy's menu, besides being good for you, cost only about one third (or less) the price Laura paid for her meal.

THE LATEST ON NUTRITION AND LACTATION

INFORMATION about nutrition and lactation that may seem obvious — knowledge that was part of traditional folklore for centuries — has recently been validated scientifically. Some of the "new" information follows.

· *Stress of lactation.* Nutritional requirements are higher during pregnancy and breast-feeding than at any other stage of your life.
· *Healthy infants.* The well-fed lactating mother is more likely to raise a healthy baby.[45]
· *Future pregnancies.* Breast-feeding days may be followed rather soon by another pregnancy, so the mother's nutritional status, as well as the quality of the milk now being produced, is of prime importance.
· *Energy output.* Lactating women require more calories. The results of a large-scale study of lactating Australians show that the mothers were getting plenty of food (more than recommended for similar non-lactating women) but still not enough. They were not compensating adequately for the energy content of the milk they were producing.[46] No wonder most lactating women are always so tired!

It is unfortunate that the nutritional demands to support adequate lactation have been studied much more carefully in dairy cattle than in humans.

You may read contradictory reports on breast-feeding. The following factors affect the content of human milk, thereby contributing to differing views:

- mother's health (both current and prior to delivery)
- the nutrient stores in the baby
- the age of the baby
- the size of the baby
- the method of milk expression
- the time of day of expression

An example of dissimilar conclusions can be demonstrated in the results of three separate studies in which protein content was examined to determine its level in prolonged lactation: one study found a decline, another a rise, and the third reported no change.[47] Presently available data on the composition of human milk are incomplete.[48]

ARRANGING FOR THE VEGETABLE SCRUBBER

REGARDLESS of life's circumstances, you usually eat three meals a day, dress in the morning, brush your teeth, and undress at night. But a new baby alters the inexorable logic of custom. Habits suddenly dissolve along with schedules. Your first reaction to Laura's and Wendy's meal plans may be, "What a fantasy. I have no time to prepare such foods, let alone shop for them. Meals are catch-can, if at all. And furthermore, I don't always undress at night, because I don't always get dressed in the morning."

The best present you can give to yourself or have anyone give to you is catering help — perhaps someone who will do no more than purchase and scrub vegetables — husband, lover, neighbor, mother, grandmother, or hired teenager down the street. Plans for food preparation must be arranged in advance. Selecting your temporary chef is as important as deciding on your obstetrician or midwife; as worthy of concern as arranging for diapers or buying your crib. It is your trump card, your masterstroke. And it doesn't have to be expensive. Arrange to have catering help for at least three weeks after your baby is born, longer if possible.

A decline in your nutritional status is an ever-present risk, given the loopholes in our foodway system, coupled with the fatigue that so frequently plagues new mothers. "I'm just too tired to get it together to have a meal," is a common refrain. Believe it or not, the solution may be as simple as adding a large mixed salad for lunch and a pot of varied steamed vegetables for dinner.

We have learned that the two main sources of interference with lactation appear to be nutrition and reflexes that control milk ejection. They are not mutually exclusive. Although the reflexes can be circumvented emotionally, the production of key hormones that play a role in the reflex actions may be diminished or enhanced by the food you eat.

Here is another fascinating phenomenon: better nutrition encourages an earlier resumption of menstrual and ovulatory activity. Well-nourished women often start menstruating after seven months. The baby is still sucking vigorously at this time, so one would think that the resulting high prolactin production would discourage ovulation. It doesn't.[49,50]

Nutrition for the breast-feeding woman has not been adequately emphasized in our culture, but we hope it is the wave of the future. We sifted through several thousand papers on breast-feeding before reading, "The emphasis should be in large measure on the mother.... 'Nourish the mother, thereby the infant.' "[51]

If you are low on the nutrition-awareness continuum, you may feel overloaded with too many facts that are hard to accept all at once. It is preferable to make a few changes slowly rather than to throw up your hands in despair and do nothing.

Quality breast milk is powerful. It requires energy and nutrients. The researchers know *why*. Primal food is the answer to *how*. We've had a breast-feeding renaissance. Now let's have a nutritional renaissance.

COMPENDIUM

Human milk production

Requires energy
Requires nutrients
Can be maintained on inadequate diets
Cannot be optimal on inadequate diets
May take certain nutrients from mother's stores if lacking in her diet

General information

Restricted diet for mother produces smaller babies
Infants have reduced food tolerance compared to adults
Nutrient levels in breast milk may decrease as breast-feeding continues
Well-fed mothers have healthy babies
Poorly fed mothers increase milk volume when given nutritional supplements
Mother's nutritional requirements are higher than at any other time
Few lactating women consume enough calories (940 additional calories are required for lactation)
Breast-feeding malnutrition often goes unrecognized

Milk volume is

Increased by good nutrition
Decreased by stress
Not influenced by increased quantity of mother's food
Reduced when mothers go on weight-reducing diets

Protein content of breast milk

Is not influenced by quantity of food mother ingests
Is reduced in older mothers
Improves in quality with better diet for mother

Protein values in diet can be increased by

Consuming high-protein plant foods

    legumes — peas, beans, and lentils
    Protein-Aide sesame seeds

Combining complementary foods
Adding small amounts of animal protein to plant foods

Fat in breast milk

Is the main source of calories
Contains vitamins A, D, E, and K
Matches pattern of mother's ingested fat, or
Matches pattern of stored fat if fat is limited in her diet

Comes in two varieties
    storage fat (visible)
    structural fat

Is important to baby's brain development

Fat deficiencies cause

Higher mortality in babies
Smaller body, smaller brain, smaller liver

Carbohydrates can be

Harmful if highly processed
Helpful if in primal form

Nutrients in milk immediately affected by mother's diet are

B vitamins; vitamins A, C, and K
Fat, iodine, folic acid
Protein quality

Nutrients in milk not immediately affected by mother's diet but depleted from mother's stores are

Zinc, phosphorus, magnesium, potassium, copper
Protein quantity

Nursing mothers

Have increased thirst
Should not drink sodas, fruit juices, skim milk
Should drink two and one-half quarts water daily
Do not require milk to produce milk
Should not consume processed foods

Calcium in human milk is

Independent of mother's intake
Maintained at expense of skeletal stores
Absorbed better than from cow's milk

Calcium metabolism is reduced by

Unleavened bread

Excessive protein and fat
Phosphorus foods, salt, cola drinks
Poor nutritional status
Stress, age, immobilization, lack of sunshine

Calcium metabolism is enhanced by

Fatty fish, eggs, butter, liver
Good nutritional status
The right amount of activity
Vitamin D, especially from the sun
Synergistic nutrients: magnesium, copper, zinc, manganese, silicon,
   molybdenum, vanadium

Avoid processed foods because

Frozen foods

   lose texture, color, and flavor
   usually contain additives
   lose nutrient values in the freezing process, when stored (even in
      the freezer), and when thawed

Refined sugar causes

   loss of B vitamins
   higher levels of undesirable fat
   higher risk of several disease states

Processed fat causes

   altered molecular structures
   less efficient oxygen transport
   more oxygen requirement for fat metabolism
   breast milk jaundice

To attain infant's genetic potential

Breast-feed at least one year
Eat blue-ribbon, Top Ten foods

   fresh vegetables, including leafy greens
   whole grains
   liver and other organ meats
   fertile eggs

deep ocean fish or fish with high fat content (cod, salmon, halibut, snapper, mackerel)

nuts and seeds (especially sprouted)

legumes (peas, beans, and lentils, especially sprouted)

brewer's yeast

fruit

fermented dairy products (yogurt, acidophilus, etc.)

CHAPTER

~ 5 ~

All about Nutrient Supplementation

IN WHICH WE EXPLAIN

that supplementation is the act of adding substances to your diet that should have been there in the first place

Most of us can't pick, pull, or pluck in quest for food. If that were possible, our meals would be of commendable quality, and perhaps supplementing with concentrated nutrients would not be part of the world of every day.

Nor is there much to be gained in negotiating supermarket aisles with a vitamin and mineral calculator. Computing how much of this or that type of food you should eat to meet your molybdenum requirement (even if you could pronounce it) serves no better than calorie counting. And for the same reason: there are too many variables. Supplementation is regarded as a biochemical insurance policy. But like many insurance plans, it may only weather a portion of the storm and sometimes not even that. This chapter leads you to triumph in filling nutrient gaps with supplements, so vital while you are breastfeeding.

We can give our genes full opportunity for expression, but it takes personal planning, dedication, and discipline to rise above merely surviving into the rich life that our genes are capable of creating.

— ROSS HUME HALL, PH.D.

"**M**alnutrition of breast-fed infants can occur."[1]

"Marginal intake [of nutrients] in lactating mothers is more common than assumed for a well-nourished population."[2]

"Intakes of trace elements by breast-fed infants seem to be below the recommended dietary allowances."[3]

"Milk from all mothers cannot be assumed to contain adequate amounts of vitamin A."[4]

These statements have appeared in recent medical literature. Despite the worry and the warning, very little is known about the specifics of human milk nutrients. The failure, however, has not been in the test tube. The stumbling block exists because most of the experiments have never been done. And that's because interest in breast-feeding waned at a time when knowledge of nutrient metabolism began to unfold. After years of neglect, interest in human milk nutrition is emerging. It promises to be an exciting field of study in the near future. Meanwhile, the limited prelude is the background for this chapter.

OVERVIEW: VITAMINS AND MINERALS

WE all know there is no such thing as being "a little bit pregnant," but it is not unusual to be a little bit nutrient-deficient. This fact was not understood when vitamins were first discovered and is still being denied by old-school practitioners. It's no longer enough to look for the smoking gun — we must look for the hidden hand. Insufficient intake of vitamins and minerals results in a gradual progression of disturbances.

The early symptoms of nutrient deficiencies are nonspecific in nature. A headache or fatigue, for example, may reflect a very mild slump in almost any single vitamin. The Lactation Nutrient Reference Chart at the end of this chapter details the functions of most known vitamins and minerals, with particular emphasis on their roles in nursing. Here is a quick review of a few basic facts about these nutrients.

WATER-SOLUBLE VITAMINS

Water-soluble vitamins — the B vitamins and vitamin C — are not usually stored in your body (except for vitamin B_{12} and a few complex phenomena). For the most part, there are daily losses of these nutrients through normal metabolism, thus dictating their frequent replenishment. The B vitamins are thiamin (B_1), riboflavin (B_2), niacin (B_3), pantothenic acid (B_5), pyridoxine (B_6), cobalamin (B_{12}), folic acid, choline, inositol, para-aminobenzoic acid (PABA), and biotin.

The B vitamins are widely distributed in animal and vegetable foods, but no single source of nourishment contains the full range in sufficient quantities to meet your needs. These nutrients are found in yeast, fruit, vegetables, nuts, meat, and fish. Because they are water-soluble, they go down the drain with the water in which they've been cooked; and because they are located in the outer husk of seeds and cereals, they are completely lacking in bleached flour and polished rice.

The best sources of vitamin C are citrus fruits. But citrus is high on the allergy list, so it may be preferable to use other foods for daily vitamin C rations. Apples, blueberries, Brussels sprouts, cabbage, cantaloupe, carrots, celery, chard, endive, peas, peppers, pineapple, rhubarb, spinach, tomatoes, turnip greens, and watercress all contain vitamin C.

Most water-soluble vitamins are components of enzyme systems, that is, they turn on important metabolic events.

FAT-SOLUBLE VITAMINS

Fat-soluble vitamins — A, D, E, and K — are more permanent residents in your body, relieving you of the responsibility of acquiring them on a day-to-day basis. These vitamins are found in foods in association with fats and are absorbed along with fats in the diet. Conditions unfavorable to normal fat uptake impair their absorption. Good sources of fat are found in primal foods like eggs, nuts, avocados, seeds, fish, and some vegetables. Proper absorption is disturbed with the consumption of processed oils, especially rancid salad dressings, fats that have been hydrogenated, and fats that have been repeatedly heated at high temperatures.

Fat-soluble vitamins participate in cell differentiation and growth. Their general function is to regulate the manufacture of protein.

MINERALS

Minerals, also called *trace elements*, are both interrelated and balanced against each other, like members of teams in a tug-of-war. A single mineral doesn't work by itself. Knowing the quantity of one mineral in an individual's diet has little significance without knowledge of the quantities of other minerals. Diagnostic interpretation using the amount of a single mineral is like one hand clapping.

At least thirteen different trace elements are needed by your body, and all must be derived from your diet. Whole grains, nuts and seeds, and leafy greens are good sources of minerals, including potassium, calcium, magnesium, manganese, and zinc.

WATER-SOLUBLE VITAMINS AND YOUR MILK

WATER-soluble vitamins have no difficulty finding their way from blood to human milk. Levels of these vitamins in your milk are directly affected by your diet. With few exceptions, the vitamin content of milk increases steadily with the dose used in supplementation.[5]

THE B VITAMINS

Vitamin B_{12}.   Unlike adults, infants need a more sustained intake of vitamin B_{12} because of the added requirement for growth. Vitamin B_{12} deficiency has been reported in a few cases of infants exclusively breast-fed by vegetarians.[6] Strict vegetarianism alone does not cause a vitamin B_{12} drain. Malnutrition is the lever, the mainspring. When researchers study the total diets and nutritional competency of women whose vitamin B_{12} levels are overdrawn, they learn an important lesson about the seamy side of vegetarianism (the Twinkies type) as compared to its incredible health-promoting attributes when practiced properly (the primal-foods regimen).

Vitamin B_{12} plays a unique role in cell replication. This nutrient shows up significantly in breast milk after supplements are taken.[7]

Vitamin B_6.   The concentrations of vitamin B_6 in the mammary gland and in breast milk are more sensitive to the level of vitamin intake than any other tissue. Dietary sources of vitamin B_6 are usually inadequate for lactation, and this is reflected in low levels of the vitamin in the milk.[8]

Other B vitamins.   The B vitamins have little in common except that they occur together in the same sources in varying proportions. Each has a separate function for the growing infant, but all are interdependent: a deficiency in any one leads to a deficiency in others, and an excessive intake of one increases the need for the others.

Folic acid, like B_{12} and B_6, increases significantly in milk after supplementation.[9]

VITAMIN C

Requirements for vitamin C increase during stress, but exclusively breast-fed babies maintain adequate levels. In fact, they have higher quantities than infants who are on vitamin C–supplemented formulas and solid foods. And they have more than their mothers, even when the mother's vitamin C intake is under the mark. But this built-in protection breaks down after a while.

Many lactating women exhibit marginal vitamin C deficits. The risk period seems to be at two months of lactation and in the spring.

Women who are advised to avoid citrus fruit during lactation because of allergies are also at risk.

High concentrations of vitamin C are necessary during infant growth. A variety of important reactions, which include regulating protein metabolism and potentiating iron absorption, are associated with vitamin C. Although the baby maintains a sufficient amount of the nutrient, the meager measure in the milk places the baby at risk *if the mother's shortcoming continues over a long period of time.*[10]

Archie Kalokerinos, M.D., eliminated sudden infant crib death among his patients — along with other serious but less fatal maladies — by recommending that the lactating women coat their breast nipples with ascorbic acid (vitamin C) powder just before feeding.[11] His work is well documented and has worldwide acclaim.

No woman can function with good humor and good health when she has limited allowances of vitamin C, which may cause feelings of weakness, delayed wound healing, and decreased iron absorption, among other manifestations.

Women may hesitate to increase vitamin C quantities during times of stress or the advent of a respiratory disturbance because of fear that the baby will wind up with an overdose. Amounts that exceed a thousand milligrams a day, however, do not raise the vitamin C quantity of the milk. There appears to be a controlling mechanism at work.[12] Another marvel of mother's milk!

Many experts agree that considerably greater intakes of vitamin C are required than indicated in recommended daily allowance charts in order to maintain satisfactory levels during lactation.[13]

FAT-SOLUBLE VITAMINS AND YOUR MILK

THE fat-soluble vitamins A, D, E, and K are found in foods in association with fats, or lipids. Unlike water-soluble vitamins, they are not normally excreted. Because they are stored in the body, you are not dependent on a day-to-day supply in your diet. These vitamins are found in the lipid portion of breast milk.

VITAMIN A

Most lactating women fail the vitamin A test, falling far short of having enough. Supplementation with vitamin A makes human milk vitamin A–rich.[14] Vitamin A is found in nature to a large extent in the form of its precursors in the yellow and orange pigments of fruits and vegetables. Your body then manufactures vitamin A from these precursors if all the right enzymes are present.

VITAMIN D

Historically, vitamin D has been classified as a fat-soluble vitamin, but a water-soluble fraction of this nutrient has recently been discovered in human milk. So much for classifications.

The power of cod-liver oil to stave off rickets was discovered over a half century ago, making this substance a standard for infants in your grandma's time. Your mother learned about vitamins A and D, so she discarded the bottle of cod-liver oil and bought extractions of the two nutrients. Now we find that we threw the baby out with the bath water: there are constituents in cod-liver oil, in addition to vitamins A and D, that are notably essential. So we're back to Grandma's cod-liver oil. Other than cod-liver oil, egg yolks, and liver, few foods contain significant amounts of vitamin D.

Unless you live in a sunny climate, vitamin D supplementation is recommended — not only for you but for your baby as well. Dark skin, atmospheric pollution, and skin coverage due to cold climate (or religious beliefs) increase the risk of improper calcium utilization and poor bone development.

Decreased bone mineral content shows up in infants fed human milk without supplemental vitamin D compared with those receiving 400 IU daily.[15] Vitamin D becomes progressively more important with age, indicating the necessity for vitamin D supplementation in older breast-fed infants.[16]

The medical literature reports that your baby's supply of vitamin D appears to be independent of the amount in your milk. More accurately, we really don't know the degree to which your diet influences your baby's vitamin D status. We do know that when vitamin D is in short measure, a reduced amount of milk and/or nutritionally incomplete milk is produced.[17]

VITAMIN E

A very specific amount of vitamin E is required to balance polyunsaturated fat. The balance prevents rancidity and provides proper metabolism. Another of the wonders of breast milk is that it regulates vitamin E in the appropriate ratio necessary (dependent on the polyunsaturated fat in your diet) — provided all the nutrients are available.[18]

The richest sources of vitamin E among primal foods are whole grains. Eggs, fish, all meats — especially liver — and butter contribute some vitamin E. Because processing and storage destroy a large percentage of the vitamin E content of most foods, supplementation is advisable. Many babies in this country are born with vitamin E deficiencies.

VITAMIN K

Vitamin K is produced by the intestinal flora. Because it takes several days after birth for the formation to take place, many states in the country mandate the administration of vitamin K on the first day of life. This is done to avoid hemorrhage, an apparently frequent occurrence even in full-term infants.[19] (The illness is called "hemorrhagic disease of the newborn.") The risk of hemorrhage in the baby is especially apparent with malnourished mothers.

Consuming dark green leafy vegetables the first few days after delivery will help to insure an adequate vitamin K level for you and your baby.[20]

The maxim "If a little bit is good, more is better" does not apply to fat-soluble vitamins. These nutrients can increase to toxic levels because they accumulate in the body. But unless you are eating seal liver in the Arctic, or you are overdosing on concentrated vitamin tablets, the chances are that hazardous amounts will not accrue on a primal-foods diet. It is advisable to follow instructions on the label pertaining to the dosage of fat-soluble supplements. Again, it's the *processed*-foods diet that is endangering. Synthetic vitamin D added to commercial milk, for example, can collect in the body.[21]

In summary, fat-soluble vitamin levels in your milk are affected by the length of time you breast-feed and by your diet.

TRACE MINERALS AND YOUR MILK

WHEREAS a single dose of a mineral does not alter milk content, it has been demonstrated that long-term supplementation does. Some of the limited information available on the relationship between mineral content of breast milk and the mother's diet follows.

ZINC

After three months of breast-feeding, "healthy" lactating women show lower average zinc levels than age-matched non-lactating women.[22] The zinc concentrations in milk are influenced by your diet, and the effects of low intakes are most apparent with prolonged lactation.[23] This may also be true of other minerals.

Zinc supplements that contain iron or are taken along with specific iron supplements will not raise the zinc status of your milk.[24] Regular zinc supplements are effective.

According to Dr. Martin Milner, director of the Center for Holistic Medicine in Portland, Oregon, zinc helps to induce the flow of milk.[25]

MANGANESE

Manganese serves as an activator of important enzymes. Manganese deficiency can halt the making of mucus and impair the senses of vision, hearing, and smell. Most important, manganese aids in milk production.

The use of oral contraceptives prior to conception may considerably reduce the manganese content in both colostrum and mature milk.[26] If you were on the Pill prior to conception, it is important to consider manganese supplementation.

CALCIUM

The amount of calcium in milk varies considerably. The calcium-absorption recommendations in Chapter 4 deserve special attention. Ethiopian mothers, despite low dietary intake of the mineral, have high levels in their breast milk, probably due to exposure to sunshine, enhancing their vitamin D stores,[27] plus an inborn efficiency of calcium utilization. As previously indicated, calcium supplementation, although important, is not the most significant factor in calcium balance and bone health. Calcium absorption depends on other nutrients (magnesium in particular), the right amount of exercise, and sunlight. It is inhibited by stress and by too much phosphorus.

MAGNESIUM

The amount of magnesium supplied by the American diet is marginal at best, and serious deficiencies can result when there are concomitant high intakes of nutrients that increase magnesium requirements.[28] Phosphorus and calcium are among the antagonists.

A possible link between magnesium deficiency and sudden infant death syndrome has been suggested.[29] In test animals, the survival rate of pups fed by magnesium-deficient mothers was shown to be very poor.[30] The type of heart problems frequently seen in infants resembles that produced in animals on diets lacking in magnesium. Breast-feeding creates the need for additional amounts of this mineral.[31]

SELENIUM

Selenium levels show geographical variations. You can't depend on values printed in food charts. Soil quality and environmental factors influence the selenium uptake of foods. Animal studies show a relationship between the selenium content of food and the amount in the milk. Too much selenium is detrimental to the teeth. But most of the soil in this country is selenium-deficient. Vitamin E and selenium work together, accomplishing jobs that neither could do alone.

IRON

Iron in human milk is quite bioavailable, which means it's easily absorbed by the baby. Iron also has a special anti-infective property. Interference with this guardian role occurs when iron supplements are given to the baby. In fact, this intrusion further aggravates iron depletion, because without the protective aspect of natural iron — now destroyed by the iron supplements — the baby is at risk for disease-causing microorganisms. This leads to gastrointestinal inflammation, which causes bleeding, which in turn reduces iron.[32] Supplements given to the mother, however, do not affect the anti-infection process.[33] But there are other disadvantages associated with iron supplementation for you. Iron supplements that are easily assimilated often have unpleasant reactions; those that have fewer side effects are not as readily metabolized.[34] Iron supplements can also mask folic acid deficiency. Consequently, serious diseases may go unnoticed.[35]

Despite the efficiency of iron absorption from human milk, babies may begin to suffer iron drains between three and six months.[36] Limited iron in your diet coupled with low storage tendencies creates an iron inadequacy — so that your iron levels are insufficient to meet lactation demands. In addition, consuming foods with both phosphorus and high protein levels interferes with iron absorption. (A hamburger and soft drink would be a high protein–phosphorus combination. A cheeseburger would be even worse.)

Our recommendation for making sure you and your baby get enough iron is desiccated liver tablets for you (a natural concentrated food source containing iron), along with vitamin C which, as noted, facilitates the absorption of iron.

So you see that the latest research does not support the advisability of iron supplements for you or your baby. (Small amounts already incorporated in multinutrient preparations, however, should not concern you.)

You have one advantage as long as you are not menstruating. Blood loss through menstruation causes further iron losses. But if you are in excellent health and have menstruated by six or seven months after the birth of your baby (as very healthy women are prone to do), chances are you have no iron deficit.

FLUORIDE

Fluoride supplementation for protection against cavities is not recommended for two reasons: First, allergic reactions to fluoride have been reported, some of them serious. Second, the use of therapeutic measures to counteract a problem caused by poor nutrition perpetuates the foolish-food myth, which suggests that you can continue to consume corrupt foods and get away with it. Horace said it best: "You may drive out Nature with a pitchfork, yet she still will hurry back."[37] Protection against cavities is dependent on your baby's diet and method of feeding. Teeth exposed to unprocessed primal-food meals rarely get holes in them.

It is significant to note that there is far less fluoride in human milk than in cow's milk.

THE VITAMIN REGIMEN FOR YOU

MANY women who breast-feed longer than six months show definite signs of vitamin deficiencies, indicating that the nutritional status of breast-fed infants is maintained at the expense of their mother's reserves.[38,39] If you are the wonderful mother of a lucky baby enjoying the benefits of breast-feeding beyond six months, you know that the right diet and a few supplements can be protective.

It's no surprise that many of us have lost faith in our food protection system. Too many environmental factors (pollution, pesticides, preservatives, and processing) wash away the frail natural protection of foods. Since most of us can't gather berries, dig for roots, or chase wild animals, supplementation is not unwarranted.

Concentrated Food Supplements

The best supplement is one that is a concentrated food rather than extractions of nutrients from that food. Our list of such supplements includes brewer's yeast, desiccated liver, special oils, acidophilus (carrot-grown, in particular), some form of sea plant or algae, and a few botanicals. Each of these food-type supplements offers benefits that are unique. Ideally, natural food concentrates should be taken prior to conception and continued forevermore — or until our food system improves.

Brewer's yeast. Ruth A. Lawrence, M.D., reports that "prescribing brewer's yeast as a dietary supplement has been observed to provide improvement in milk production beyond that accounted for by mere addition of the same nutrients. Some mothers report a feeling of well-being from taking yeast that they do not obtain from taking daily vitamins."[40]

Brewer's yeast is an excellent source of B vitamins and nucleic acids. Nucleic acids (RNA and DNA) are the genetic life force of each of your trillions of cells.

Brewer's yeast should be taken in very small increments at first and the quantity built up gradually. This food supplement is required in large amounts to be effective. It is best to use a preparation of brewer's yeast that is not fortified with any vitamins or minerals. If you take the equivalent of two tablespoons daily, you don't want to be concerned about an overdose of vitamin B_{12}, or iron, or minerals, often added to brewer's yeast.

Again: to avoid sensitivity reactions, start your doses slowly. Don't consider it unreasonable to build up to eight or ten tablets with each meal. Think of brewer's yeast as *food*. You wouldn't hesitate to consume an extra tablespoon or two of ice cream or an additional lamb chop, would you?

Note the frequency with which brewer's yeast is listed as a good food source for specific nutrients in the Lactation Nutrient Reference Chart on pages 109–125. For those concerned about yeast infections (candida), it has been ascertained that brewer's yeast does not fit into the category of substances causing candidiasis problems. The strain of bacteria in brewer's yeast is different from the strain causing candida.[41]

Desiccated liver.   Desiccated liver is nothing more than a concentrated source of liver. *Desiccated* means dried. Surely you have eaten desiccated apricots or desiccated apples. Of course, dried fruit is more appealing than dried liver, but that's why (like brewer's yeast) it has been prepared in powder, tablet, or capsule form.

And like brewer's yeast, desiccated liver is effective if taken in quantity — the equivalent of about a tablespoonful a day. The same warning applies: start slowly and build gradually.

This supplement is a rich source of natural iron, complete protein, and B vitamins. The lining, connective tissues, and external fat are removed from the liver, which is then dried at low temperature in a vacuum chamber, a process that preserves nutrients. A hundred years ago, large quantities of brewer's yeast and desiccated liver were given to diabetics to control the disease. It worked!

DHA (an omega 3 oil).   Chapter 4 provides a brief explanation of fatty acids. The most abundant fatty acid utilized in brain development and function is DHA.[42] Your consumption of oils containing DHA during lactation influences your baby's brain development and learning ability. The oil is obtained from fish or from encapsulated supplements referred to under the brand name Max-EPA. (DHA is not a constituent of fish liver, so cod-liver oil does not contain DHA.) The professionals suggest increasing your intake of DHA during this critical period of brain growth for your child. Even small amounts can elevate the level in your milk.[43]

A base for niacin and other B vitamins that regulate neurological pathways is also provided by these newly discovered omega 3 fatty acids. In addition to their brain-promoting attributes, supplements of DHA in your regimen encourage more relaxed attitudes for both you and the baby.[44] Present-day refining and food-selection patterns deplete both B vitamins and omega 3 fatty acids.

GLA (an omega 6 oil). An extensive and detailed survey was carried out by The Hyperactive Children's Support Group, an organization with more than seventy branches in Britain devoted to helping such children and their families. The group concluded that many of these children have a deficiency in essential fatty acids. Several reasons for the deficiency were cited, among them: deprivation of essential fatty acids in the diet; inability to convert the acids to their useful form (gamma-linolenic acid, or GLA); an inborn higher requirement for this nutrient (especially in boys). The more common problem is the lack of GLA formation, the result of eating too many processed trans fats (hydrogenated vegetable oils), described in Chapter 6, or sensitivity to cow's milk and wheat. The World Health Organization recently issued a report recommending that pregnant and lactating women increase their intake of essential fatty acids.

David Horrobin, renowned for his research on fatty acids, believes it might be better to give GLA, the converted form of the oil, directly to the mother. There are only a few major sources of the already converted form of GLA. One is human milk — in itself strong evidence that nature believes essential fatty acids to be vital for growing infants. Other sources are black currant–seed oil (the latest exciting discovery because of its high concentration of GLA and other important fatty acids) and borage. (In sixteenth-century Europe, borage had a reputation for making people happy.) GLA extracted from these plants is available in supplemental form.

The report from Britain stated that many hyperactive children have eczema, allergies, and asthma, and announced that some of these problems were alleviated with the use of essential fatty acids.[45]

Cod-liver oil. Most pediatricians recommend a modest vitamin D supplement for all lactating women: 400 IU (10 micrograms of vitamin D) or 5 milliliters (one teaspoonful) of cod-liver oil daily.[46] Our preference is cod-liver oil, which is more effective than taking vitamins A and D alone. We suggest that you purchase cod-liver oil in a natural food store because this product is more likely to have a higher turnover there than in a drugstore. Your supply must be fresh. You don't want a bottle that has been sitting on a shelf collecting dust and becoming rancid. After opening the bottle, refrigerate it. And if you haven't managed to finish it in four months, discard the bottle and get another one. Cod-liver oil is not expensive, and even if it were, it would be worth the cost in terms of your health.

Cod-liver oil is available in capsules, but the capsule preparations are often too concentrated. Cod-liver oil capsules are inconvenient — you need too many to equal a teaspoonful of the liquid.

There is one caveat: if you have a tendency to bleeding (frequent nose bleeds, excessive bleeding when you get a cut, and so on), don't take cod-liver oil.[47]

Chlorella — the one-celled wonder.   The Japanese eat marine plants in many forms and in great quantity because they know that algae are healthful. Algae harbor nutrients in percentages not commonly found in most of the foods sold in your local supermarket. A one-celled organism called *chlorella* (*chlor* for green; *ella* for small) is among the most popular of marine plants in Japan (there are many major companies that grow and distribute nothing else). In our country, chlorella has recently been tableted for your convenience.

Chlorella is an independent plant, containing everything it needs to maintain life in its cell. It's a raw, whole food containing chlorophyll, protein, B vitamins, nucleic acids, and even polyunsaturated fatty acids. Chlorella has been shown to enhance immune responses and liver function, in addition to containing antiviral components and cold-reducing properties.[48,49] It is especially valuable for lactating women because of its nucleic acid content.

Carrot-grown acidophilus.   Through the magic of breast milk, your baby's intestinal tract is populated with an assemblage of good-guy bacteria called *L. bifidus* (*lactobacillus bifidus*). The advantage of this mob scene in your child's gut is that it crowds out bacteria of disreputable lineage. This process has served as an example for ancient cultures for centuries and has been noted by modern-day physicians only recently. You, too, can resist enemy invasion by entrenching your normal flora with good-guy sentries.

The easiest way to provide a similar settlement of proper bacteria is with vegetarian-type acidophilus (acidophilus is a second cousin of the bifidus bacteria). Carrot-grown acidophilus — grown on carrot juice, and called carodophilus, vegedophilus, and so on — unloads a few billion acidophilus organisms per gram. Acidophilus bacteria set up housekeeping in your intestine, creating an ecological system that helps to absorb nutrients and create new ones.

Acidophilus is also available in a milk base. A similar helpful bacterium (*lactobacillus bulgaricus*, perhaps a second cousin once removed) is found in *viable* yogurt. (Note the emphasis on *viable;* not all supermarket yogurts are "live." Natural food store proprietors can direct you to the "live" yogurt.) Your great-grandmother produced another equally beneficial strain by "clabbering," or souring, milk in her kitchen.

Effective dose: one or two capsules after every meal.

Herbal or botanical support. Everyone is most comfortable with the familiar. The alphabet nutrients (vitamin A through zinc) are no longer strangers. But nature has many relay systems, and herbal or botanical suggestions should not be overlooked.

- *Alfalfa.* Alfalfa has been known to increase the supply of milk. The roots of the alfalfa plant penetrate deep into the soil, picking up valuable trace minerals. Alfalfa is also high in vitamin K and aids in iron absorption.
- *Nettle.* Nettle has the reputation of reactivating disappearing milk. It also reduces chances of allergic reactions, acting as an herbal antihistamine.[50]
- *Folk remedies from the neighbor next door.* If the lady in the next apartment offers her breast-feeding suggestions, check them out. It could be the wisdom of the ages. Use discretion, of course.

MULTINUTRITION FORMULA

Many physicians recommend multinutrient supplementation. This may be taken in addition to the food preparations. The multi-formulas cover a broad range of known nutrients and help to insure against specific deficiencies of those nutrients. The food-type supplements cover the unknown nutrients. That's why it makes sense to take both. If you think of the food supplements as food, you won't have the feeling that you are overdosing on vitamins.

Because vitamins have to be stamped out like microchips on an assembly line and our dietary needs are not all alike, the recommended intake of a particular nutrient may be higher than the actual requirements of most people, with the hope of meeting the needs of everyone in any state of health. Sometimes the doses are not high enough. Standards set for nutrient supplementation are based on averages. Variables such as heredity, disease, exercise, rate of growth, environmental contamination, and diet have an impact on individual needs.

The type of lactation formula we recommend has been well researched and is approved by many nutrition-oriented physicians. Natrol Nutrition for Breast-Feeding Mothers (produced by Natrol, Inc., Chatsworth, California) is one formula that helps to meet the needs of lactating women. Some of the nutrients in this formula safely exceed the recommended daily allowances set up as minimum guidelines by the Food and Nutrition Board. Research shows that the quantities indicated by the Board for these nutrients are not adequate. The quantities of other nutrients included adhere to limits set for safety reasons. Still other substances are part of this formula because they have been proved to be effective despite the fact that no daily allowances have been established for them.

Included in this formula's specific nutrients are vitamins A, C, D, E, and most if not all of the B vitamins, plus a full range of minerals. Natrol has simplified supplementation by adding a few of the broad-stroke food-type concentrations known to be effective for lactation. In addition to the basic formula, Natrol produces PUFA Complex, a supplement with the entire range of essential fatty acids. The combination of these two formulas was designed specifically for lactation. Check with your doctor or natural food store for availability.

For those concerned with budgets, relatively inexpensive supplements are brewer's yeast, ascorbic acid powder, and sprouts. But remember, any diet deficient in nutrients is costlier in the long run.

THE VITAMIN REGIMEN FOR YOUR BABY

YOUR milk is not the sole source of nutrients for your baby. Fetal stores acquired during pregnancy are significant if your diet was satisfactory during those nine months. Sunshine, providing vitamin D, is another contributor.

There is no evidence that additional vitamins are needed for solely breast-fed offspring in the first six months of life *if mothers have been well nourished in pregnancy and lactation.*[51] We have cited that a possible exception is the need for vitamin D in relatively cloudy and/or cold areas. Vitamin D supplementation administered with an eyedropper is definitely recommended for older breast-fed babies. Another conditional circumstance may be the period of time following an infection. When the baby is weakened by illness, your milk may not be adequate to compensate for his or her increased nutritional requirements.

If you have been eating only primal foods and plan to continue consuming them, there is little reason to give your baby supplements for the first half year. Supplementation should be considered if:

· you cannot resist cheesecake (or other sweet desserts) — frequently
· you party with friends often
· you eat in restaurants several times a week
· you cannot let go of the convenience of using processed foods
· your diet lacks a variety of fresh raw vegetables (in salads) plus lightly steamed vegetables
· you consume soft drinks and/or other nonfood products
· you work or live with someone who smokes

FIRST-YEAR FORMULA

An excellent infant multivitamin mix formula has been prepared by Freeda Vitamins in New York City, called LKV Drops. The formula is administered in increasing doses as the baby grows. This vegetarian formula includes:

Vitamin A	5,000 IU	Vitamin B_6	2 milligrams
Vitamin D	400 IU	Vitamin B_{12}	6 micrograms
Vitamin E	2 IU	Niacinamide	10 milligrams
Vitamin C	50 milligrams	Panthenol	2 milligrams
Vitamin B_1	1.5 milligrams	Biotin	50 micrograms
Vitamin B_2	15 milligrams		

Note: the values indicated for the individual nutrients are based on the full dose, achieved when the baby is about six months old.

SECOND-YEAR FORMULA

The Freeda company has also developed a chewable multivitamin-mineral supplement for children (called Vitalets). This is a raspberry-flavored vegetarian formula that includes:

Vitamin A	5,000 USPU
Vitamin D	400 USPU
Vitamin E	5 IU
Vitamin C (sodium ascorbate)	60 milligrams
Vitamin B_1 (thiamine HCL)	2.5 milligrams
Vitamin B_2 (riboflavin)	0.9 milligrams
Niacinamide	20 milligrams
Vitamin B_6 (pyridoxine)	2 milligrams
Vitamin B_{12} (cyanocobalamin)	5 micrograms
Calcium pantothenate	3 milligrams
Biotin	25 micrograms
Iron (fumerate)	10 milligrams
Manganese gluconate	1.0 milligrams
Calcium phosphate	200 milligrams

Other excellent formulas for infants and older babies are available from Babyco. (See Resources list in Appendix B.)

Remember, no amount of supplementing can compensate for poor food habits. Administration of concentrated nutrients is a secondary (but necessary) effort to improve your nutrition during lactation. Animals malnourished during the period from birth to weaning, no matter how superb their subsequent nourishment, remain small for the rest of their lives.[52] That's just one consequence of undernourishment.

After extensive research, including interviews with scientists and physicians who specialize in pediatrics, we have discovered that most of the studies regarding breast milk and nutrition have yet to be done. But the nutrition-aware experts are in full agreement, based on their clinical experience: *nourish the mother, thereby the baby.*

COMPENDIUM

Breast-fed infants can be malnourished if

Mother's nutrition during pregnancy was inadequate
Mother's nutrition during lactation is inadequate
They are not exposed to sunlight and do not get sufficient vitamin D

Nutritional deficiencies

Can be partial
Are nonspecific in early stages
Can be without overt symptoms

Water-soluble vitamins

Are not stored by the body (except B_{12})
Affect the quality of human milk
Have little functional similarity
Are widely distributed in same sources
Are interdependent

Fat-soluble vitamins

Are stored in body
Are absorbed with fats
Regulate and manufacture protein
May be affected in human milk by mother's diet
Are affected in human milk by length of lactation

Minerals

Are interrelated
May be affected in human milk by supplements
May be affected in human milk by diet

Concentrated food supplements include

Brewer's yeast, which

    increases milk production
    contributes to well-being
    contains B vitamins
    contains nucleic acids
    should be taken in small doses at first
    is significant only if taken in large amounts
    contains different bacteria strain than those causing yeast infections

Desiccated liver, which

    is important for quality breast milk
    contains bioavailable iron

is high in B vitamins
is a good source of iron, B_{12}, vitamins A, C, and D, and minerals

DHA (or omega 3), which is

important for brain development
important for retinal development
depleted in food refining
related to mother's diet in breast milk
a base for niacin and other B vitamins
in short supply in average American diet
a relaxant

GLA (or omega 6), which is

commonly in short supply in average American diet
not converted when in competition with processed foods
available and recommended in supplemental form
depleted in hyperactive children

Cod-liver oil, which is recommended as an important daily supplement

Carrot-grown acidophilus, which

provides healthful bacteria
crowds out infectious bacteria
is recommended as supplementation

Herbal/botanical support, such as

alfalfa (increases milk supply and provides vitamin K and trace minerals)
nettle (reactivates disappearing milk and reduces allergic responses)

Vitamin supplements for mother

Are recommended at levels based on average requirements
Improve nutrient values in breast milk

Vitamin supplements for baby

May be necessary if child is ill

Are not usually necessary, except for vitamin D, required if
baby lives in cloudy, cold area
baby is always covered when outdoors

LACTATION NUTRIENT REFERENCE CHART

The following chart is a reference list of known nutrients.* It enables you to tell at a glance how the foods and supplements you consume influence the breast milk you produce. Sources for each specific nutrient are designated and biological functions are explained. We have included information concerning nutrient depletion caused by harmful methods of food storage or preparation, the kinds of foods or additives that detract or inhibit nutrient utilization, and how your personal environment may contribute to deficiencies. The effects of deficiencies are noted, and situations that require special attention are indicated. Finally, the status of each nutrient in human milk is described.

Note that foods other than those cited may contain some of the nutrients listed. We have included as sources only foods that are beneficial for the breast-feeding process.

VITAMINS

VITAMIN A

SOURCES	Liver, fish-liver oils, kidney, eggs, yogurt; provitamin sources: carrots, apricots, broccoli, cantaloupe, parsley, other yellow vegetables, leafy greens
FUNCTION	Fights infection, maintains mucous membranes, repairs cells, necessary for protein metabolism and night vision
ANTAGONISTS	Air pollutants, exposure to glare or strong light, mineral oil, high temperatures
DEFICIENCIES	Can cause poor growth, anemia, blindness, dry skin, faulty tooth development, mental retardation
SPECIAL NEEDS	Helpful for lactation and pregnancy, women on oral contraceptives, stress

*The nutrient fluoride is intentionally omitted because we strongly oppose fluoride supplementation.

IN HUMAN MILK   Usually in short supply; dependent on mother's diet; colostrum contains twice as much as mature milk; supplementation helpful in raising status

VITAMIN B$_1$ (*Thiamin*)

SOURCES   Brewer's yeast, organ meats, whole grains, fish, fruits, eggs, legumes, nuts and seeds, green vegetables

FUNCTION   Helps maintain health of nerves and heart muscle, promotes growth and repair, helps create food energy

ANTAGONISTS   Caffeine, stress, food additives (particularly nitrites and sulfites), baking soda, air pollution, alcohol, refined carbohydrates, antibiotics, overcooking, high temperatures, milling of grains, food preparation, antacids

DEFICIENCIES   Can cause insufficient carbohydrate oxidation with accumulation of lactic acid, loss of appetite, insomnia, irritability, impairment of cardiovascular and nervous systems, fatigue, weight loss, poor reflexes, memory loss, edema

SPECIAL NEEDS   Helpful for lactation and pregnancy, fever, allergy, cardiac problems, recovery from surgery

IN HUMAN MILK   Levels increase with duration of lactation; deficient in diets largely based on polished rice; increased deficiency in lower socioeconomic status

VITAMIN B$_2$ (*Riboflavin*)

SOURCES   Organ meats, fish, brewer's yeast, eggs, leafy greens, broccoli, yogurt, whole grains, legumes, intestinal bacterial flora

FUNCTION   Significant in newborn in whom intestinal tract bacterial synthesis is minimal; aids in growth, vision, and metabolism; necessary in release of energy; helps regulate hormones; helps in wound healing

ANTAGONISTS   Antibiotics, the Pill, light, increased protein in diet

DEFICIENCIES   Can cause lesions of lips, mouth, eyes, skin, and genitals; fatigue; loss of appetite; severe personality disturbances; anxiety; digestive upset; hypertension; photophobia; seborrheic dermatitis at nose and scrotum; magenta tongue

SPECIAL NEEDS — Helpful for lactation and pregnancy, increased protein in diet, liver damage

IN HUMAN MILK — Good source if maternal diet is adequate; correlates in quantity with mother's diet; deficits corrected with supplementation

VITAMIN B₃ (*Niacin*)

SOURCES — Liver, poultry, halibut, legumes, whole grains, butter, yeast, nuts

FUNCTION — Converts food to energy, aids nervous system, necessary for metabolism of protein and carbohydrates, aids digestion of fats, involved in more than forty enzymatic reactions, helps wound healing

ANTAGONISTS — Alcohol, stress, antibiotics, high corn diets, the Pill

DEFICIENCIES — Can cause pellagra, dermatitis, gastrointestinal and central nervous system disorders, diarrhea, irritability, headache, memory loss, loss of appetite, insomnia, red and painful tongue

SPECIAL NEEDS — Helpful for associated B₆ deficiency, stress

IN HUMAN MILK — Values increase over time; generally better levels with higher socioeconomic status

VITAMIN B₅ (*Pantothenic Acid*)

SOURCES — Organ meats, eggs, nuts, legumes, whole grains, broccoli, cauliflower, cabbage

FUNCTION — Proper red blood cell production; important for synthesis of essential body fat, including cholesterol; important in stress and adrenal function; necessary for synthesis of antibodies

ANTAGONISTS — Insecticide fumigants used in storing foods, stress, alcohol, dry heat, acid or alkali medium, high-temperature frying, freezing

DEFICIENCIES — Can cause infection, loss of appetite, apathy, depression, constipation, neuromotor disorders, fatigue, sleep disorders, abdominal pain, impaired adrenal function, tingling of hands and feet, muscle cramps, impaired coordination, loss of antibody production

SPECIAL NEEDS — Helpful for lactation and pregnancy, healing of wounds or infections, marginal diabetes, stress

IN HUMAN MILK — Quantities affected by mother's diet; amounts decrease as lactation progresses; additional quantities required for lactation

VITAMIN B$_6$ (*Pyridoxine*)

SOURCES	Liver, poultry, whole grains, eggs, yeast, soybeans, walnuts, cantaloupe, leafy greens, bananas, prunes, raisins, herring, salmon
FUNCTION	Involved in metabolism of nerve tissue, necessary for synthesis of protein, important for red blood cells and antibodies, essential to healthy teeth and gums, regulates body fluids and almost all enzymatic reactions
ANTAGONISTS	High-protein diet, marijuana, milling of grains, high temperatures, food processing, light, alkalis, cortisone, the Pill, blood-pressure medication, penicillamine, alcohol
DEFICIENCIES	Can cause anemia; neuronal disorders; dermatitis of the eyes, nose, mouth, and back of ears; edema; depression; kidney stones
SPECIAL NEEDS	Helpful for lactation and pregnancy; faulty blood, nerve, or growth development in infancy; those on the Pill; increased fat or protein in diet
IN HUMAN MILK	Usually inadequate; acutely affected by dietary sources; increased levels in higher socioeconomic status; must be supplied daily because virtually no storage in mother's body

VITAMIN B$_{12}$ (*Cobalamin*)

SOURCES	Liver, kidney, fish, shellfish, eggs, crab, oysters, algae, tempeh, intestinal bacterial fermentation
FUNCTION	Unique role in cell replication; necessary for bone marrow, nervous system, and myelin formation; contributes to integrity of gastrointestinal tract and red blood cells; prevents certain forms of anemia; assists in synthesis of nucleic acids (RNA and DNA); needed for normal blood ascorbic levels
ANTAGONISTS	Aspirin and aspirin substitutes, codeine, the Pill, alcohol, heat (especially severe heating of meat), nitrous oxide, poor vegetarian diet, surgery
DEFICIENCIES	Can cause pernicious anemia, nervous disorders, disrupted carbohydrate metabolism, memory loss,

paranoia, ataxia (interference with bodily movements)

SPECIAL NEEDS   Helpful for poor vegetarian diets, surgery, those on the Pill, eye problems, those with inadequate stomach absorption, liver disease

IN HUMAN MILK   Adequate amounts in well-nourished mothers; requirements high when baby's growth is rapid; inadequate levels on poor vegetarian diet, but more than adequate on real-foods vegetarian diet; amounts increase significantly after supplementation; drained through malnutrition

VITAMIN C

SOURCES   Acerola berries, rose hips, berries, cantaloupe, tomatoes, potatoes, papaya, parsley, peppers, cabbage, green vegetables (raw or minimally cooked), black currants

FUNCTION   Part of enzyme and hormone systems and intracellular chemical reactions, essential to collagen synthesis, regulates amino acid metabolism, potentiates iron absorption, antihistamine effect, heals wounds and burns, functions as antioxidant

ANTAGONISTS   Improper food preparation, exposure to air and heat, storage and processing, cortisone, the Pill, air pollution, industrial toxins, smoking, alcohol, aspirin, anticoagulants, antidepressants, diuretics, copper, stress

DEFICIENCIES   Can cause scurvy, bacterial infection, cell deterioration, bruising, edema, hemorrhaging, tooth and gum problems, anemia, lethargy, sudden infant death syndrome, delayed wound healing

SPECIAL NEEDS   Helpful for lactation and pregnancy, stress, smoking, infections, burns, infant growth

IN HUMAN MILK   Dependent on mother's diet but does not increase further when mother takes more than 1,000 grams; widespread marginal deficits; greater quantities required than indicated by recommended daily allowances

VITAMIN D

SOURCES   Sunshine, liver, fish-liver oils, eggs, yeast, shrimp, salmon, avocados

FUNCTION   Aids calcium absorption, kidney function, heart action, nervous system, and blood clotting

ANTAGONISTS   Laxatives, antacids, cortisone, inadequate sunshine, aflatoxins (mold found on nuts)

DEFICIENCIES   Can cause skeletal malformation, rickets, osteoporosis, tooth problems, fluoride toxicity, diminished muscle tone

SPECIAL NEEDS   Helpful for lactation and pregnancy, heavy metal toxicity, lack of sunlight

IN HUMAN MILK   Appears in both fat and water fractions; higher in colostrum than mature milk; supplementation recommended where sunshine not available; deficiency reduces quantity and quality of milk

VITAMIN E

SOURCES   Whole grains, eggs, avocados, sweet potatoes, leafy greens, asparagus, broccoli, cabbage, yeast, nuts

FUNCTION   Aids in muscle integrity, necessary for red blood cells, protects against air pollution, helps to withstand stress, protects essential fatty acids, helps intestinal absorption of fat, prevents topical scar formation, acts as antioxidant

ANTAGONISTS   Food processing, rancid fats and oils, inorganic iron, the Pill, mineral oil, thyroid hormone, oxidizing agents

DEFICIENCIES   Can cause reproductive disorders, anemia, red cell destruction in premature infants

SPECIAL NEEDS   Helpful for lactation and pregnancy, increased polyunsaturated fat intake, air pollution, stress, burns, menopause, increased E (the more you take, the less efficient the absorption), premature infants, anemia

IN HUMAN MILK   Levels rise quickly at birth; requirement related to polyunsaturated fatty acid of mother's diet; acts to protect polyunsaturated fatty acids against rancidity; prevents hemolytic anemia and myopathy; amount usually adequate; the smaller the infant, the greater the degree of deficiency at birth, but term infants attain normal values; in greater quantity in colostrum and transitional milk than in mature milk and cow's milk

VITAMIN K

SOURCES	Leafy greens, alfalfa, eggs, intestinal bacterial flora, cauliflower, cabbage
FUNCTION	Important for blood clotting, implicated in mineral transport
ANTAGONISTS	Aspirin, aspirin substitutes, mineral oil, anticoagulants, antibiotics, sulfonamides
DEFICIENCIES	Can cause prolonged blood coagulation time, increased incidence of hemorrhage
SPECIAL NEEDS	Helpful for women in labor, infancy, surgery, major medical problems, celiac disease
IN HUMAN MILK	Present in small quantities; larger amounts produced by intestinal flora several days after birth; most women are not sufficiently nourished to supply adequate amounts the first few days of baby's life; administered at birth in most hospitals; not known whether human milk facilitates absorption or promotes growth of flora

BIOFLAVONOIDS

SOURCES	Red peppers, tomatoes, apricots, rhubarb, buckwheat, onions with colored skins, grapes, black currants, cherries, cantaloupes, rose hips
FUNCTION	Strengthens artery walls, maintains blood capillaries, effective in treating cardiovascular disease, helpful for viral and bacterial infections, aids fungal infections, serves as antioxidant, has anti-inflammatory activity
ANTAGONISTS	Air pollution, industrial toxins, smoking, alcohol, anticoagulants
DEFICIENCIES	Can cause edema, spontaneous hemorrhaging, bruising, inflammation of mucous membranes
SPECIAL NEEDS	Helpful for reproduction, menstruation, bruises, hemorrhoids, varicose veins, smoking
IN HUMAN MILK	Not established; possibly similar to actions of vitamin C

BIOTIN

SOURCES	Brewer's yeast, liver and other organ meats, mushrooms, corn, eggs, legumes, nuts (especially peanuts), intestinal flora, cauliflower

FUNCTION | Metabolizes fats; releases energy from carbohydrates and proteins; maintains bone, bone marrow, sweat glands, skin, nerve tissue, blood cells, and hair tones

ANTAGONISTS | Raw egg white (avedin), choline, antibiotics, sulfonamides, processed food

DEFICIENCIES | Can cause mild skin disorders, lassitude, anorexia, anemia, muscle pain, nausea, depression, high cholesterol, alopecia, conjunctivitis

SPECIAL NEEDS | Helpful for dry hair, those on antibiotics, those consuming large quantities of raw egg whites

IN HUMAN MILK | If deficient, delayed infant motor development; readily made by intestinal bacteria

CHOLINE

SOURCES | Lecithin, eggs, liver, brains, legumes, leafy greens, brewer's yeast, whole grains

FUNCTION | Helps fat and cholesterol metabolism, aids in nerve impulse transmission, helpful in preventing arteriosclerosis

ANTAGONISTS | Water, food processing, alcohol, sulfa drugs

DEFICIENCIES | Can cause loss of memory, anemia, heart and circulatory disease, muscle weakness, chronic liver disease, cirrhosis, toxic exposures

SPECIAL NEEDS | Helpful for high cholesterol levels, weak or thin nails, lactation and pregnancy, circulatory problems, toxic exposures

IN HUMAN MILK | Important in support of early growth; has cholesterol-lowering effect for both mother and baby, which is advantageous

FOLIC ACID

SOURCES | Leafy greens, asparagus, whole grains, nuts, legumes, yeast, liver, kidney, intestinal bacterial flora, broccoli

FUNCTION | Works with B_{12} in production of red blood cells, aids metabolism and development of nerve cells and cell division, helps skin, acts as antidepressant, involved in production of choline and methionine, maintains intestinal activities, essential for nucleic acid production

ANTAGONISTS | Alcohol, stress, the Pill, sulfonamides, aspirin, anticonvulsant drugs, air, light, moderate heat, processing, storage at room temperature

DEFICIENCIES | Can cause certain anemias, inflamed tongue, depression, nervousness, cell and tissue disruptions

SPECIAL NEEDS | Helpful for lactation and pregnancy, psoriasis, cancer, blood disorders, those on the Pill, intestinal problems, depression, low white cell count, sickle cell disease

IN HUMAN MILK | Along with B_6 and B_{12}, increases significantly after supplementation; increases milk flow; more easily absorbed from milk than other food sources

INOSITOL

SOURCES | Whole grains, organ meats, brewer's yeast, seeds, nuts, lecithin, vegetables, fruits

FUNCTION | Involved in reactions controlling metabolism of fats, necessary for brain metabolism, lowers cholesterol, regulates oil glands

ANTAGONISTS | Antibiotics, mineral oil, diarrhea, cholesterol, pesticides, water, food processing, caffeine, toxic chemical exposure, alcohol

DEFICIENCIES | Can cause hardening of the arteries, fatty degeneration of liver; may be related to nerve damage of muscular dystrophy

SPECIAL NEEDS | Helpful for heavy caffeine users, toxic chemical exposure, heart conditions

IN HUMAN MILK | Important in support of baby's early growth; has cholesterol-lowering effect

PABA (*Para-Aminobenzoic Acid*)

SOURCES | Brewer's yeast, whole grains, yogurt, liver and other organ meats, seeds, nuts, leafy greens

FUNCTION | Protects against rancidity, aids in utilization of proteins, aids in formation of red blood cells, regulates oil glands, blocks sun

ANTAGONISTS | Food processing, alcohol, estrogen, sulfonamides

DEFICIENCIES | Can cause some anemias, skin disorders

SPECIAL NEEDS | Helpful for excessive sun exposure, vitiligo and other skin conditions, burns, high-protein diet, ozone toxicity

IN HUMAN MILK | As with all B-complex nutrients, amount contingent on mother's diet

MINERALS

CALCIUM

SOURCES	Yogurt, shellfish, eggs, sardines, salmon with bones, soybeans, tofu, leafy greens, broccoli, kale, bone marrow, bone
FUNCTION	Major regulator of bone growth, helps regulate many body processes, aids in blood clotting, regulates heart rhythm, contributes to vitality and endurance, involved in contraction and relaxation of muscles, essential for nervous function, buffer for acid/alkaline balance
ANTAGONISTS	High-phosphorus diet, high-protein diet, stress, inactivity, magnesium deficiency, vitamin D deficiency, cortisone, antacids containing aluminum, laxatives, diuretics, aging, anticonvulsants
DEFICIENCIES	Can cause osteoporosis, tooth problems, heart palpitations, menstrual cramps, hypertension
SPECIAL NEEDS	Helpful for lactation and pregnancy, smokers, inactive people
IN HUMAN MILK	Levels vary widely in well-fed women, but concentration in milk doesn't change; large amounts drained from mother to support infant; long-term shortage causes economy of usage; amount in milk independent of mother's diet, but required by mother for replacement; significant amount found in fat fraction of breast milk; absorbed more readily than from other milks, perhaps because of high lactose content

CHROMIUM

SOURCES	Brewer's yeast, black pepper and other condiments, liver, whole grains
FUNCTION	Important in insulin metabolism and glucose conversion, involved in synthesis of fatty acids and cholesterol in liver, associated with RNA
ANTAGONISTS	Air pollution, stress, food refining, average American diet (this is the only country with chromium deficiencies), glucose metabolism problems, high cholesterol levels
DEFICIENCIES	Can cause diabetes, hypoglycemia, atherosclerosis,

retarded growth, high cholesterol levels, aortic plaques, corneal opacification

SPECIAL NEEDS — Helpful for low–birth weight infants, glucose metabolism problems (diabetes or hypoglycemia), high cholesterol levels

IN HUMAN MILK — Term infants start life with substantial amounts; tissue levels decrease through childhood; little is known about status during early beginnings except that it is lower in premature infants

COPPER

SOURCES — Oysters, liver, nuts, legumes, avocados, leafy greens, seaweed, raisins, blueberries, whole grains, fish

FUNCTION — Helps form myelin sheath, involved in RNA production, calms nerves, involved in storage of iron to form hemoglobin, necessary for blood cell production, contributes to bone formation, vital to enzyme system

ANTAGONISTS — Excess zinc, calcium, cadmium, iron (competition from other minerals); intravenous feeding

DEFICIENCIES — Can cause pernicious anemia, respiratory problems, retarded growth, edema, bone demineralization (until recently, deficiency was rare)

SPECIAL NEEDS — Helpful for premature infants, intravenous feeding, tropical and nontropical sprue

IN HUMAN MILK — Levels fall as lactation progresses; not clear what proper levels should be; significant amount found in fat fraction of breast milk; better absorbed than from cow's milk

IODINE

SOURCES — Seaweed and other plants grown near the sea, seafood, mushrooms, fish-liver oil (negative sources are iodized salt, sea salt, drugs, food additives)

FUNCTION — Necessary for proper function of thyroid (which regulates rate of oxidation within cells); essential for proper growth, energy, and metabolism; needed to convert carotene to vitamin A; important for metabolism of all nutrients

ANTAGONISTS — Lithium, PCBs (polychlorinated biphenyl, toxic environmental pollutants)

DEFICIENCIES — Can cause apathy, sensitivity to cold, goiter, thyroid cancer, metabolic problems, enlargement of thyroid, increased weight, thickening of skin, lethargy, hair loss, mental retardation

SPECIAL NEEDS Helpful for lactation and pregnancy, people living in iodine-deficient areas, patients on lithium

IN HUMAN MILK Dependent on mother's dietary content

IRON

SOURCES Liver, legumes, whole grains, potatoes, eggs, leafy greens, oysters and other shellfish, blackstrap molasses, seaweed, nuts, cherries, tofu

FUNCTION Required in manufacture of hemoglobin; helps carry oxygen to blood; important in protein metabolism, bone growth, disease resistance, and preventing fatigue

ANTAGONISTS Zinc, excess phosphorus, coffee, tea, bleeding, intestinal parasites, lack of hydrochloric acid, antacids, oxalates, phytates, high protein

DEFICIENCIES Can cause anemia, weakness, fatigue, headaches, palpitation, heartburn, colitis, leukemia

SPECIAL NEEDS Helpful for lactation and pregnancy, nosebleeds (or any blood loss), excessive menstruation, rapid growth; consumption of iron-rich foods essential for mother, especially after three months of nursing

IN HUMAN MILK Easily absorbed by baby, perhaps because of milk's high lactose and vitamin C levels; contains anti-infective properties; deficiency not usual in breast-fed babies; supply reduced after three to six months of feeding, and continues to drop as lactation proceeds; amount in milk not affected by mother's diet, but required by her to replace her stores; is not helped by iron supplementation (supplements are not usually well absorbed and may have unpleasant side effects); purely breast-fed infants show no iron deficiency at six months, and even at twelve to eighteen months; significant amounts of iron found in fat fraction of breast milk; bioavailability superior to that of other milk

MAGNESIUM

SOURCES Dates, leafy greens, figs, nuts, whole grains, molasses, seaweed, legumes, seeds, fish, raisins, miso, beans, tofu, buckwheat, avocado, banana, potatoes, spinach

FUNCTION   Involved with brain and spinal cord, necessary for enzyme energy conversions, required for calcium and vitamin C metabolism, vital to carbohydrate metabolism, important component of bones and tooth enamel, helpful for neuro-muscular contractions, may protect against sudden infant death syndrome

ANTAGONISTS   Alcohol, diuretics, high cholesterol levels, high calcium, high phosphorus, barbiturates, anxiety

DEFICIENCIES   Can cause tooth problems, muscle tensions, bone problems, accelerated heartbeat, exhaustion, kidney stones, convulsions, ear noises, loss of hearing, dizziness; linked to sudden infant death syndrome

SPECIAL NEEDS   Helpful for lactation and pregnancy, recurrent spontaneous abortion, low–birth weight infants, anxiety, alcoholism, arterial edema

IN HUMAN MILK   Usually deficient; supplementation suggested

MANGANESE

SOURCES   Nuts, whole grains, legumes, tea, cloves, sweet potatoes, eggs, leafy greens, carrots, beets, celery, liver, pineapple

FUNCTION   Synthesizes fatty acids and cholesterol; involved in growth; activates enzymes; aids in utilization of vitamins B_1 and E; important to brain, pancreas, heart, spleen, bones, and lymph fluids; essential to central nervous system

ANTAGONISTS   High calcium-phosphorus ratio, bran, food refining, hydralazine (hypertensive drug)

DEFICIENCIES   Can cause ataxia (lack of muscle coordination), diabetes, hearing loss, convulsions, glandular disorders, growth retardation, infertility, skeletal disorders, disturbed fat metabolism, disturbed blood clotting, mild dermatitis

SPECIAL NEEDS   Helpful for lactation and pregnancy, professional athletes; essential for any woman who has been on the Pill

IN HUMAN MILK   Reduced if oral contraceptives used prior to conception; levels decrease slightly as lactation progresses

MOLYBDENUM

SOURCES	Yogurt, legumes, organ meats, grains, leafy greens
FUNCTION	Promotes growth, mobilizes release of iron from liver stores, helps prevent cavities
ANTAGONISTS	Food refining, milling of grains, sulfur, copper, tungsten
DEFICIENCIES	Can cause decreased liver and intestinal enzyme activity, lethal defect in sulfur metabolism
SPECIAL NEEDS	Helpful for anemia, poor dentition (those with lots of cavities), gouty arthritis
IN HUMAN MILK	Very little known to date

PHOSPHORUS

SOURCES	Whole grains, leafy greens, seaweed, poultry, legumes, nuts and seeds, fish, organ meats, eggs, brewer's yeast (negative sources include almost all processed or canned meats — hot dogs, ham, bacon — processed cheeses, baked products using phosphate baking powder, soft drinks, instant soups and puddings, phosphate food additives)
FUNCTION	Works with calcium and vitamin D to give strength and rigidity to bones and teeth; important in muscle and nerve function; essential in all cell metabolism and cell repair; has more functions than any other mineral element
ANTAGONISTS	Magnesium, iron, sugar, fats, aluminum, antacids
DEFICIENCIES	Can cause bone and tooth problems, fatigue, nervousness, loss of appetite or overweight
SPECIAL NEEDS	Helpful for sepsis (poisoning), Reye's syndrome
IN HUMAN MILK	Concentrations change rapidly; may become a limiting factor in older breast-fed infants

POTASSIUM

SOURCES	Bananas, oranges, fruit, meat, fish, poultry, cereals, vegetables, seaweed, nuts and seeds, legumes
FUNCTION	Works with sodium to maintain body fluids; involved in nervous and muscular systems; necessary for normal muscle tone, nerves, heart action, and enzyme reactions; aids glucose absorption; aids growth

ANTAGONISTS | Excessive sweating, caffeine, stress, alcohol, laxatives, diuretics, sugar, salt, high cholesterol levels, diarrhea

DEFICIENCIES | Can cause edema, high blood pressure, nervousness, depressed heartbeat, insomnia, constipation, impaired glucose metabolism, general weakness, poor reflexes, acne

SPECIAL NEEDS | Helpful for heavy physical exertion, sweating in hot environments, diarrhea, excessive vomiting, hypertension

IN HUMAN MILK | Sodium-potassium ratio is more crucial at this stage of baby's life than at any other time; level in milk decreases with ongoing lactation

SELENIUM

SOURCES | Brewer's yeast, organ meats, seafood, whole grains, brown rice, garlic, cabbage, eggs, broccoli, tomatoes, onions

FUNCTION | Used in protein matrix of teeth, helps maintain liver and muscle function, important for tissue elasticity, acts as antioxidant of fats, contributes to growth and hair, may protect against cancer and heart disease

ANTAGONISTS | Mercury, cadmium, air pollution

DEFICIENCIES | Can cause growth retardation, cancer, arteriosclerosis, cataract formation, toxicity of oxidants, liver damage

SPECIAL NEEDS | Helpful for those who live in low-selenium areas, any antioxidant needs, toxic metal poisoning, infertility, radiation toxicity

IN HUMAN MILK | Dependent on mother's diet; varies with amount in soil; levels at three months are within recommended limits only in breast-fed infants; content is higher in hindmilk (milk released in latter part of a feeding)

SODIUM

SOURCES | Seafoods, poultry, leafy greens, kelp, vegetables (negative sources include salt shaker, processed foods, smoked meats, soft water)

FUNCTION | Important for bone mineralization during first year of life, maintains normal fluid levels in cells and osmotic pressure of fluids outside the cell, necessary for muscle contractions, vital for acid/alkaline balance

ANTAGONISTS   Hot weather, dehydration, diuretics

DEFICIENCIES   Can cause alkalosis, muscle cramps, nausea, edema, high blood pressure, irritability, intestinal gas, weight loss, impaired conversion of carbohydrates into fats, weakness, lassitude, aches in skeletal muscles (chronic sodium deficiency is uncommon)

SPECIAL NEEDS Helpful for diarrhea, vomiting, fever, any fluid loss, intense perspiration, adrenal cortical insufficiency

IN HUMAN MILK Reaches low levels in a few months; when sodium level changes, potassium level changes; breast-fed babies adapt easily to low-sodium diets; too much sodium is not beneficial; amount contingent on mother's dietary intake, but values don't vary significantly unless very low

VANADIUM

SOURCES   Fish, vegetable oils, fats, whole grains, water

FUNCTION   Can substitute for molybdenum in certain processes, works with zinc in cell reproduction, helps prevent tooth decay, influences metabolism of fats, may reduce excess sodium levels, depresses manufacture of cholesterol and triglycerides, necessary for normal infant growth

ANTAGONISTS   Food processing

DEFICIENCIES   Can cause slow healing, hair loss, premature aging, excessively lowered cholesterol

SPECIAL NEEDS Helpful for lowering cholesterol

IN HUMAN MILK Research incomplete

ZINC

SOURCES   Oysters, herring, liver and other organ meats, eggs, brewer's yeast, legumes, nuts and seeds, paprika, whole grains, mushrooms, leafy greens

FUNCTION   Many diverse functions, ranging from manufacture of DNA to wound healing; facilitates release of vitamin A stores; necessary for normal skeletal growth and repair of body tissues; important to brain, thyroid, liver, kidney, hair, skin, prostate, and phosphorus metabolism; nearly every function depends on an adequate supply

ANTAGONISTS   Unleavened bread, grain processing, high phytates, oral contraceptives, parasites, alcohol, excess calcium, iron supplements

DEFICIENCIES   Can cause slow healing, retarded growth, baldness, delayed sexual maturation, fatigue, decreased alertness, retarded mental development, stretch marks during pregnancy, white spots on fingernails, sterility, loss of smell and taste senses

SPECIAL NEEDS   Helpful for healing wounds, burns, surgical incisions (will help heal episiotomy); poor appetite; failing smell and taste sensations; growth failure

IN HUMAN MILK   Levels are lower than normal after three months of breast-feeding (attributed to insufficient intake by mother); iron supplements reduce absorption; helps induce flow of milk; deficiency exists in most lactating women and in most human milk, but superior bioavailability from breast milk; found in fat fraction of milk; better absorbed than from cow's milk

CHAPTER
～ 6 ～

Keeping Contaminants at Bay

IN WHICH WE DISCUSS

drugs — medical and recreational — and other ingested hazardous substances

THE QUESTIONS:

"Will the drug be excreted in my milk?"
"Will my baby be at risk?"
"Will the adverse effect, if there is one, be serious?"
"Is the damage reversible?"
"Will the benefit outweigh the risk?"

THE ANSWERS:

Yes.
Maybe.
Perhaps, but maybe not.
Sometimes.
Maybe, but perhaps not.

Most drugs and unnatural substances wend their way from a mother's bloodstream to her breast milk. But there are safety valves.

*Only within the moment of time represented
by the present century has one species —
human — acquired significant power to alter
the nature of the world.*

— RACHEL CARSON

Once upon a time, but not too long ago, breast-feeding women were given cause for alarm. They were told that chemicals leaped into their breast milk at will and endangered their babies. Overlooked was the fact that drugs and environmental contaminants are also present in milk from nonhuman sources. Or in any food product selected to feed their infants. Nothing and no one escapes. Breast-feeders, however, have two advantages. Their babies have the best possible defense system *because* they are breast-fed, and their mothers can exert control over some of the ensnaring hazards.

It is an established fact that toxins enter your breast milk. Some you take yourself; others are thrust upon you. Among contaminants you appropriate of your own volition may be some you are unaware of. The inadvertent transfer of harmful substances from you to milk to baby can be insidious. These poisons are almost always eliminated from milk more slowly than they are from blood.[1]

PRESCRIBED AND OVER-THE-COUNTER DRUGS

A doctor may advise you to wean your baby because of a categorical need you have for drug intake. The decision to curtail breast-feeding should not be made lightly. Your baby has a savage disregard for your needs. Sudden weaning will have that child asking in wordless (but most expressive) language, "What happened?" An infant views change as betrayal. Temporary weaning may place your baby at risk of infections after milk withdrawal. The baby may develop allergies from artificial feeding.

Needless to say, if you're on the sick list, therapy for cure must be considered. But don't let anyone force your hand. Nature provides many relay systems. Embrace that fact with joy, and ask your doctor these questions:

"What are the consequences if I do nothing?"

"Is there another way I can be helped exclusive of taking drugs?"

"What are my chances for getting better if I take a reduced dose of the drug?"

"Do you know how the drug will affect my baby?"

"How long will I have to remain on the drug?"

"Will you have your laboratory check my milk for drug concentrations?"

If your doctor cannot find a less harmful solution, you may want to get a second opinion.

Obviously, ongoing therapy or more potent medications are usually more deleterious than minor remedies administered briefly. But not all drugs are dose-related. Allergic drug reactions are often unpredictable, having nothing to do with quantity.

Immediate adverse effects are more easily recognizable, whereas long-term damage is often difficult to define. And the small-dosage concept, although convenient, could be dangerous because of oversimplification. Everyone remembers the tragedy of thalidomide, the "harmless" nausea-suppressing pregnancy drug of a few decades ago that caused serious birth defects.

You can assume that some level of excretion into your milk will occur with most drugs. Although there is a paucity of knowledge on the subject, we are beginning to accrue bits and pieces. A summary of some of the known drug effects follows.

AMPHETAMINES

If you want your baby to be jittery, have tremors, and wake frequently, try dieting with amphetamines while you are breast-feeding.[2] For a regimen that will benefit both you and your baby, depend on primal foods and the breast-feeding process for weight loss.

ANALGESICS

Aspirin is the most common among drugs used to relieve pain. Aspirin penetrates mother's milk, causing intestinal bleeding tendencies in both mother and baby.[3] If you must take aspirin (assuming the natural pain-relief bag of tricks suggested later in the chapter has failed), ask your pediatrician about adequate vitamin K stores for your child. Include vitamin K foods in your diet, listed in the Lactation Nutrient Reference Chart at the end of Chapter 5.

ANTIBIOTICS

Antibiotics are drugs that destroy or inhibit microorganisms. They, too, enter breast milk. Antibiotics affect the normal flora of the gastrointestinal tract, thereby affecting the immune system. To restore the natural, healthful flora, anyone taking antibiotics is urged to eat yogurt or acidophilus.

Penicillin appears to be safe initially, but problems may arise as a result of this exposure when your baby is older.[4] Allergic reactions to the drug are common. Tetracycline, another antibiotic, causes discoloration of baby's teeth. The devastating aftermath of antibiotics is so severe that mothers for whom they are a necessity are told to discontinue breast-feeding for the duration of therapy. They are advised to express and discard their milk until the drug is withdrawn.

ANTICOAGULANTS

Some drugs that delay or prevent blood clotting are transferable to your nursing baby, others are not. Check with your physician, or do the research yourself. Every library has a *Physician's Desk Reference*, which includes information on excretions of drugs into human milk and their effect on the infant. Current labeling for prescription medicines carries warnings against use of the product whenever the potential for harm during lactation has been determined.

DIURETICS

From the point of view of the mother, the major concern with drugs that increase secretion and flow of urine is their power to decrease or even suppress lactation.[5] The effect on the baby could be dehydration and mineral loss.[6]

HORMONES

Preparations of substances normally secreted by glands of the body are agents that are almost always transferred to breast milk. And you are not the only carrier of these substances. See the report on meat later in this chapter.

Oral contraceptives should never be a partner to breast-feeding. The long-term effects have already been documented.[7] Estrogen-containing contraceptives diminish milk volume and alter milk composition. Feminization of male children has been reported.[8] Females may be affected fifteen to twenty years later, when they mature.

LAXATIVES

Drugs that relieve constipation contain ingredients (aloe, calomel, cascara, and danathron) believed to have an effect on baby's bowels.[9] Why consider a drug remedy when the cure may be as simple as a slight change in your breakfast habits? Several hints for relieving constipation appear later in this chapter.

SEDATIVES

Drugs that relax may soothe you and the baby — undesirably. Relaxants are definitely not to be used during lactation.[10] Try pleasant music, warm baths, massage, or meditation.

OTHER MEDICATIONS

Anticonvulsants, radiopharmaceuticals, psychotherapeutics, anti-neoplastics, cardiovascular agents, and other drugs for serious disease states are beyond the scope of this book. Check with your doctor.

Helpful Hints When Drugs Are Necessary

· Minimize reactions by carefully scheduling medication and feeding times. The concentration of the drug will be lowest just prior to repeating drug intake. So nurse, then dose. Don't dose and then feed.
· Consider these variables: frequency of nursing, your kidney function, other foods you have eaten, plus health and age of your baby. An older, healthy child can handle contaminants better than a younger, under-the-weather baby.
· If you have an allergic reaction, discontinue the drug at once.
· Look for these symptoms in your baby: fever, nausea, increased activity, lethargy. (Your baby may also experience dizziness or headache, but how would you know?)
· Don't be taken in by reports of "minimal secretion into breast milk." Despite seepage of only small amounts, significant accumulation could be the result of slow elimination from your baby.
· Consider drug-nutrient reactions. Refer to the chart at the end of this chapter.

SAFE HOME REMEDIES FOR COMMON PROBLEMS

YOU may be accustomed to magic-bullet cures. Here is an opportunity for you to learn about less invasive methods that could be used when you feel as though a butterfly collection was let loose in your stomach. Or fifty Boy Scouts tied knots in your colon. Or the Music Man's seventy-six trombones are parading in your head.

Headache

Headaches are often caused by tension. A warm bath or the simple relaxation techniques outlined in Chapter 3 could be helpful.

Traditional herbal remedies include peppermint, rosemary, or sage tea.

Calcium is a relaxant. Nutrition-oriented physicians recommend four to six calcium tablets, taken all at once, for headache relief. A single dose of six tablets often does the trick. If it doesn't, repeat in half an hour, but not more than twice.

A simple neck or body massage relieves the muscle pain of headache. For more persistent agony occurring with frequency, explore the possibility of acupressure or acupuncture. These ancient non-toxic methods of relief should not be left behind by the years. They can be very effective.

Herbal medicine books supply many recipes for liniments and ointments that help to reduce discomfort. They're worth trying before risking drugs.

CONSTIPATION

Improper diet is the main cause of constipation. People on primal-food diets (high fiber, complex carbohydrates) rarely suffer from this torment. There are subtractions and additions to your daily food intake that help if constipation persists. Avoid eating:

· overrefined and starchy foods — white bread, white rice, bakery products, and so forth — foods that you should have thrown overboard by now anyway
· hard-boiled eggs, cheese, meat, and milk
· hot drinks
· foods containing tannin — red wine, nonherbal teas, and cocoa
· iron supplements

Add to your diet:

· foods that absorb moisture readily — celery, radishes, carrots, lettuce
· foods that are slightly laxative — strawberries, watermelon
· lots of fluids
· herbs and other high-nutrient foods such as garlic (prescribed for constipation by Hippocrates); agar-agar, taken with lots of water (agar is extracted from a marine algae); herb teas, especially dandelion leaf, fern, caraway, chamomile, and golden seal (drink them at room temperature); brewer's yeast; rice polishings
· high-fiber foods such as vegetables and cereals
· fruits such as raw apples, pears, fresh pineapples, and the seeds of fresh figs
· grated carrots in a salad — an excellent anticonstipation measure
· foods with polyunsaturated oils — avocados, sunflower seeds, Protein-Aide sesame seeds, psyllium seeds, and flaxseeds
· acidophilus in capsule form, called carodophilus, carrot acidophilus, vegedophilus, or similar designations (check the label, which

should indicate carrots as source; carrot-grown acidophilus is discussed in Chapter 5)

Here are two effective anticonstipation recipes: (1) Three dried prunes soaked overnight in water with a splash of lemon juice. (2) Place in blender: 1 tablespoon pumpkin seeds, 2 ounces sesame seeds, 1 cup soaked raisins. Add enough warm water to make 1 quart; blend until smooth. Sip through the day.[11,12]

Because your milk may be affected by an overdose of any of these anticonstipation remedies, try moderate changes at first. The rebuttal to constipation may require no more effort than eating a small bowl of millet every day.

BACK PAIN

You may have back pains left over from your pregnancy, and new ones from lifting your baby. Have a family member — or a friend who cares — gently rub your back with two tennis balls placed in an old sock. If you are lucky enough to have a professional massage, ask your masseuse to use an alternative for oil. Rancid-free virgin oil is extinct, and you don't want the variety that has a bumper crop of preservatives. Oil penetrates skin.

Dry heat is often an effective measure for relaxing tight, sore muscles. Try an electric heating pad for twenty minutes.

Sleep on your back with a pillow placed under your knees, another at the nape of your neck, and one under each outstretched arm.

Contrast baths are glorious for back relief. Alternate hot and cold water in the shower: hot water at about 125 degrees for ten minutes, and cold water at about 55 degrees for five minutes. Wind up with a towel rub, preferably administered by the baby's father.

All of these measures help to strengthen muscles and to stimulate the natural analgesic responses in your body.

STOMACH UPSET

Bellyaches or indigestion (including diarrhea) are usually the result of poor eating habits, tension, or allergies. When you strike processed foods from your diet, especially very sweet and fatty foods, you eliminate a major cause of digestive disorders.

Before resorting to commercial aids, explore a nonallergenic, easy-to-digest food regimen for a few days. Such a diet includes millet, brown rice, buckwheat groats (kasha), buttermilk, sweet potatoes, string beans, tofu, deep-water fish, and viable yogurt. (Viable yogurt contains live bacteria. Many supermarket brands do not contain active strains of bacteria because of overprocessing. Homemade yogurt is ideal.) Meals made up of several (or even all) of these foods in small amounts, repeated a few hours apart, almost always relieve distress. (To clarify: two tablespoons *each* of nonallergenic foods can be consumed at one meal, and then eaten again — in the same limited quantities — three hours later.)

The outranking natural supplement for bellyache relief is acidophilus. Acidophilus culture grown on carrot juice works wonders. You may never need a digestive remedy again after adding this fermented food supplement to your regimen.

TOOTHACHE

There are several temporary measures that help relieve toothache torture. A drop or two of hot-pepper extract applied on cotton to a sore tooth was recommended in 1850 as an instant remedy. More than a century later, we understand why this works. The pungent agent of hot paprika or chili peppers is capsicum, which selectively stimulates and then blocks the sensitive sensory nerves of the skin and mucous membranes. The chemical structure of capsicum is similar to that of eugenol, the active substance in oil of cloves, which can also induce a long-lasting local anesthesia. Additional tricks for relieving toothache are: chewing on cloves from the condiment box and chewing on a vitamin E capsule. Another pain reliever is the application of aloe vera because of its anesthetic properties.[13] (Remember — you need a plant that's at least three years old.) And finally, Grandma's potato trick: place a slice of peeled potato on the affected area. Keep it there until the potato becomes warm; reapply.

VAGINITIS

Acidophilus culture comes to the rescue again. Double your usual dose while vaginitis is present, and also dissolve a capsule of carrot-grown acidophilus in a small amount of water and use as a douche. This procedure can be repeated several times a day. The topical and internal applications usually relieve the problem.

BREAST MILK AS HEALER FOR VARIOUS AND SUNDRY PROBLEMS

Human milk has been used medicinally through the ages — by mouth, as an enema, or for external applications.[14] Take advantage of its easy access during your lactation months, and try it out on eye infections, skin irritations, or nasal congestion (via an eyedropper).

RECREATIONAL DRUGS

THERE are no simple solutions to the problem of drug abuse. But as a lactating woman, you cannot, must not, should not use recreational drugs.

CAFFEINE AND RELATED STIMULANTS

Caffeine and other stimulants are found in coffee, tea, chocolate, and cola drinks. Your baby joins you at the coffee klatch, present or not, because significant amounts of caffeine are secreted in breast milk.[15] Caffeine exposure is usually continual, so accumulation in the baby occurs even when your use is moderate. Because caffeine is a stimulant, the caffeine-intoxicated infant may be irritable, jittery, and wakeful.[16] Reduced growth is another consequence.[17]

Coffee is not the only vehicle for this type of drug. In addition to cola drinks, tea, and chocolate, over-the-counter pep pills, many brands of aspirin, diuretics, and antihistamines may also contain caffeine.

NICOTINE

Nicotine interferes with the let-down reflex and diminishes milk secretion.[18] The effect on the milk itself of chronic elevation of blood carbon monoxide levels caused by smoking is unknown. We don't expect good news when the jury is in. Twenty cigarettes a day can produce high levels of nicotine in the milk. Penalties for fewer cigarettes depend on variables such as the mother's health in general and nutrient intake in particular.

The widespread use of socially acceptable mood-changing substances cannot always be avoided. You may become a passive recipient through inhalation if you live or work with a smoker.

People who smoke often drink alcohol; and a cigarette frequently goes with a cup of coffee. Please, not while breast-feeding.

MARIJUANA

Marijuana use may affect a mother's ability to care for her baby. The baby gets a double dose — through ingestion and through inhalation — and presents the following disorders: structural changes in brain cells; impairment of DNA, RNA, and judgment; disturbance of proteins essential for growth; behavioral abnormalities.[19]

ALCOHOL

Prolonged high intake of alcohol is risky. Although small single doses — a glass of beer or wine, for example — encourage milk ejection reflexes for the neophyte nurser, higher doses are inhibiting.[20] A recent statement from the American Academy of Pediatrics' Committee on Drugs advises that drowsiness, excessive perspiration, deep sleep, weakness, decrease in growth, and slow weight gain have been reported in infants of breast-feeding mothers who consume alcohol.[21] Test animals given alcohol have offspring who are more emotionally reactive.[22]

Reports relating alcohol and its effects in breast-fed babies are sparse, but there is a plethora of information on alcohol in pregnancy. Insults may be greater for the baby than for the fetus because the fetus has the benefit of the detoxifying and eliminatory systems of the mother — systems yet to be developed in the young infant who is "out on its own."

During pregnancy, drinking as little as two ounces of alcohol on a routine basis increases the risk of giving birth to an infant with defects. At lower levels of exposure, the baby's abnormalities are behavioral.[23] Moderate consumption of alcohol is especially damaging if it accompanies moderate malnutrition. Until we know more about breast milk and alcohol consumption, these examples should serve as red flags.

HEROIN

The news media have made us aware of infant heroin addiction as a result of the mother's use of the drug during pregnancy. A heroin baby has an especially uncoordinated and ineffective sucking reflex.[24] Heroin abuse during lactation may result in general debilitation and malnutrition of the mother. It is illogical that anyone reading this book would use heroin during lactation. (For the sake of the babies, we hope this is not a Victorian view.)

COCAINE

Cocaine use has become an increasingly frequent problem in this country. Cocaine has been gaining popularity faster than any other drug. According to Dr. Lester Luz, renowned pediatrician of San Francisco, a woman taking cocaine would not be able to produce milk.

TOXIC TRANSFER THROUGH FOOD AND THE ENVIRONMENT

IMAGINE substances that are virtually indestructible, difficult to dispose of, widely distributed, slow to leave your body, cumulative in their effects, and potentially harmful. No, they're not machinations of the Devil (unless you feel the name fits some industrial and food-processing moguls). They're environmental contaminants. In the real world of multiple exposure, toxic effects don't add, they multiply. Like the animal noises on Old MacDonald's farm — here a toxin, there a toxin, everywhere a toxin, toxin.

These crouching tigers are usually beyond your control. You can, however, select foods that are the least outrageous in the supermarket's Pandora's box. (Diogenes said it best: "Only one good, namely, knowledge; only one evil, namely, ignorance.")

MEAT

Antibiotics, hormones, insecticides, and herbicides accompany meat purchases. These contaminants have been known to lodge in the fat of human milk. They are stored in your fat too. Because dieting involves the mobilization of fat stores during lactation, women are advised not to diet while nursing.[25]

Reports of infant females developing premature breasts, and "feminized" grade-school boys afflicted with the same problem, have been gaining in frequency. Researchers have traced the source of these problems to hormone residues in meat products.[26]

In spite of the meat industry's claims, any nutrient benefit that meat might offer loses its dazzle in light of these facts.

PEANUT BUTTER

Commercial nut butters usually contain partially hydrogenated fats as well as sugar. Hydrogenation of vegetable oils produces fatty acids with unusual structures, called *trans* fats. Breast milk yields to these acids, and they make themselves quite at home as unwelcome guests. They alter metabolic pathways involving essential fatty acids, the nutrients discussed earlier as paramount for brain development. These distorted molecules also wipe out vitamin E reserves. The quantity of trans acids in your milk is directly related to the amount of partially hydrogenated food fats in your diet.[27]

In addition to nut butters, these transgressors come from an assortment of processed foods: margarine, shortening, french fries, potato chips, crackers, baked goods, cakes, frosting mixes, baking mixes, frozen dinners, sauces, frozen vegetables, breakfast cereals, salad dressing, cooking oils, and any rancid fat.

IODIZED SALT

Contrary to popular belief, goiter (thyroid gland enlargement) can result from iodine overdose as well as deficiency. We have already cited that iodized salt is related to the high iodine content of breast milk.[28] Primal foods supply all the sodium you require, plus the right amount of iodine.

The American diet is supplemented with iodine from other foods, too, coming primarily from processed offenses, including bread and cow's milk derivatives. The amount of iodine in our food is far higher than it was a number of years ago. When checked for iodine content, breast milk among a group of women was found to contain about four times the recommended daily allowance for infants.

The best solution is to fill your salt shaker with kelp. Learn to use natural condiments. Iodized salt is not in this category.

ADDITIVES

Fifteen hundred different chemicals in more than sixty thousand formulations are poured and sprayed on our foods. The first additives are ushered in before seeds are planted. They progress as food grows, persist at the processing plant, and continue in the market-place. You keep the ball rolling in your very own kitchen with the use of your salt shaker, charcoal grill, aluminum or copper cook-ware, aluminum foil when used with heat, plastic bags, sprays in your frying pan, or bicarbonate of soda to "green" your vegetables.

A wide range of long-lasting patterns of symptoms may result from sensitivity to these myriad substances. Additives confer no nutritional benefit.

Label reading is not much help for two major reasons:

· Secondary additives do not have to be listed on finished products. If, for example, vitamin D-2 (irradiated ergosterol) is added to milk, you have no way of knowing that the preservatives BHA or BHT may already be included. The dairy does not actually add the preservatives — they are in the vitamin D.[29] Another example is the use of monosodium glutamate (MSG), which often accom-panies hydrolyzed vegetable protein. This is not revealed on the label.

· More than 350 food items are "Standards." Standard formulas are exempt from label listing. The manufacturer has the option of listing all, some, or none of the ingredients. Standards include macaroni, cheeses, flour, mayonnaise, bread, ice cream, canned fruits, fruit juices, tomato products, cornmeal, and salad dress-ings.[30]

As far as labeling is concerned, additives in Standard foods and secondary additives are swept under the rug, as though they don't count and as though it's none of your business what's in the food you buy.

In addition to the problems that may be caused by allowable ad-ditives, disclosures of disreputable use of illegal substances fill vol-umes. (About ten years ago, for example, it was discovered that arsenic was being poured into some French wines as a preservative. Arsenic, via breast milk, accumulates in baby's blood.[31] A more re-cent example is the addition of sugar to "sugar-free" foods.)

SINGLE-FOOD OVERDOSE

Consuming a variety of foods is essential. Lactating women in Japan who eat ten to twenty tangerines daily during summer months (when the fruit is cheap and popular) produce orange-colored milk.

In turn, their babies' skin and mucous membranes become stained. This is due to high levels of beta-carotene, the vitamin A precursor in the tangerines. Whether or not this is undesirable is not fully understood. But it demonstrates the susceptibility of human milk to ingested substances.[32]

DETOXIFYING FOODS

Your baby's detoxification mechanisms are not fully developed. These involve enzyme systems and kidney function. Absorption rates of toxins are significantly higher in the very young. A little goes a long way. We don't know yet whether these poisons will be less inclined to invade your milk if you consume detoxifying foods. The very least effect will be an increase in your general health status, because these are healthful foods. In addition to a varied diet, use these foods:

- one cup of peas or beans daily (string beans, green peas, lentils, etc.)
- one cup of alfalfa sprouts daily
- lots of raw vegetables
- vitamin C

We do know that if your baby has optimal nourishment and maximum development, milk-tainting hazards are mitigated, if not eliminated. For this reason healthful, detoxifying foods should be the center, rather than the margin, of your food plan.

When a group of lactating women learned that they had been exposed to toxic doses of a dangerous chemical, most of them refused to accept the fact that their milk was contaminated. The potential of chemicals and pollutants to enter your milk should not be denied, nor should you feel guilty about their presence. It's the state of the art, the world we live in. The ideal world you would like for your child cannot be.

Perhaps you can help to initiate change so that the world becomes a better place for all new life we bring into it. One way to accomplish this is to cast your vote in the supermarket: *don't buy products that are overprocessed.* Use primal foods — foods as close to their natural state as possible — vegetables that push through the earth and find their way directly to your kitchen without being mushed, mashed, and mangled, and then crammed into boxes and bottles, cans and cartons. In your effort to shield your baby, you can outwit the food-processing juggernaut. It is not a totally irresistible force.

Just now, most of your energies need to be directed toward moment-to-moment nurturing. Although long-term effects remain basically unknown, any immediate toxic reactions may be overcome by the nutritional advantages of superior breast milk. One woman, learning that she had been dangerously exposed to PBBs (polybrominated biphenyl) because of a manufacturer's mistake, said, "You can't cry over spilled milk."[33] You can't, and you shouldn't. But you can make the next portion better.

COMPENDIUM

Questions to ask when drugs are prescribed

Is there another way?
What if I do nothing?
Will reduced dosage work?
How will the drug affect my baby?
Do I have to stop breast-feeding?
How long will I have to remain on the drug?
Will the doctor check my milk for contamination?

Medicinal drugs that may affect human milk

Analgesics may cause intestinal bleeding in baby
Antibiotics may cause allergic reactions later on
Anticoagulants (reactions not known)
Diuretics decrease or suppress lactation, cause dehydration and mineral loss in baby
Hormones diminish milk volume, alter milk composition, may cause feminization of male children
Laxatives affect baby's bowels
Sedatives sedate baby, may metabolize other drugs

If you must take drugs

Schedule doses away from feeding time
Consider variables such as

your kidney function
other foods consumed
health and age of baby
allergic reactions

Look for symptoms in baby such as

fever
nausea
increased activity
lethargy

Recreational drugs that may affect human milk

Caffeine affects baby by causing

irritability, wakefulness, jitteriness
reduced growth

Nicotine affects mother and baby by

suppressing let-down reflex
diminishing milk secretion
reducing nutrient quality of milk

Marijuana affects baby by causing

structural changes in brain cells
impaired RNA, DNA
impaired judgment
disturbed protein metabolism
behavioral abnormalities

Alcohol affects mother and baby by causing

altered milk-ejection reflex
excessive perspiration in baby
deep sleep in baby
weakness, decreased growth, slower weight gain in baby
emotional reactivity in baby

Heroin affects mother and baby by causing

general debilitation
malnutrition

Foods with toxic substances

Hormone-treated meat
Peanut butter and other hydrogenated fatty foods
Iodized salt
Possibly *any* food, if consumed in excess

Detoxification diet includes

Raw vegetables
Vitamin C
Peas, beans, and lentils
Alfalfa sprouts
Kelp
Varied primal foods

Natural remedies

Headaches

relaxation techniques (see Chapter 3)
herbal teas (peppermint, rosemary, sage)
calcium tablets
neck or body massage
acupressure, acupuncture

Constipation

don'ts: white bread, white flour, baked products; eggs, cheese, milk; meat; hot beverages; tannin drinks (red wine, nonherbal teas, cocoa)

dos: moisture foods (celery, radishes, carrots, lettuce); laxative foods (strawberries, watermelon); lots of fluids; herbs and high-nutrient foods (garlic, agar-agar, herb teas, brewer's yeast, rice polishings); high-fiber vegetables and cereals; fruits; grated carrot; acidophilus

Back pain

two tennis balls in old sock, rolled on back
dry heat
pillow under knees, neck, each arm (you lie on back)
contrast bath

Stomach upsets

> caused by: poor eating (sweet and fatty foods), tension, allergies
> solutions: nonallergenic foods (millet, brown rice, buckwheat, yogurt, buttermilk, sweet potato, string beans, fish); acidophilus

Toothache

> paprika, chili peppers, hot-pepper extract, oil of cloves
> vitamin E
> aloe vera, potato slices

Vaginitis

> carrot-grown acidophilus, internally and topically

Mother's milk as healer

> eye inflammations
> skin irritations
> stuffy nose

DRUG-NUTRIENT INTERACTIONS

Drugs are important causes of malnutrition. This problem must be considered particularly with respect to lactation. Knowledge of nutrients affected by drugs can be helpful in efforts to avoid deficiencies.

DRUG/MEDICATION	NUTRIENT ADVERSELY AFFECTED
Alcohol	Water-soluble vitamins (especially B_1), magnesium, potassium, zinc
Antacids	Water-soluble vitamins, calcium, iron, phosphorus
Antibiotics	Vitamins A, B_1, B_2, B_3, B_6, K; biotin; inositol; PABA
Anticoagulants	Vitamins B_1 and K, folic acid
Anticonvulsants	Vitamins D and K, calcium, folic acid
Antidepressants	Vitamins B_6 and C
Antigout medication	Vitamin B_{12}
Anti-inflammatory medication	Folic acid
Aspirin	Vitamins B_1, B_{12}, C, K; folic acid
Barbiturates	Vitamins B_5, B_{12}, C; magnesium
Black tea	Iron
Blood-pressure medication	Vitamin B_6, manganese
Caffeine	Vitamins B_1 and B_5, iron, potassium
Codeine	Vitamin B_{12}
Cortisone	Vitamins B_6, C, D; calcium; magnesium; potassium; zinc
Digitalis	Magnesium, potassium
Dilantin	Vitamins B_{12} and D, folic acid
Diuretics	Water-soluble vitamins (especially biotin), calcium, magnesium, potassium, sodium
Estrogens	Water-soluble vitamins, vitamin E, iron
Hypoglycemics	Vitamin B_{12}
Hypotensive medication	Vitamin B_6, manganese
Laxatives	Calcium, potassium
L-Dopa	Vitamins B_6 and B_{12}, folic acid
Licorice (natural)	Potassium
Lithium	Iodine
Marijuana	Vitamin B_6
Mineral oil	All fat-soluble vitamins

DRUG/MEDICATION	NUTRIENT ADVERSELY AFFECTED
Nicotine	Vitamin C
Oral contraceptives	Vitamins B₂, B₃, B₆, B₁₂, C; copper; folic acid; iron; zinc
Oral hypoglycemics	Vitamin B₁₂
Potassium chloride	Vitamin B₁₂
Sedatives	Folic acid
Sulfa	Vitamins B₂, B₃, B₅, K; folic acid; PABA
Tetracycline	Vitamin C, calcium, magnesium
Thyroid hormones	Vitamin E
Tuberculosis medication	Vitamins B₃, B₆, B₁₂; folic acid

CHAPTER
~ 7 ~

Problem Solving: The Preemie, the Colicky, the Non-Sleepy

IN WHICH WE DISCUSS

What to do when your baby arrives too soon

What to do when your baby won't be pacified

Being awake from dusk to dawn

A sick, crying, or tired baby quickly slams a heavy door between you and the outer world. When you walk into a supermarket for the first time after the birth of your baby — especially if there have been problems — you will probably be surprised that life should be going on in the old way, when your reactions to it have changed so much. You may wonder if any of the mothers escorting preschoolers up and down the aisles endured similar agonies. Life seems so normal for them now.

*The newborn infant must have the capacity
for many adjustments in order to survive in
extrauterine life.*

— THOMAS K. OLIVER, JR., M.D.

W hen you've been a good girl and done all your chores, you're accustomed to a reward. Well, you did all the right things when you were pregnant, but the sunshine has dwindled and gone under a cloud. Your baby was born too soon, or maybe he won't surrender to sleep, or is it that she just cries and cries?

BORN TOO SOON

THE preterm or very small infant has a requirement for nutrients that outranks that of any other individual in our society. The greatest vulnerability to nutritional deficiency occurs during periods of rapid growth.

A significant area of difficulty for a premature baby stems from the immature gastrointestinal tract. Because the absorption of nutrients is impaired, a preemie may be deprived of important nutrients even when apparently thriving and healthy-looking.

We explained earlier that deficiencies can be nonspecific. If, for example, your baby does not have enough zinc, the shortcoming may not be severe enough to cause the skin problems symptomatic of zinc deficiency. But the lack could be grave enough to promote irritability. The fact that the manifestation of diminished zinc is not classic (or may even be silent) does not mean it is not serious.[1]

CHOOSING THE RIGHT MENU

Feeding the average premature baby formula or term milk (milk from a mother who delivered her baby after nine months of pregnancy), or even intravenously, is losing popularity. Formula-fed infants regain their birth weight more slowly than infants fed human milk.[2] Milk feeding from the mother remains the principal means of nourishing preterm infants in Europe, particularly in Scandinavia, where it is used exclusively for premature infants. The results have been excellent. Any nutritional inadequacy is considered small in relation to benefits. Hormones stimulate the production of milk as early as the fourth month of pregnancy. Nature seems to adapt mother's milk to meet the premature baby's needs. Premature milk has:

· substantially higher concentrations of protein, sodium, and chloride than term milk, offering a significant growth advantage[3]
· slightly higher overall calcium content
· higher immune factors, crucial at a time when the baby is extremely defenseless against both infection[4] and absorption of ingested food antigens[5] (all the more reason not to feed formula)
· higher levels of nitrogen, which provides the rapidly growing premature infant with compounds necessary for building tissue protein[6]
· properties of colostrum and transitional milk for a longer period of time than is present in milk of mothers who deliver at term[7]
· higher fat content, which is more appropriate for premature babies[8]

The milk produced by the mother of the preterm infant is uniquely suited to her baby's increased nutritional and immunologic requirements. It more than compensates for the limitation imposed by the reduced volume of food the baby can tolerate. The infant's own mother's milk is the ideal source of nutrition and protection, irrespective of birth weight or birth date.

HOW YOU CAN HELP

If you are the mother of a preterm infant, your milk must be of transcendent quality. The dramatic call for excellence in your diet precludes cheating. *Any kind of cheating.* To help yourself resist cheesecake, picture your child's immature stomach lining. When you see french fries, think of cell-destroying free radicals (highly reactive unbalanced molecules) created by reheated oil. If someone offers you ice cream, announce: "My baby's too good for that." Envision your skeleton disintegrating, if that's what you need to do, to rescue yourself from soft drinks. Create a vivid image of a tiny skull and crossbones attached to whatever you think processed sugar and fat molecules look like, and watch these enter your milk in your mind's eye.

Here are a few specific suggestions for making sure your diet contributes to the optimal development of your child. In Chapter 10 you will find recipes particularly rich in many of these vital nutrients.

Fat. Fat malabsorption is a major problem for the preemie because enzyme systems are not fully developed. The absorption of fat, as well as the kind of fat, is influenced by the type of fat in your milk. As previously stated, the fat content in your milk is contingent on what you are eating. The fats that are more easily absorbed are those described earlier — EPA, DHA, and GLA, plus cod-liver oil.[9] You should be eating lots of fish, Protein-Aide sesame seeds, chlorella, and sprouted sunflower seeds.

Vitamin D. The preterm or low–birth weight baby has a higher requirement for vitamin D on a body weight basis than the full-term infant, not only because the velocity of growth is greater but because the vitamin D stores may be less. The pathways necessary for vitamin D metabolism may not be fully operational because of the immaturity.[10] Vitamin D absorption is limited when fat is malabsorbed. The list of recommended substances echoes that of the previous paragraph: fish, Protein-Aide sesame seeds, EPA, GLA, DHA, and cod-liver oil. And walk on the sunny side of the street — with the baby — whenever possible.

Phosphorus. High intakes of phosphorus interfere with vitamin D metabolism, already at risk for your small baby. The phosphorus foods to avoid are: all sodas, meat, hot dogs, ham, bacon, processed cheese, baked products (with phosphate baking powder commonly used), instant soups and puddings, commercial dessert toppings, and mixed herbal seasonings.[11] Reject any foods with labels reading phosphoric this or phosphoric that.

Phosphorus also interferes with absorption of iron, another nutrient in jeopardy at this time.[12]

Vitamin A. Mothers of premature and low–birth weight infants have lower levels of vitamin A in their blood, suggesting that vitamin A status is one of the correlates of prematurity.[13] Again, the twice-told tale: cod-liver oil. Reminder: the amount of vitamin A in your milk is reflected by the vitamin A in your diet.

Calcium. Calcium deficiency is common among premature babies. Because calcium absorption is generally lower, we suggest you review the section on this subject outlined in Chapter 4.[14]

Zinc. A progressive decline in the concentration of zinc in premature babies is prevalent.[15] Zinc deficiency is thought to be due to the high requirement for rapid growth plus a poor zinc supply in food.[16] Whole grains and seeds, anyone?

Other minerals. There is strong evidence that latent mineral deficiencies are common among premature infants. The progression to overt symptoms may occur in later months under unfavorable dietary conditions. This is another reason for you to monitor your nutritional status during breast-feeding, and to abide by the tenets on weaning set forth in Chapter 9.[17]

Vitamin E. Vitamin E malabsorption in preterm infants results in one of the few recognized deficiency states of this vitamin, causing a form of anemia.[18]

Toxins. Premature babies don't handle drugs as well as their full-term peers because of immature activity of liver enzymes and other mechanisms that normally detoxify, inactivate, or excrete such agents. Review Chapter 6, and watch those toxins.

Quantity. High-volume milk feeds for preterm infants are desirable, which means feeding as often as you and your baby can possibly get together.[19]

Bottle feedings. Small or even slightly premature infants who start on bottle feedings have difficulty relearning proper sucking motion. The baby has to work harder to obtain milk from your breast after using the soft rubber nipples in the hospital. Discourage all bottle feedings if possible, unless of course the procedure is life-saving. In such cases mothers are asked to express milk manually and contribute the colostrum to the baby. Patience is required when baby comes home until the breast-feeding sucking action is established.

Supplementation. Because the smaller baby requires higher intakes of nutrients, it is advisable to consult your physician about administering the vitamin formula outlined in Chapter 5. The regimen recommended for lactating women should also be considered.

In addition to improved health status for you and your child, your careful food selection confers very positive psychological benefits. By assuming responsibility for the good nutrition of your child, you are actively participating in providing a quality foundation for your baby's tomorrow.

If you follow these recommendations, your milk should be able to support catch-up growth in the first two to three months.[20] Think of all those children negotiating the supermarket aisles. Just a year or two ago, a significant number were also preemies. The rate of premature births has decreased minimally, if at all, in the past thirty years.[21]

THE COLICKY CRIER

WHEN you were in junior high, most of your girlfriends started to menstruate; some started earlier, others later on. One or two got their "periods" in sixth grade, and a few didn't join the crowd until senior high. The menarche starting gun goes off at various ages because of *biochemical individuality.* The maturation of infants' digestive systems is no different. Not all babies have completely developed intestines at the same age. The potential for hypersensitive reactions is a consequence of immature intestinal linings. The less developed they are, the more susceptible,[22] and the greater the child's risk of developing allergies. Because your baby's gastrointes-

tinal tract will be stressed by the demands of rapid growth, colic
may occur more readily.

Biochemical individuality doesn't answer all the sensitivity questions. If it did, infantile colic would not be the almost exclusive right
of modern Westernized cultures.

THREE MONTHS' COLIC

"Three months' colic" is the name given to the syndrome that
usually begins at about two weeks of age and stops by four months
but may occasionally persist somewhat longer. The baby screams,
draws up its legs, and cannot always be comforted by milk, by being
picked up, with diaper changes, or even by being rocked or walked.
The baby is suffering from an abdominal spasm. You are willing to
do anything possible, and nothing works. You say please, but, like
all other efforts, please doesn't do any good. The baby's weakness tries your strength. And you join the Holy Fellowship of
Martyrs.

When you attempt to comfort your baby, the child may be frantic
unless nursed because of the smell of your milk. But the baby is not
really hungry. Daddy or a grandparent may be more successful
when placing the baby against his or her warm shoulder and at the
same time gently rubbing the baby's feet.

Although the eruptions can occur at any time, they characteristi-
cally happen in the early evening, when you thought you were
going to get the evening meal ready, and everyone is tired and hungry. The outbreak could last three or four hours. The insistent message of grief is relentless.

Some researchers believe that colic is *iatrogenic* (doctor-caused),
initiated by increasing interference with normal labor. Despite the
natural-childbirth movement, few women escape the administration
of drugs during labor or delivery. A fascinating study shows that
the effects of obstetric medication influence a child's behavior up to
at least seven years of age.[23] As for short-term effect: babies born
after significant exposure to maternal medication during labor are
more likely to develop colic than babies born after normal, unmedi-
cated labor.[24] D. B. Thomas, M.D., explains the phenomenon:

> Early onset of colic and its disappearance by three months
> after birth would fit in with these findings. Considerable
> neurobehavioral maturation occurs in the first three months of

life, and colic might well represent disturbances of development subsequent to drug administration during labor.

If this hypothesis is correct, it would seem unlikely that medications, such as antispasmodics, would have much effect in the relief of colic. Encouragement of more natural forms of childbirth, together with a reduction in the amount of drugs given during labor, would perhaps go a long way towards a reduction in the incidence of colic.[25]

Does this mean that colic is the inevitable fate for a sensitive child or one whose mother has been subjected to drugs? Or for a child whose parents are allergy-prone, because that, too, is a factor? The single answer to the questions is *no!* If you are susceptible to the sun's rays but stay out of the sun, you don't get sunburned.

It is widely accepted that potentially allergenic macromolecules (large, undigested molecules) are absorbed by the normal adult gut and may pass from mother to infant through breast milk. These substances could produce adverse reactions in susceptible babies. They not only cause colic, they can also be responsible for runny nose, vomiting, diarrhea, eczema, and asthma. The macromolecules that kindle the damage usually come from cow's milk or milk derivatives *in the mother's diet.*[26] When mothers are placed on a cow's milk–free diet, colic (and other symptoms) almost always disappear. Although different people are allergic to a vast range of unrelated substances, the list of common allergens is curiously consistent, and milk is at the top of the chart.

Note the frequency rate of the five most common food allergens found in one thousand food-allergic adults:[27]

Food	Food-Allergic People with Sensitivity (in 1,000)
Milk	679
Chocolate	400
Cola	400
Corn	302
Citrus fruits	272

Having read a report in a medical journal on cow's milk as a cause of infantile colic in breast-fed infants, the entire pediatric care team

of a medical facility sought out colicky breast-fed babies. They reported:

> We advised the mothers to stop drinking cow's milk to see if
> their baby's behavior improved. If the colic did not disappear
> we then advised the mothers to cut out other dairy products as
> well. Within 24 hours most mothers reported a welcome im-
> provement in their baby's behavior. The babies became less
> fractious, less jittery, and more amenable, and the agonizing
> colic which had caused screaming and feeding problems disap-
> peared. A further challenge that we advised to confirm the
> diagnosis nearly always reproduced the original behavior.
>
> We often find mothers consuming three, four, or even five
> pints of milk in a day, in the belief, often fostered by advisers
> elsewhere, that cow's milk helps the breast milk supply.[28]

Statements of success with the elimination of cow's milk and its
products have appeared in prestigious medical journals all over the
world. A diet totally free of cow's milk is suggested for the mothers
as a first trial of treatment of infantile colic in breast-fed infants.[29] It
usually works!

If this regimen is not successful, check your diet for any of the following foods, which have obvious or hidden milk products in them:
buttermilk, cream, sour cream, butter, sherbet, evaporated milk,
powdered milk, puddings, bakery products made with any of these
items, creamed soups, creamed sauces, gravies, all cheeses, nondairy
products that may have milk solids added, nondairy substitutes
containing caseinate, such as Coffee-mate, Cereal Blend, Preem,
Rich'ning, Cool Whip. (Casein is a milk protein.) Cultured products such as yogurt may be more easily tolerated. Pancakes, waffles,
omelets, puddings, and creamed dishes may have milk products in
them.[30] At the department of pediatrics, University of Lund Hospital in Sweden, doctors reported that mothers' intake of capsules
containing whey protein initiated colic.[31]

Colicky breast-fed infants who are weaned to formula are usually
much worse.

TRANSIENT COLIC

Transient colic is caused by occasional consumption of a food eaten
by Mom for the first time since she began breast-feeding. Beans,
onions, garlic, curry, and rhubarb have been known to cause tran-

sient colic. Other foods not well tolerated are fruits (especially citrus), gassy foods (cabbage, turnips, broccoli, Brussels sprouts), apricots, and prunes. Additional demons may be chocolate and tomatoes. In the summer, a heavy diet of melons, peaches, and other fresh fruits may cause colic and possibly diarrhea.[32] Offensive beverages are carbonated drinks, coffee, or tea. Fluoridated water, calcium lactate tablets, or iron pills may be other sources of trouble.

Symptoms appear within twenty-four hours following ingestion. But then there's biochemical individuality: colic-promoting foods are different for different babies.

In times past, long lists of foods, such as spicy items, were prohibited during breast-feeding. In sixteenth-century Europe, mothers were warned against ". . . bad air, bad smells, salty or spiced foods, garlic, mustard, stale cheese, roast meat and raw fruit."[33] Your baby's genetic imprint hasn't changed since the sixteenth century. Nor for sixteen hundred centuries, for that matter.

Some infants may have distinctive breathing patterns associated with periods of colic. Parents report rapid and congested or "snuffly" breathing preceding the big fuss.[34]

Confidence in the future should have a steadying effect on the present. While this disconcerting rite is in progress, it may be difficult to remember your previously tranquil life before the war or the flood or the colic. But the cloud will lift. Colic is self-limiting: eventually it goes away.

NIGHT LIFE IN THE NURSERY

WAS it another life or only a few months ago when you were led from glamor to reality, when the security of habit fell away, when night began to creep over you in uneasy pauses rather than in sound sleep? When you discovered what was on TV at 1:00 A.M.? At 2:30 A.M.? 5:00 A.M.?

No baby ever died from lack of sleep. (As for the parents, well . . .) And in the early months, the waking is not an appeal for attention. The requests for frequent night feeds may even be genetic! Theory has it that cavewoman wandered about gathering food by day, with baby lulled to sleep on her back. When she returned to her shelter at night, feeding began, and it went on — and continued — through the night. That's how the anthropologists say it started.

In many cultures it is common for infants and young children to share their parents' bed. Where this occurs the infants do not get suffocated (a concern of parents who consider the measure), and night-waking problems are not reported. Many babies reach out for their mother's breast in the night and suck while she goes on sleeping. More and more parents are adopting this pattern in our "developed" world. Unless you or your husband takes strong exception to "three's company," the professionals agree that this may be an acceptable solution to the problem. It almost always works. But the sleep problem is clearly an interactive one, affecting the entire family.[35] The decision to have the baby sleep with you should be discussed as a family.

There is no easy solution to the dilemma, but knowing a few facts may help to cushion some of the unpleasantness. Here are a few of nature's unfolding secrets about night life in the nursery:

· Night feedings disappear more slowly in breast-fed babies. Among the reasons: (1) There is an inverse relationship between protein content and frequency of feedings. Human milk has far less protein than modified formulas.[36] (2) Breast-feeding promotes a more liberal and permissive attitude, while bottle-feeding mothers are more likely to see night wakings as a problem and to apply any necessary negative reinforcement.[37]
· In traditional or more primitive cultures, as much as one third of the daily intake of breast milk can occur during the night.[38]
· Night waking is described as a problem in infant boys more often than in infant girls.[39]
· Sucking frequency is one factor that affects the length of infertility during breast-feeding. So night feedings may extend your infertile period.[40] (Any consolation?) But don't forget the caution: breast-feeding is *not* a totally reliable contraceptive measure.
· Twenty percent of young children wake up at night during the first two years of life. But only one in five of these night-lifers will be waking up at age three.

Check with your pediatrician for his or her bag of tricks. Dr. Lester Luz of San Francisco recommends tryptophan for the mother.[41] (Tryptophan is an amino acid that has a calming effect on many people.) Children's Hospital Medical Center in Boston suggests a tiny dose of tryptophan for the baby.[42] Dr. Michael Gerber of Reno, Nevada, advises mothers to take five or six calcium tablets two or three hours before the last evening feeding.[43] (These elixirs may be used briefly but not as ongoing therapy.) Dr. Robert Mendelsohn councils mothers to call La Leche League for moral support. ("My daughters take their kids to bed with them," he says.) The why's overrun the how's and we wish it were the other way around. Sorry about that!

JAUNDICE, COLITIS, AND OTHER TROUBLES

IT is not in the scope of this book to discuss home care of sick infants, but a brief note or two on common problems may help to chase some of the lions out of the path.

JAUNDICE

Jaundice is an accumulation of bile pigments in the infant's blood, causing the baby to look yellow. Not all newborns have sufficient liver reserves to help correct the problem. The incidence of jaundice in full-term infants has increased. Inappropriate hospital feeding practices have been suggested as one cause.

Jaundice occurring in the first week of life (which peaks on the third day and then begins to drop) is different from breast milk jaundice (which rises after the third day and peaks as late as the fifteenth day). Mild jaundice seems to cause no difficulties.[44] Here are a few hints:

· Policies that are good for lactation are also effective in minimizing jaundice. Try to shorten your hospital stay, and insist that any tests performed on the baby be done in your presence. Reject schedules and go for demand feeding.
· Your dietary intake influences the development of breast milk jaundice through the triglyceride content of the milk. Eliminate all processed fats.[45]
· Ideal room temperature for the newborn is 75 degrees Fahrenheit with at least 60 percent humidity.[46] (Small portable humidifiers are easily available.)
· Water-and-glucose solutions should be forbidden. There is no evidence that they reduce jaundice.
· Infants suffering from jaundice are depressed and lethargic and may not nurse well.[47] Be patient.

COLITIS

Colitis is an inflammation of the colon, the lower part of the large intestine. Colitis occurs occasionally in an exclusively breast-fed infant. The symptoms are constipation alternating with watery diarrhea. Elimination of cow's milk protein and other dairy products from mother's diet usually solves the problem.[48]

STUFFED NOSE

Try clearing baby's stuffed-up nasal passages with an eyedropper full of your own breast milk. If your baby has frequent nasal congestion, try eliminating all milk and milk products from *your* diet. Consider changing the linens in the crib to 100 percent cotton — including the bumpers. You will be amazed at how your baby's congestion can be eased if you follow these two suggestions.

The usual flawless execution of an infant's functions is appreciated only when you have to cope with problems.

Nature tends to the normal. Nature-nursed infants have fewer problems than bottle-fed babies. But that's not much solace for the caretaker of an ill child. Sick babies don't soften your captivity with smiles to flood your heart.

You have a lot of power. You can offer the best of the two most controllable factors in normal development: love and good food.

COMPENDIUM

The premature baby

Requires more nutrients than any other individual
Has an immature gastrointestinal tract
May be nutrient-deficient even when gaining weight
Thrives best on its own mother's milk

Suggestions for mothers of premature babies include

Consuming

essential fatty acids (EPA, DHA, GLA, cod-liver oil; Protein-Aide sesame seeds; sprouted sunflower seeds)
fish

Getting enough sunshine
Avoiding phosphorus foods
Increasing vitamin A intake
Increasing calcium absorption
Eating whole grains and seeds for zinc and vitamin E
Avoiding toxins wherever possible
Taking supplements

Care of premature baby includes

Feeding as often as possible
Avoiding use of bottled feedings
Checking with doctor for supplements for baby

Babies who have colic

May scream for many hours
Draw up their legs
Cannot always be comforted
Usually cry late in afternoon or early evening
Can often be cured if mother

　　eliminates cow's milk from diet
　　eliminates all other dairy products from diet

Transient colic

Caused by foods eaten by mother for first time
Such foods include

　　beans, onions, garlic, curry, rhubarb
　　fruits (especially citrus)
　　gassy foods (cabbage, turnips, broccoli, Brussels sprouts)
　　fluoridated water
　　calcium lactate tablets
　　iron pills

Waking at night

May be genetic
Is not an appeal for attention in early months
Can often be remedied by taking baby into your bed
Occurs more frequently in breast-fed than bottle-fed babies
Occurs more frequently in boys than girls

Jaundice

Is increasing in full-term babies
Can be reduced or cured by

    eliminating processed fat from diet
    keeping temperature of baby's room at 75 degrees
    exposing baby to light
    maintaining humidity at 60 percent
    omitting all water-and-glucose solutions

CHAPTER

8

Breast-Feeding in the Late Twentieth Century: Milk, Emotions, and Emancipation

IN WHICH WE DISCUSS

Milk expression — preparation of a healthful convenience food

Milk storage — storing this healthful convenience food

Stress, which is to be expected in the late twentieth century, and which we should hope to greet with humor and patience

New feelings, new family — anticipating the change

Sex — getting it together again

There must be something sadly amiss with a society that encourages pornographic pictures in newspapers, movies, and TV, but looks askance at (or even arrests) a mother for indecent exposure when she discreetly nurses her baby in public.

Breast-feeding is not always more convenient than bottle-feeding in today's world. It may be expedient for the camping trip, and it beats heating bottles when you are summoned out of bed at the wrong hour on a cold night. But for the ancestors who say, "It was convenient for me, it should be for you," the answer is, "You didn't live in this time." That doesn't mean the end doesn't justify the means. Having dedicated yourself to motherhood, you want to do what's necessary to give your child the best of all possible worlds, and breast-feeding heads that list — even though it's not always opportune.

*After several months of breast-feeding, most
mothers will admit to both physical pleasure
and psychological satisfaction.*

— SIDNEY R. KEMBERLING, M.D.

One of the powerful symbols of the emancipation of women
was bottle-feeding. After so much preparatory demolition,
times are a-changin'. It is now entirely possible to return to
work and breast-feed. It's not always convenient or easy. You have
to be committed and creative: in addition to establishing a solid
support system, you need to express your superiority over household chores. You may have to forgo the pleasures of a lover's week-
end or a night out at the three-star restaurant. But your baby's time
to be a baby is so short, you'll come out way ahead if you cling to
every propitious moment.

We hope that some of the ideas we suggest will help to turn
things around — that you will find breast-feeding more of a joy and
less of a burden or frustration than many young women today. For
the dedicated breast-feeder who is also a career woman, we even
offer healthful formula preparations that may be substituted on
occasion in an emergency or for lack of expressed milk (see Chapter 9).

FAST-FOOD BREAST MILK: EXPRESSING AND STORING

SEPARATION of mother and child is not unique to the twentieth century. The influence of urbanization on breast-feeding practices first became apparent during the Middle Ages. Mothers could not attend to the needs of babies as they had been able to in a rural milieu. In extreme cases this went as far as abandonment. Temporary abandonment describes the practice of turning a child over to a wet nurse, and this dates back to A.D. 787. It continued to the end of World War I.[1]

Now that your baby has arrived, you may desire time away from it more enthusiastically than you wanted to become pregnant. Perhaps you want to leave your baby with a caretaker to go to school, to go to work, to go shopping, or to meet the needs of older children in the family. In the late twentieth century, *your baby can feed on your very own milk in your absence.*

GETTING BACK TO WHATEVER

Ideally, a six-to-eight-week leave of absence should be planned before returning to your job (or to any other prior involvements). Once you are back at work, night nursing is a necessity. So is devoting weekends and holidays to full-time mothering. You may at times feel that the world is flowing past you, but it's not forever. What is lasting is the extraordinary array of benefits your child receives.

Your midmorning break will never be the same. Instead of coffee and doughnuts, you'll be nibbling carrot sticks and hard-boiled eggs. Your colleagues may spend their lunch hour pumping iron. You will be pumping milk.

NUTRIENT LOSSES OF CONVENIENCE MILK

Nothing can fully match the quality of milk transported directly from breast to baby's mouth. There's no spoilage, no contamination, no temperature change, no nutrient loss! Second best is milk expressed and stored by you. This is far better than formula or any other proprietary food, despite the shortcomings listed below. Expressing milk gives you an opportunity to get back to work, to have an afternoon off, to join friends for dinner, or to sleep through a night while Daddy or baby-sitter takes over. But there is a small price to pay.

Decreased immune content.   Freezing milk affects its cellular content. Pasteurizing annihilates both the cellular and immunity components.[2] Pasteurization takes place at 160 degrees Fahrenheit (72 degrees Celsius) for fifteen seconds. To give you a basis for comparison, boiling occurs at 212 degrees Fahrenheit (100 degrees Celsius).

Not only are cells of human milk unlikely to function well after exposure to temperatures that vary greatly from 98.6 degrees Fahrenheit, but they are known to stick to both plastic and glass and, therefore, may be lost in the milk containers.[3] So polyethylene, polypropylene, and Pyrex containers influence key immunologic components of expressed milk, as do storage temperatures.[4]

Fat.   Human milk fat is best absorbed if the milk has not been heated.[5]

Fragile vitamins.   Heat-labile vitamins such as vitamin C and folic acid are also wiped away by heating.

Protein.   Most proteins are denatured when exposed to heat.

Enzyme activity.   When milk stands at room temperature or in a refrigerator or is subjected to freezing and thawing, wide fluctuations are observed in enzyme activity. Heating to various temperatures between 100 and 130 degrees Fahrenheit (40 to 55 degrees Celsius) results in further progressive losses of enzyme action.[6]

Collection problems.   Ordinarily, there is an ordered variation in the fat content of breast milk during the course of a single feeding. When the entire feeding is placed in a bottle, the advantages of fat variations from start to finish are lost. (Water-soluble constituents remain the same.)

In summary, freezing causes loss of cellular quality but not enzymatic action. Heating is destructive on both counts. Freezing and thawing are generally less harmful than heat treatment, but consumption of milk that has been frozen may decrease the baby's resistance to disease.

EXPRESSING THE MILK

It's helpful to start expressing and storing milk at least a week before you return to pre-baby activities.

Your first milk expression should be done between feedings. If, however, you find the process works better at any other time, that's okay too. It is tempting to express milk for storage following a feeding if you have a plentiful supply, but the latter part of a feeding is high in fat and offers little else in the way of nutrients.[7] Again, try for the ideal time, and settle for whatever lightens the job.

Each bottle should contain the amount of milk about equal to one feeding. Once you are away, express milk at the time of a customary feeding. You will find that your milk supply gathers when you would ordinarily be feeding. If you choose not to express this milk, production will decrease at those particular times in a few days. But it is advisable to express small amounts of milk when your breasts are full to help maintain your comfort and to keep ducts open.

Hand pumps designed for milk expression are like bicycle pumps in reverse — they suck out instead of pumping in. The pump creates suction as you apply pressure to your breast with your hand. The action of the pump simulates sucking and stimulates the letdown reflex that starts the milk flowing. When you stop pumping, the release of the pressure terminates the flow of milk. If your breast is overfull, leaking may occur after you remove the pump. Each pump comes with clear instructions and diagrams to facilitate its use.

Most women find it necessary to try a few different models before settling on the one that feels most comfortable. The pumps are inexpensive, lightweight, and portable. Some models are electric- or battery-powered. These are larger and heavier, more costly, and cumbersome to transport.

Check Appendix A for information on pumping equipment; for additional hints on milk expression, see Chapter 11.

STORING MILK

Either glass or plastic bottles may be used to store your expressed milk. As indicated earlier, neither one is totally without its problems. The bottles can be sterilized by heating in a pot of boiling water for a few minutes. Avoid residues of detergent on the bottles by keeping them out of the dishwasher.

Buy a few packets of chemical ice and keep them in your freezer. An insulated bag with these frozen packets inserted provides a portable refrigerator. This setup keeps milk properly refrigerated while in transit, maintaining adequate cold temperatures all day.

Refrigerated breast milk remains safe at about 40 degrees Fahrenheit (4.4 degrees Celsius) for forty-eight hours, and milk in the freezer can be kept for about two weeks. There is no harm in keeping the milk frozen longer, but you pay for the time with lost nutrients.

INSTRUCTIONS FOR THE BABY-SITTER

Obviously, if the milk has been frozen or refrigerated, it is too cold for the baby. Warn your baby's caretaker not to heat beyond "taking the chill out." Try to imagine what body temperature feels like. You should be able to hold the bottle in your hand without a sensation of heat, nor should the bottle feel cold. Post a large note on the refrigerator reminding everyone to set a timer when warming the milk to avoid overheating. Overheating and recooling is highly nutrient-destructive. Thawing frozen milk in boiling water may cause curdling.

Any milk left in the bottle after a feeding should be discarded. Bacteria multiply much more rapidly when added to heat-treated human milk than to raw milk.[8]

Make your points by telling the sitter that overheating milk significantly reduces its protective effect. (We know one mother who told her sitters that warm milk made her baby cranky and restless. The sitters were sure not to overheat the milk.)

FEEDINGS AND FEELINGS: MOTHER, FATHER, FAMILY

PRESCRIPTIONS for love and joy and tranquillity abound — for all stages of life. Few prepare anyone for the sudden change of interactions that takes place between mother and father when the baby arrives, or for the new feelings that each develops toward the baby. We hope that knowing what to expect will give you a better chance of having it all together.

MOTHER

Breast-feeding is the very essence of mothering. It offers the unique opportunity for unmatched emotional and physical closeness between you and your baby. You become the strong, life-sustaining force for someone more helpless.

Unlike bottle-feeding, in which the mother has control, breast-feeding makes both mother and baby responsible for ending bouts of sucking. It's more of a togetherness act.

For some women, however, trying to resolve the fear of lost freedom and comfort causes conflict. Many express guilt, confusion, and anxiety because of sexual arousals stimulated by nursing. Physiological similarities between the reactions to breast-feeding and sex explain these feelings. Neurohormonal reflexes are similar during coitus and breast-feeding.[9] Women should know that the sensual relationships they share with their babies are normal, and these feelings should not be denied. In addition to the biological process, there is a cultural aspect: it is not unusual to sexualize feelings about breast-feeding in this country, where breasts have become a sex symbol.

Women report that they get little help from discussing their emotional breast-feeding reactions with professionals. This apparently is an unexplored area. More understanding of the feelings involved would be of help.

Despite the difficulty you may have in discussing your feelings with a professional, and the limited information in print on the subject, you will find that you require little experience to adapt your reactions to your baby's behavior.

FATHER

The greatest value attributed to involving fathers in caretaking is not the relief it offers you, or even the bonding of father and baby. *It serves to reduce feelings of inadequacy and exclusion for Dad.* How fortunate that men are taking a more active role in child care, even with infants.[10] Actually, breast-feeding women see their husbands as more supportive of their mode of feeding than do bottle-feeding women. More conflict is reported among bottle-feeding couples than breast-feeding parents.[11]

And what about the father's feelings? He is no longer the sole recipient of your attentions. More than one popular book on breast-feeding addresses the problem. An example of the advice follows: "You may seem so capable in carrying out your maternal responsibilities and, as a nursing mother, so self-sufficient, that he underestimates your need for him. . . . He needs your assurance that he has not slipped to second place in your life."[12]

Mature men usually experience pride in response to their nursing wives. New feelings well up among the intricate ties of your relationship. But even among "grown-up" men, negative attitudes may be present. They are asked to give more than they get at this crucial time. They need to readjust, understand, and sympathize.

MOTHER AND FATHER AND SEX

You won't have to tell your husband you have a headache. He may have one too. Seriously, you will both find yourselves very tired. (We assume that your husband will be participating in household chores and baby care.)

Sexual frustration goes back to abstinence in pregnancy. Vaginal lubrication may be poor due to the absence of the menstrual flow for so long a time. Breasts may be sore from initial breast-feeding efforts. The best solution is clear and open discussion of feelings between you and your partner.[13] Frank talks and creative solutions can precede and replace storm signals.

Eventually, the fatigue disappears, but forget the norm of the past. New precepts are created with the presence of a child. This is the fabric of family life.

Surely you can be creative about working through sexual encounters. Time together — alone — should be given priority. If the baby is asleep, let the dishes in the sink wait for tomorrow. Or use paper plates, as often as you like, for as long as you like.

About a third of couples resume intercourse after six weeks, and nearly all do by three months. However, frequency (compared to the month prior to conception) is diminished, even a year later.[14] Catch-up time will occur. We promise!

COPING WITH THE LIFESTYLE CHANGE

Dr. Serafina Corsello, a noted New York psychiatrist with a string of prestigious titles, says that when she talks to breast-feeding parents, she quotes her grandmother, who was a midwife:

"Your milk won't be any good if you don't relax," said Grandma. I always knew that if Grandma said it, it must be true. And now I know why.

Stress begins its destructive action at the level of the mid-brain. The image of unpleasantness travels from your cortex (the outer layer of gray matter in your brain which receives stimuli) to your brain's deeper structures.

One of the most important of these deep structures is the hypothalamus, which works like a dispatching station of a tele-communications center. Once it receives the message of an uncomfortable situation, it sends stimulating impulses to its entire territory.

The hypothalamus is top kingpin of your brain's relay setup. It alerts *all of you* to unpleasant situations. That's the stress effect. All of you reacts, and does so with the speed of an electronic messenger. Your hypothalamus is in command of activating, empowering, and integrating those mechanisms which are self-controlled and which function without conscious effort (like the release of milk).

So your ability to release milk is a correlate of your mood. Your hypothalamus sends the warning message to your pituitary, which then refuses to release prolactin. No prolactin release, no milk release. The process is more complex, of course, involving neurotransmitters and even endorphins, but in general that's the way it works.

Relaxation and good nutrition. That's what my grandma advised. When stress mechanisms are well nourished, they don't break down as readily. When you are relaxed, there is no interference with hormone release.[15]

COPING HINTS FROM NURSING MOTHERS

Here are a few suggestions to ease the emotional strain from women who have "been there":

· Get a telephone answering machine. You won't have to feel tense about missing a call.
· Be sure to invest in a rocking chair. Your baby will love it and so will you.
· If you haven't purchased a crib yet, consider one that rocks.
· Supplement with formula if you have to. It's better than "going

crazy." And don't feel guilty about it. Your baby is well nourished most of the time.

· Don't be discouraged by other women's tales. Do what's best for you and your child.
· Stay in a nightgown the first six weeks. Visitors will treat you like a patient and offer more help.
· Watch TV while pumping.
· Beautiful music is relaxing for you and the baby. It also helps with let-down reflex.
· If people ask what you need for the baby, tell them you can use:

    · a fully cooked dinner for two
    · a housecleaning service for a day
    · enrollment in postnatal exercise classes
    · an afternoon or evening of baby-sitting
    · a masseuse for a session or two
    · a house call from a beautician

If you think you have problems now, wait until your son or daughter is sixteen and is picked up for a date by a friend who just got a driver's license. These will be "the good old days."

COMPENDIUM

Nutrient losses in expressed milk

Freezing affects cellular structure
Pasteurizing affects

    cellular structure
    immunoglobulin content
    fat absorption
    heat-sensitive vitamins
    enzyme action

Expressed milk should be

Pumped between feedings if possible
Poured into bottle with amount for one feeding
Refrigerated for no more than two days

Frozen for no more than two weeks
Heated to no more than 98 degrees Fahrenheit
Discarded if not finished

Mother-baby interactions

Breast-feeding is a togetherness act
Lost freedom may cause conflict
Sensual feelings aroused by breast-feeding are normal

Father-baby interactions

Caring for baby reduces feelings of exclusion
Negative attitudes are not unusual

Mother-father interactions

Sexual frustration is to be expected
Open discussions are helpful

Getting from Breast Milk
to Table Food

IN WHICH WE DISCUSS

the introduction of solid food, a process that should not start until your baby bangs on the high chair with a spoon and demands some of *your* food

Here we are in the late 1980s with extensive literature available to us on weaning, but literature that is chaotic and without clear guidelines. There appears to have been better direction in the Elizabethan era, when weaning was considered a time of anxiety and danger. Weaning concomitant with teething was known to lower resistance to infection. So doctors recommended introducing solid foods after all the teeth were through. Once the teething and weaning periods were over at around two years of age, the Elizabethan child stood a much better chance of survival than at any previous time.[1] Maybe there's a lesson here. Space Age parents report, almost unanimously, "The first time my child got sick was just after he (or she) was weaned."

... and Abraham made a great feast on the day that Isaac was weaned.

— GENESIS 21:8

The word *weaning* as used in our language and culture has taken on the meaning of "no more breast-feeding." Derived from the Anglo-Saxon *wenian*, meaning "to accustom," the word has as its actual textbook definition "the process by which the milk-fed infant gradually becomes accustomed to the wide range of foods characteristic of the society into which that child was born." For the purpose of clarity, we are using the term in its true meaning, rather than the popularly accepted definition. Weaning should indeed be gradual!

New foods should be introduced slowly, and not too soon. Early feeding of solid food is comparable to landing an airplane before putting the wheels down. Humans are the only animals who govern weaning time instead of allowing the process to be natural.[2]

Premature weaning interferes with the development of various functions, having both immediate and delayed effects. Some of these effects increase the risk of

- allergies
- eczema
- obesity
- inadequate vitamin intake

- loss of protective immune factors
- incomplete tooth enamel development
- affluent malnutrition
- prolonging baby's sucking desire[3,4]

WHEN TO WEAN

THERE is absolutely no validity in statements made suggesting that early weaning will encourage varied diets, result in more rapid growth, or have your baby sleeping through the night.

You've probably joked about your baby having sovereign power in your household. Here is one time you want your baby to reign supreme: it is more important than ever to allow the baby to dictate his or her weaning time. The average age for the start of weaning in response to the child's interest in table foods is about eight and a half to nine months.

One of the advantages of slow weaning is that the food antibodies in human milk are needed more than ever to influence the baby's immune response to foreign food proteins now being introduced.[5] Babies who are weaned after the age of six months have higher protective immune factors than infants weaned before that age. *The later the cessation of breast-feeding, the higher the protective antibodies.*[6] So weaning doesn't mean "no more breast milk." Not just yet.

The following renowned pediatricians comment on the first stage of weaning and the termination of breast-feeding:

Dr. Ruth Lawrence: "The time considered proper for weaning has gradually shortened from 2 or 3 years to as little as 6 to 8 months. Public opinion has overlooked the infant's needs in favor of what is considered the mother's rights. Weaning should be done with the infant's needs as a guide."[7]

Dr. Lewis A. Barness: "Early introduction of supplemental feedings has no known nutritional basis. . . . Human milk alone apparently contains sufficient nutrients until the infant reaches 9 to 12 months of age."[8]

Dr. Emory Thurston: "The mother who is truly concerned for the present and future welfare of her child will breast feed for at least six months. A year or more is better."[9]

Dr. Alvin Eden: "For those few mothers who are still breast feeding [when the child is 18 months to two years old], there is no reason to stop. If you and your baby are still enjoying the breast-feeding experience, then by all means continue it. You will find that your child will usually 'tell' you one way or another when [he or] she has finally had enough of breast feeding."[10]

Dr. Lendon Smith: "Separation fear or anxiety is common and is to be expected at about eight to twelve months of age.... Because this is a mild and short-lived problem in breast-fed babies, it seems wise to nurse a baby well into and after the months when the condition is at its peak. Try to nurse beyond one year of age."[11]

Professor Derrick B. Jelliffe: "In traditional societies, including the Western world until the present century, breast feeding was usually continued for two to three years or more."[12]

Dr. Sidney Kemberling: "A completely breast-fed infant will maintain adequate iron stores up to twelve to eighteen months of age. Breast milk alone is adequate for nutritional needs. Additional foods are not necessary."[13,14]

WHY BREAST-FEEDING SHOULD CONTINUE
PAST THE AGE OF ONE YEAR

AROUND six months of age some intestinal enzymes mature. This makes the baby increasingly capable of digesting complex proteins and starches. But remember *biochemical individuality.* Maturation time varies from baby to baby. Your baby may develop these enzymes earlier or later.

According to Dr. C. T. Smith of the American College of Clinical Nutrition, the enzyme ptyalin, present in saliva, plays an important role in the digestion of starches. The power of this enzyme to perform its function is not fully generated until one year of age. It remains at optimum efficiency from about the first birthday until old age. For this reason, breast-feeding is essential for at least one year.[15] Cereals are starchy foods. This is a major reason not to introduce cereals until after the first birthday.

Folic acid metabolism serves as an excellent model demonstrating the need to continue breast-feeding for longer periods of time than is commonly practiced. This nutrient is required for the manufacture of DNA and RNA, initial events in cellular division and growth. Breast-fed babies have higher blood levels of folic acid than formula-fed babies.

Folic acid is absorbed far better from mother's milk than any other food. This strong effect of milk folate intake indicates that the use of milk should not be discouraged during late infancy. For this reason, continued breast-feeding at least until your baby's brain is developed — and that takes eighteen months — is highly recommended. Longer breast-feeding is even better, provided other quality foods are offered in conjunction with your milk.

Other nutrients, including minerals, are also far better absorbed from breast milk than from most other foods.

NO COW'S MILK — NOT EVEN AS A WEANING FOOD

THINK of soft, fluffy clouds. Think of flocculent tufts of wool. Think of feathery pillows. Think of your baby's stomach. The texture of human milk protein in that stomach is velvety, facilitating digestion. The primary protein of cow's milk forms a tough, rubbery curd, not so easy to digest. Human milk protein is composed of a large amount of whey, and cow's milk contains more casein. That makes the difference.

Cow's milk should never be substituted for breast milk, at any age.[16] During the first year of a baby's life, cow's milk may cause gastrointestinal bleeding, iron deficiency anemia, and cow's milk allergy. Blood loss occurs with whole milk ingestion in those who are anemic, even when older. Cow's milk plays a potential role in a variety of disorders, including atherosclerosis, recurrent abdominal pain of childhood, cataracts, milk-borne infections, and juvenile delinquency.[17,18] (The association between cow's milk and juvenile delinquency may sound exaggerated. Several prominent researchers have documented the correlation, relating antisocial behavior to brain allergies caused by excessive cow's milk consumption.)

The longer whole cow's milk feeding is delayed, the less chance of developing iron deficiency. Skim milk and 2 percent milk may also lead to an unbalanced diet.[19] (The American Journal of Public Health reported that children over age one year taking low-fat milk have a fivefold risk of acute gastrointestinal illness compared to children on whole milk.)

Study after study confirms the potential problems associated with cow's milk consumption. Here are a few more reports:

· A large percentage of children, aged five to seventeen years, with recurrent abdominal pain of childhood were relieved of symptoms when placed on a milk-free diet. These were children who had not had previous intolerance symptoms.[20,21,22,23]

· There is a higher incidence of cataracts among people who consume large quantities of milk and dairy products.[24,25]

· The onset of colitis in children under two years of age usually commences soon after weaning. The offending food is most often cow's milk protein. Food allergy is considered to be the major cause of colitis in infancy. Excluding the offending food is the treatment of choice.[26]

· The avoidance of cow's milk by prolonged breast-feeding has been shown to reduce the prevalence of asthma as well as eczema.[27]

Lactase is the enzyme that digests milk sugar, which is called lactose. This enzyme disappears in most of the world's populations between the ages of two and five years. The persistence of lactase to the age of five suggests that it might be a genetic remnant from a time when weaning occurred later in life.[28] Until recently, it was believed that the milk-intolerant adult was abnormal. It is now postulated that adults who have lactase activity beyond childhood are the aberrant ones.

No single test, short of milk challenge, presently exists that can accurately predict milk hypersensitivity. (Milk challenge means eliminating all milk, and then reintroducing it after a period of time.) If you even suspect difficulties caused by milk, don't include it in your child's menu in any form. That means no cheese, whipped cream, or other dairy products. It is not necessary to restart milk products when your child is older. A variety of healthful foods should supply all necessary nutrients.

OTHER FOOD SENSITIVITIES

Celiac disease. Celiac disease is highly familial. If you or the baby's father have been sensitive to wheat, chances are that your child will have similar difficulties. Increased duration of breast-feeding is associated with decreased risk of developing celiac symptoms.[29]

Celiac disease is characterized by flatulence and by large, foul-smelling, bulky, frothy, and pale-colored stools containing much fat. There may be recurrent attacks of diarrhea, with possible accompanying stomach cramps, alternating with constipation. Stomach distention is another symptom.

In 1903 a brilliant scientist suggested that bacterial decomposition of protein in infants with celiac disease created a substance responsible for the depression commonly seen with this disease. That substance has recently been identified.[30] Early use of wheat in your baby's diet is inappropriate, especially where genetic predisposition to celiac exists.

Celiac responses to oats have also been noted. Watch for this.[31]

Citrus fruit sensitivity. Citrus is the fifth most common food allergen in this country. The worst offender is citrus fruit juice. A sign in the office of our grandson's pediatrician's office says it all: "Please do not feed your children fruit juice. This is not much better than soda pop."

Additive allergy. Foods can cause allergic responses and changes in behavior as a result of specific chemicals added to them.[32]

Children who inherit allergic tendencies are inclined to have dermatitis and frequent runny nose in their first twelve months, with wheezing occurring later and increasing in prevalence with age.[33] Extended breast-feeding and elimination of cow's milk and its products usually solves the problem.

FOODS TO AVOID

Allergens. Here's a summary of the list of common allergens to be avoided for a minimum of eighteen months:

- cow's milk and its derivatives (cheese, etc.)
- wheat and wheat products (cereals and breads made with wheat)
- oranges and other citrus fruits, including pineapples
- commercial eggs (as opposed to fertile eggs)
- nuts
- tomatoes
- chocolate

Oxalic acid foods. Spinach, chard, rhubarb, and unhulled sesame seeds are very high in oxalic acid. Moderate amounts are found in peanuts, pecans, wheat germ, and baking and bitter chocolate.[34]

Oxalic acid is a calcium thief. Because some of these foods are nutrient-dense, they should be served later on in small quantities when your child is eating a variety of foods. (The wheat germ and chocolate should never be served. These are not primal foods.)

Sweet foods. Berries and melons are too high in carbohydrates for small, sensitive stomachs. Your child has a lifetime ahead to enjoy these treats. The less sweet the early foods are, the more interest your child will have in vegetables during these fast-growing months.

Honey, in addition to its high carbohydrate content, poses another problem. Honey sometimes contains bacteria that produce botulinal toxin once they are in the intestine of children under one year of age. This is a poison that can cause intestinal disease and sometimes respiratory failure. The American Medical Association has published a press release advising parents against feeding honey to babies under one year of age.[35] It is best to avoid honey at any age because of its very high carbohydrate content. Honey's small offering of minerals can be obtained from foods that have additional benefits as well.

Fruit juices. We have already cited the disadvantages of fruit juices. If used at all, they should be highly diluted with water and fed from a cup, not a baby bottle. Because they are largely carbohydrate in content, fruit juices may contribute to "nursing bottle cavities," cavities caused by the sugar that bathes the teeth when taken in from a baby bottle. *No fruit juice* is a better choice than diluted fruit juice.

Dangerous foods. The following foods are to be avoided because they have been reported to cause choking: peanuts, grapes, round slices of frankfurter (not on our diet anyway), raw carrot, and large pieces of apple.

Microwave-cooked foods. We do not recommend microwave ovens for baby food preparation. In addition to molecular distortion of food proteins, microwave heating can create hot spots in food. Many incidents of burning of the mouth and throat have been reported.

Commercial baby foods. Sugar and starchy fillers are often used in prepared baby foods. Tapioca and modified food starches are commonly added as gelling agents. These, along with excessive use of sweeteners, are undesirable. The heating process required to preserve food in cans or jars for shelf storage destroys nutrients. It is this destruction of enzymes that enables food to remain at room temperature for endless periods without spoiling.

Hydrolyzed vegetable protein is about 40 percent MSG by weight, a fact unknown to most label readers. Hydrolyzed vegetable protein is a totally unnecessary and potentially hazardous substance.[36]

Dried baby foods are not much better. Restoring water to concentrated flakes or granules does not bring the food back to its original value.

Grains.   People who are sensitive to cow's milk are often sensitive to wheat. These two foods have a common peptide (linkage of protein molecules) that alters intestinal transit time (the time it takes to digest and eliminate food).[37,38] As a point of interest, doctors around the country are reporting that when patients comply with the suggested no-milk, no-wheat diet, the patients check back with glowing reports of feeling better than ever before.

PREPARATION OF FIRST FOODS: INTRODUCING SOLIDS

WEANING should be introduced as a *complement* rather than as a *supplement* to breast milk. New foods should be offered slowly and sequentially until a wide variety of foods is accepted. Texture is a critical factor during early weaning. Regardless of flavor, infants tend to accept very smooth foods and reject any that are gritty or coarse.

The first few trials should be presented after the milk feed is completed. Nurse, then introduce the new food.

It is best to introduce one new food at a time, preferably every two to four days. Possible allergic reactions to look for are sneezing; runny nose; rash around mouth, anus, or urethra; a change in stool or personality. Nonallergenic foods should be rotated every five to six days to minimize sensitization. Sensitization may occur when the same foods are eaten once or twice daily for five to seven consecutive days.

If a particular food is rejected, offer it again a little later on. Persistent rejection, however, may indicate an adverse reaction, and that food should be abandoned.

The sequence in which solid foods are added is not critical. Combination foods should be introduced only after tolerance to single ingredients is established.

Offering a variety of foods over a period of time provides nutrient balance and encourages acceptance of a wider selection of foods later.

Breast milk contains sufficient water for most infants. Babies may require additional water during hot weather and when they are not feeling well. But after introduction of solids, there may be times you think your baby is hungry when in fact the complaint is a call for water. Solid foods may increase water needs, particularly when new foods contain high protein such as found in strained meats and egg yolks. (Fertile eggs are healthful, but we do not recommend strained meats until your child is past a year. It has been suggested that the manufacturers reduce the meat content of commercial baby foods from the usual 40 to 50 percent to amounts closer to the infants' requirements.[39])

SUGGESTED WEANING SCHEDULE AND FOOD PREPARATION HINTS

This suggested sequence is a guide for the gradual introduction of solid foods, taking into account common sensitivities. Preparation suggestions are indicated with a bullet (·).

First Level

Age: Preferably begin at eight and a half or nine months, but absolutely no younger than six months.

Type of food: Hypoallergenic, puréed, mashed foods containing iron.

Quantity: Start with one teaspoon of a single food on the first day. Offer two teaspoons the next day, working up to one or two tablespoons a day. After three days, introduce a second food from this category.

Food choices: Carrots, squash, yam, broccoli, cauliflower, banana, apple, apricot, sprouts (blended in water), Jerusalem artichoke.

• Adding breast milk to ground vegetables sweetens the mix and imparts a familiar taste. This is a masterstroke for introducing new foods.

• Vegetables should be lightly steamed and mashed. Other foods should be ground.

• It's very tempting to make additional quantities of mashed or ground foods and freeze them for future use. Freezing destroys nutrients, and although most home refrigerator freezers are cold enough to maintain frozen foods, they are not cold enough to freeze foods properly. If you do freeze foods, use them within two weeks.

• Do not season with salt and sugar. Other seasonings (listed below) may be used later on.

Second Level

Age: Begin at about twelve months.
Type of food: Foods high in zinc and good for the immune system.
Quantity: Two to four tablespoons a day.
Food choices: Sweet potato, cabbage, papaya, string beans, split pea soup, blackstrap molasses, millet, brown rice cereal, potato, lima beans, tofu.

• Lima beans, potato, and millet may be too difficult to digest. Watch for signs. The addition of papaya mashed into the foods is often helpful. Papaya aids digestion.

• Serve wheat cereals and oatmeal later on; at least wait until *after* the first birthday. Brown rice and millet are better cereal choices.

Third Level

Age: Begin at about fourteen months.
Type of food: Foods high in zinc and/or fiber.
Quantity: Four to six tablespoons a day.
Food choices: Acorn squash, barley, parsnips, asparagus, yogurt, eggs, avocado, goat's milk, brewer's yeast powder (sprinkled lightly on foods).

• The best way to prepare eggs is to steam them in the shell for six minutes.

• Grind small amounts of raw vegetables into cooked vegetables.

• When your child has enough teeth to chew well, offer small bits of soft raw vegetables on a platter, such as cucumber and tomato.

Fourth Level

Age: Begin at about eighteen months.
Type of food: Foods high in B vitamins and calcium.
Quantity: According to appetite.
Food choices: Tahini, lamb, greens, kelp, eggplant, rye, beets and greens, chicken (organic), rutabaga, beans, fish, buckwheat, liver.
   • We recommend Protein-Aide tahini, which is made from the mechanically hulled sesame seeds.
   • Serve raw vegetables on platters. Children love little bits of veggies that are easy to chew. They enjoy watching you open green pea pods, and they love the peas.

Fifth Level

Age: Begin at about twenty-one months.
Type of food: Additional primal foods.
Quantity: According to appetite.
Food choices: Walnuts, turkey, organic chicken, pineapple, wheat (in very limited quantities), sunflower seeds (preferably sprouted), and other seeds listed below.
   • Soak nuts or seeds in pure water (nuts for twenty-four hours, seeds for twelve hours) and allow to sprout for one day. (See more detailed sprouting instructions in next chapter.) Grind into foods. These seeds can be used: pumpkin, sunflower, sesame, squash, chia, alfalfa, mung, red clover, and fenugreek.
   • The following seasonings can be added to foods: ground celery seed, kelp powder, dulse powder, miso, tamari, and mixed vegetable powders.[40]

Final Level

Age: Two to three years.
Type of food: All primal foods.
Quantity: According to appetite.

Food choices: Lamb, liver, duck, clams, soy, lentils, kiwi, blackberries, blueberries.

• To make wheat cereal: sprout wheatberries for two days; steam slightly, grind, and serve with a bit of yogurt. Remember, do not use wheat products frequently. That means limiting breads too. Occasionally, use a multigrain sprouted bread. Try to get the varieties that do not have flour added to the sprouted grains.

• Empty a capsule of carrot-grown acidophilus into any mixed vegetable or grain preparation.

• Add assorted sprouts to all dishes.

• By this age, your child has probably already been sharing family meals. We can only repeat: *children learn best by example.* You cannot preach good nutrition while your hand is in a bag of potato chips.

HOMEMADE EMERGENCY FORMULAS

THERE is nothing more frustrating than opening the freezer on the night you are ready to go to your best friend's surprise birthday party only to find that the supply of expressed milk has been unexpectedly depleted or that a bottle has burst. Or maybe in your haste it crashes to the floor. Emergencies do come up now and then, and there are solutions. The following formulas may be used on occasion.

Raw goat's milk.   Find a safe source for certified raw goat's milk. (If your local natural food store doesn't carry it, ask the people who shop in the store. Someone is bound to lead you to a source.) Dilute with pure bottled spring water in the amount specified by your doctor, depending on the age of your baby. Usually, goat's milk is diluted two parts milk to one part water. Add lactose (milk sugar) to sweeten to about the same taste as mother's milk — about three tablespoons to each quart of formula. (Milk sugar is sold in drugstores without a prescription.) If the baby is over three months of age, a small amount of blackstrap molasses and brewer's yeast powder may be added to the above (one-half teaspoon of each per quart).

When your baby is a year old, no dilution or addition of lactose is necessary. Goat's milk is a satisfactory occasional substitute for breast milk because its composition is closer to human milk than cow's milk. Goat's milk has even been used as a substitute for formula, but not exclusively because it interferes with folic acid and may lead to anemia. If fresh raw goat's milk is unavailable, keep a box of powdered goat's milk on hand.

Fresh goat's milk can be used more frequently than powdered goat's milk. If you must be away for an extended period of time, one teaspoon of vegetable oil, such as sesame or olive oil, should be added along with regular infant supplements.

Yogurt emergency formula. If there is absolutely nothing else on hand and your baby requires a milk feeding to fall asleep, the sitter can strain a good quality yogurt and dilute it with water.

Simple soy formula. This is a convenient, inexpensive backup, developed by Dr. Lester Luz. The ingredients can always be on hand.

1 tablespoon soy powder
1 teaspoon safflower oil (fresh, refrigerated supply)

½ teaspoon blackstrap molasses

Add these ingredients to 3 ounces of pure spring water, and blend.

Soy formula number 2. This soy formula has additional nutrient-dense ingredients.

1 cup soy flour or powder
4 cups water (pure bottled spring water)
3 tablespoons lactose
1 tablespoon vegetable oil (preferably virgin cold-pressed olive oil)
1 tablespoon brewer's yeast (or nutritional yeast, if baby prefers taste)

¼ teaspoon calcium lactate powder
⅛ teaspoon magnesium oxide powder
½ tablet of kelp or equivalent in powder

Mix soy flour in 4 cups water and boil for 20 minutes. Cool and mix with other ingredients in blender. Bottle and store in refrigerator.

When soy formula is given, the infant should receive these additional supplements daily:

· ascorbic acid — 50 milligrams in liquid form
· cod-liver oil — ¼ to 1 teaspoon (depending on age)
· vitamin E — 30 IU

Milk-free formula. If your child is sensitive to goat's milk, or if you know that allergies to milk exist in the family, you may want to try this milk-free, vegetable broth formula, which is nutritious and satisfying. Although not recommended for long-term bottle-feeding, it's okay for occasional or supplementary use.

1 medium carrot	4 cups water (pure bottled spring water)
2 medium potatoes	
½ small beet	3 tablespoons lactose
2 stalks celery	1 ounce raw almonds
1 medium zucchini	1 ounce Protein-Aide sesame seeds
3 large sprigs parsley (or other greens, such as comfrey)	

Chop vegetables and place in large pot with 4 cups water. Cover and bring to boil. Lower heat and simmer for 20 to 30 minutes. Strain vegetables out and discard; add lactose (milk sugar, sold in drug-stores) to broth. Grind almonds and sesame seeds fine in a seed grinder. Then pour vegetable broth in blender and add ground seeds. Blend at high speed for 1 to 3 minutes and liquefy well. Strain through fine cloth. Refrigerate strained broth immediately. Shake well and heat to body temperature before feeding. Yield: approximately 18 to 20 ounces (one day's feeding).

Caution: In no way are any of the above formulas intended for extensive or frequent use. They are once-in-a-while substitutes for breast-feeding. If you choose to use these formulas before your baby is nine months old, consult with your physician.

We have introduced food changes to you, and now you are introducing food changes to your baby. Since children learn more by what you do than what you say, this is the time to set an example. Despite the promise of health and intelligence, maintaining the optimal diet is easier said than done. We are not so naive as to think that you will forevermore resist (or that your child will not be exposed to) high-fat, high-sugar, high-calorie, high-salt, and low-fiber foods. But the more prominent your provision of *low-fat, low-*

sugar, low-calorie, no-salt, high-fiber foods during your child's first eighteen months, the better the chances that your child will like vegetables for the rest of his or her life.

And the later your child is exposed to the worst of foods, the more protective will be the past exposure from the best of foods. For the moment, you have a captive audience.

COMPENDIUM

Premature weaning

Is only practiced by humans
Interferes with many metabolic functions
Reduces immunity to disease

Weaning should be

Gradual
Started no sooner than six months
Started when baby demands it

Cow's milk is not a suitable weaning food because it

Is hard to digest
May cause

> gastrointestinal bleeding
> iron deficiency anemia
> abdominal pain of childhood
> allergies
> milk-borne infections
> antisocial behavior
> cataracts
> colitis
> eczema

Baby may also be sensitive to

Wheat gluten (celiac disease)
Citrus fruit
Additives

Foods to avoid are

Common allergens

    cow's milk and derivatives
    wheat and wheat products
    citrus fruit
    commercial eggs
    nuts
    tomatoes
    chocolate

Oxalic acid foods (spinach, chard, rhubarb, unhulled sesame seeds)
Sweet foods (berries and melons, honey, fruit juices)
Dangerous foods (peanuts, grapes, frankfurters, carrots, apple pieces)
Microwave-cooked foods
Commercial baby foods

Introduce solid foods to baby's diet

Slowly
With nonallergenic choices at first
By offering only a teaspoonful at first
By offering food after the milk feed
In ground or finely mashed form

CHAPTER
∾ 10 ∾

Table Talk: Family Recipes

IN WHICH WE OFFER

food power

If we had our way, recipe books would be no more than a few pages long. The more you do to food — the more "gourmet" you make it — the less it will do for you. That doesn't mean food has to be bland or uninteresting. Food can be both straightforward *and* exciting.

For example, a dinner of lightly steamed vegetables (steamed only until the vegetables reach prime color and are still crispy) and steamed fish or chicken, or perhaps a grain dish, plus a large tossed salad containing ten or twelve raw ingredients (including sprouts) and embellished with a rainbow of herbs and spices can be a royal feast.

The pleasure in eating is not in the costly flavor, but in yourself.

— HORACE

If you are a gourmet chef, your direction in the kitchen has taken a 180-degree turn since the arrival of your baby. Forget soufflés and Peking duck. (I'm sure you already have.) Your new modus operandi in the kitchen is speed, convenience, and *nutrient density*. Wait — don't go away! This doesn't mean that your meals won't be tasty; they'll just be different.

To meet the requirements of your modified cooking style, you need:

· a new repertoire of recipes using easily obtainable fresh foods that store well (grains, for example; harvest time is but once a year)
· a vegetable bin stocked with fresh vegetables, replenished every few days with in-season selections in a variety of colors, shapes, and sizes
· a fish dealer with whom you have a good working relationship who will supply the catch of the day, or at least the catch of yesterday (fresh fish doesn't smell and is *always* delicious)
· sprouting jars for your kitchen garden
· a natural food store for your purchase of organically grown poultry, organ meats, fertile eggs, whole-milk viable yogurt, grains, seeds, sprouted-grain breads, and nutrient supplements (if such a

store is not easily accessible, refer to Appendix B for sources offering mail-order delivery)

SHARING LUNCH WITH YOUR WEANLING

WHEN your baby approaches weaning age and graduates from level
to level, you can begin to plan family meals. Here are a few suggestions to help you get started. (The levels referred to here corre-
spond to the weaning stages described in the previous chapter.)

Carrot Lunch
(FIRST LEVEL)

2 carrots
1 tablespoon sprouted sunflower seeds

¼ avocado
a few leaves green Bibb
  lettuce

For Baby: Lightly steam ½ carrot; grind. Add some breast milk to
liquefy and sweeten.
For Mom: Grate 1½ carrots; place on bed of lettuce with remaining
ingredients. The natural oil of the avocado and the sunflower seeds
should be all the "salad dressing" you need.

Delicious Millet
(SECOND LEVEL)

1 cup millet
2 cups water
2 tablespoons Protein-Aide
  sesame seeds

½ teaspoon tamari
3 walnuts, chopped

Bring water to boil; add millet and simmer covered on low heat for
about 15 minutes, or until grain absorbs all the water.
For Baby: Add breast milk to 2 or 3 tablespoons millet; mash.
For Mom: Add remaining ingredients to balance of millet. (If any
millet is left over, refrigerate it and toss into salad for your next
meal; the addition of any cold grain to a salad adds to its flavor, texture, and protein quality.) Optional: add ¼ cup lightly steamed
tempeh.

Potato Surprise
(THIRD LEVEL)

1 large sweet potato   ½ cup yogurt

Bake large potato until fork pierces it easily (40 to 60 minutes at 400 degrees).
For Baby: Scoop out about 5 tablespoons potato, and mash with 1 tablespoon yogurt.
For Mom: Embellish rest of potato with remaining yogurt.

Easy Fish Salad
(FOURTH LEVEL)

The greatest timesaver for lunch today is yesterday's leftovers.

leftover broiled fish, about 1
  cup
¼ cup diced celery

1 tablespoon garlic mayonnaise (homemade or additive-free)

For Baby: Serve small pieces of leftover fish.
For Mom: Blend remaining fish with other ingredients, and use as filling in a pita pouch or as a salad on green lettuce leaves.

Easy Turkey (*or Chicken*) Lunch
(FIFTH LEVEL)

leftover turkey (or chicken)
raw vegetables, cut up (carrot,
  zucchini, and beets)

green lettuce
sprouted-grain bread

For Baby and Mom: Slices of turkey (or chicken), with cut-up vegetables, lettuce leaves, and sprouted-grain bread.

Liver Slivers
(FINAL LEVEL)

½ pound liver
1 medium onion, sliced thin

1 teaspoon butter or oil
1 apple, sliced thin

Place liver in freezer for 10 minutes. (This facilitates the cutting process.) Slice liver into thin, spaghetti-sized strands. Simmer onions in butter until translucent, add liver and apple slices. Stir-fry quickly over medium heat, moving pieces about while cooking. (Do not overcook. This is a very fast process.) Serve with baked sweet potatoes and assorted steamed vegetables.
For Baby, Mom, and Dad: Enjoy!

Tofu Omelet
(FINAL LEVEL)

1 green pepper, diced
½ cake tofu, cut into ½-inch
   cubes
½ cup mushrooms, diced

1 small onion, diced
1 teaspoon butter
5 eggs, beaten

Sauté pepper, tofu, mushrooms, and onions in butter until vegetables are crisp-tender. Add beaten eggs. Cook until bottom is done. Lift around edges to let egg run to bottom of skillet. Finish under broiler. Serve with alfalfa sprouts.
For Baby, Mom, and Dad: Enjoy!

CONVENIENCE COMPROMISE

IF all you can show for your day's activities is a pile of diapers, fatigue, and housework undone, here are a couple of easy dinner plans.

Homemade-Storebought Nice-Rice Dinner

1 cup brown rice
2 cups water

1 tablespoon tamari
2 cloves garlic, minced

Bring water to boil; add rice and seasonings. Simmer covered for about 30 minutes or until rice absorbs all the water. Yields about 3 cups cooked rice.
   Meanwhile, call local Chinese take-out restaurant and order an

MSG-free dish of cashew chicken, or shrimp and vegetables, or braised tofu and vegetables. Add take-out dish to brown rice.

The basic premise of preparing your own high-fiber grain and adding a portion of an already-prepared tasty dish has endless variations. See how creative you can be.

Lunch-Dinner-Meal-in-a-Bowl

A large pot of soup has many virtues. With the proper seasonings, it lends the entire house a homey, warm ambience. The pot sits atop the stove, always at the ready, providing fare for a day or even two.

2 quarts water	2 tablespoons tamari
½ cup rice, barley, or millet	1 clove garlic, minced
½ cup each, diced: onion, green pepper, celery, carrot, sweet potato, zucchini, mushrooms	black pepper oregano thyme

Bring water to boil. Add rice (or barley or millet). Reduce heat and cover. Cook on low heat for ½ hour. Add vegetables, tamari, garlic, and seasonings to taste. Barely simmer for 1 to 2 hours, or until you are ready to eat. Yields about 10 cups soup.

NUTRI-FOOD RECIPES

THESE recipes contain nutrients that have been recommended as essential for the production of top-quality breast milk.

RECIPES HIGH IN ESSENTIAL FATTY ACIDS

Avocado Salad

1 ripe avocado	1 ripe tomato, cut in wedges
green lettuce leaves	1 slice onion
½ cup alfalfa sprouts	

Slice avocado and place on lettuce leaves. Smother with alfalfa sprouts. Ring plate with tomato wedges. Dice onion onto top. Serves two, as a small salad.

Broiled Salmon Steak

2 slices fresh salmon steak,   1 clove garlic, minced
   about one inch thick   lemon wedges
1 teaspoon butter

Top fish with butter and fresh garlic. Broil about 5 minutes on each side. Do not overcook. Squeeze lemon on fish before serving. Eat the skin — that's where the DHA and EPA hang out. Serves two.

Tofu-Sesame Dressing

1 cup tofu   1 tablespoon chopped
1 cup water   parsley
2 tablespoons tamari   2 or 3 cloves garlic, minced
¼ cup Protein-Aide tahini   ½ cup lemon juice
                                    1 teaspoon kelp powder

Place all ingredients in blender and whirl until smooth. Yields about 2 cups dressing. This dressing can embellish salads or fish.

RECIPES HIGH IN VITAMIN D

Bird's Nest

2 slices sprouted-grain bread   1 teaspoon butter
                                    2 eggs

Remove a 3-inch circle from center of each slice of bread. Melt butter in frying pan and add bread. When bread is toasted on one side, flip it over and break an egg carefully into the hole in each slice. Continue cooking until egg looks "just right." Season to taste. Or cook until bottom is done, flip over, and cook "easy" on other side. Serves one or two.

Also see Liver Slivers (p. 199).

RECIPES HIGH IN VITAMIN A

Cream of Carrot Soup

10 medium carrots, chopped
2 ribs celery, chopped
1 to 2 quarts water
3 teaspoons garlic, minced
1½ cups Protein-Aide tahini

2 tablespoons fresh parsley,
  minced
¼ cup unsalted cashew nuts,
  crushed
tamari to taste

In large kettle, simmer vegetables in water until barely tender, or about 5 minutes. Add garlic and place in blender; purée soup. Add tahini and parsley, blend thoroughly. Stir in cashew nuts and season to taste with tamari. Serve warm but not hot. Makes 10 cups soup.

Also see Liver Slivers (p. 199) and Lunch-Dinner-Meal-in-a-Bowl (p. 201).

RECIPES HIGH IN CALCIUM

Egg and Tofu Salad

3 hard-boiled eggs, chopped
1-inch slice of tofu, mashed
1 tablespoon lemon juice
1 teaspoon sesame oil

dash of black pepper
¼ cup celery, chopped fine
1 teaspoon Protein-Aide
  sesame seeds

Combine eggs and tofu. Add other ingredients, and mix well. Serve with sprouts and sprouted-grain bread. Serves two.

Mung Bean Sprout Salad

½ cup mung bean sprouts
½ cup finely chopped celery
¼ cup diced tofu
½ cup grated carrots

¼ cup chopped pine nuts
½ tablespoon Protein-Aide
  sesame seeds
leafy green lettuce

Combine first six ingredients and serve on lettuce leaves with Sesame Dressing (recipe follows). Serves two.

Sesame Dressing

¼ cup ground sesame seeds   2 tablespoons lemon juice
½ cup water   ½ clove garlic, crushed

Blend all ingredients until smooth. Yields ¾ cup dressing.

RECIPES HIGH IN ZINC AND VITAMIN E

No-Bake Granola

1 cup Protein-Aide sesame   ½ cup chopped almonds
  seeds   ½ cup sunflower seeds
2 tablespoons sesame oil   ¼ cup pumpkin seeds
2 cups fine rolled oats   ½ cup unsweetened coconut
¼ cup sprouted wheat-   meal
  berries   ½ cup chopped raisins

Grind sesame seeds. Blend in oil. Add remaining ingredients; mix
thoroughly. Store in covered container in refrigerator. Serve with
yogurt or juice. Add fresh fruit pieces if desired. Makes 5 to 6 cups
granola.

The Whole-Grain Basic

So easy! Just boil 2 cups water and add 1 cup grain (brown rice,
millet, buckwheat, oatmeal), and simmer until done. Add one or
more of the following: cinnamon; chopped nuts; seeds; sprouts;
small bits of vegetables, raw or quickly stir-fried; cubed tofu; sliced
banana; chopped apple; unsweetened coconut. Optional: add 2
scrambled eggs.

RECIPES HIGH IN VITAMIN C

Fresh fruit platters require little preparation. For special treats, cut
up pieces of assorted fruit (include cantaloupe and berries when in
season), add a dollop or two of yogurt, and Protein-Aide sesame
seeds or sprouted nuts. Top with 1 tablespoon grape juice.
    Keep a bottle of grape juice on hand to embellish yogurt and fruit
platters. Just a small amount adds flavor.

RECIPES HIGH IN B VITAMINS

This recipe is for a later date, perhaps the kind of dish you'll have time to prepare when your child is two or three years old. Children adore the purchase and preparation of a whole coconut.

If you offer liver to your child at an early age, he or she will grow up loving it. Not many foods available to us are as nutrient-dense.

Indonesian Liver

2 tablespoons sesame oil
1 medium onion, finely
  chopped
1 garlic clove, crushed
½ teaspoon turmeric
1 tablespoon ground peanuts or
  cashew nuts
¼ teaspoon cayenne pepper

freshly ground black pepper
1 pound calves' liver, thinly
  sliced
1 cup Thick Coconut Milk
  (recipe follows)
1 bay leaf
1 onion, thinly sliced and
  stir-fried

Heat oil in skillet; stir-fry chopped onion and garlic until onion is translucent. Stir in turmeric, ground nuts, cayenne pepper, and freshly ground black pepper. Cook for 2 minutes, stirring constantly. Add liver and cook, turning pieces over, for 1 minute. Pour in coconut milk; add bay leaf. Cook, stirring often, for 2 to 3 minutes, or until sauce is thick and liver cooked. Remove bay leaf.

Spoon liver and sauce into serving dish. Garnish with stir-fried sliced onions. Serves three or four.

Thick Coconut Milk

1 fresh coconut
2½ cups water

Remove coconut meat from shell. One way to do this is to pierce the "eyes" to drain out juice, then place whole coconut in 400-degree oven for 15 minutes. Remove from oven and place in plastic bag. Place bag on hard surface and crack coconut with hammer or meat mallet. Shell will fall away, leaving large chunks of meat. Peel off brown skin with paring knife. (For added nutrients, leave skin intact.) Cut meat into chunks and grate in blender or food processor. Bring water to just under boiling; pour over grated coconut. Set aside for 30 minutes.

Drain water and push softened coconut through strainer lined with cheesecloth or muslin, squeezing cloth to extract as much "milk" as possible.

FROM SEED TO SALAD: HOW TO SPROUT

THERE is an ideal way to beat the food-processing establishment. Growing sprouts on your kitchen counter will save you money and provide tasty food of high nutrient quality. The bonus is that home-grown sprouts are devoid of additives. It is our opinion that of all of the hints we have offered to improve the quality of your breast milk, the use of sprouted seeds is among the best.

Combine a half dozen sprouts (alfalfa, mung, radish, azuki, sunflower, and lentil are possibilities), add herb seasonings, a dash of apple cider vinegar, and a few slices of avocado, and enjoy the medley for lunch with a chunk of sprouted grain bread. The cost of the sprout salad potpourri is less than a quarter if you grow the sprouts yourself.

SPROUTING EQUIPMENT

The best equipment for sprouting is the one-quart canning jar. These jars are widemouthed, withstand boiling water for thorough cleansing, and are quite durable. You can, however, use any mason jar. Canning jars range in cost from one to three dollars each, depending on whether you are shopping in John's bargain basement or Bloomingdale's. Discard the glass tops, rubber rings, and metal wires. All you need is the jar.

Buy nylon mosquito netting at a hardware store. Cheesecloth works too, but it's harder to use and to keep clean. Dig out some short, thick rubber bands. (You must have some in that "catch-all" drawer in the kitchen.) Cut the netting into squares large enough to cover the tops of the jars with enough of an overlap to secure with the rubber bands. This is the best and cheapest sprouting equipment available.

SPROUTING INSTRUCTIONS

Seeds may be purchased in any natural food store. They should sprout whether they are sealed in fancy packages labeled "For Sprouting," or whether they come from a bulk barrel. If the seeds don't sprout, chances are the supply you used was not fresh or was stored under adverse conditions. If you have trouble with seeds from a local source, check the Resources list in Appendix B for the address of Walnut Acres, a mail-order company that always has the best of everything.

Start your sprouting experience with only one or two varieties. Alfalfa, lentil, and sunflower seeds are among the easiest. These three together provide a nice combination of nutrients: the tiny green leaves of the alfalfa contain chlorophyll and B vitamins; the lentils add a chewy texture; and the sunflower seeds provide the polyunsaturated fatty acids. Alfalfa and lentils are legumes, so you are even using the protein complementarity principle of mixing legumes and seeds.

The recommended quantities and germination time for some commonly sprouted seeds and beans:

Seed or Bean	Recommended Quantity	Germination Time
Alfalfa	1 tablespoon	4 days
Azuki	2 tablespoons	2 days
Buckwheat	2 tablespoons	3 or 4 days
Chick-peas	3 tablespoons	1 day
Clover	1 tablespoon	4 days
Lentils	2 tablespoons	2 days
Mung	2 tablespoons	3 days
Radish	½ tablespoon	4 days
Rye	1 tablespoon	2 days
Sesame	1 tablespoon	1 or 2 days
Soybeans	1 tablespoon	1 or 2 days
Sunflower seeds	2 tablespoons	1 day
Wheatberries	2 tablespoons	2 or 3 days

Soak each variety of seed or bean in one cup of water in a jar overnight. (Seeds that take the same amount of time to germinate can be placed in the same jar; for example, lentils and wheatberries can be sprouted together.) In the morning, pour the water off. (Use this water for your plants — they'll love it! Or save the water to use in soups.) Dumping the seeds into a strainer facilitates the washing process. Rinse thoroughly under the faucet. Return seeds to jar after shaking strainer by tapping against side of sink. Cover jar with mesh netting and tight rubber band.

Place jar upside down at slight angle in dish rack so that remaining water can run off. Sprouts appreciate moisture, but not puddles. Rinse seeds again in the evening. If you can also rinse them in the middle of the day, that's an advantage. Continue rinsing and draining at least twice daily. Now that the seeds are no longer soaking in water, they can be rinsed directly under the faucet in the jars. Replace on rack until ready for use. The mesh netting, held in place with the rubber band, prevents the seeds from escaping when the water is poured off. (Be sure the rubber band is tight enough.)

Many people start the sprouting procedure in a dark place because this expedites growth. You may find, however, that when you hide the jars in a closet, you forget about them. When you unveil them a week or so later, it is not unlike Pandora's box. Another possibility is to place the jar in a paper bag and leave it on the kitchen counter as a reminder. We skip this procedure because sprouts that germinate in daylight develop with more nutrients.

Seeds may be consumed at any stage of sprouting, but harvesting at peak offers the most value. Vitamin C is synthesized during germination, and the concentrations of some of the B vitamins is also increased, along with other nutrients.

Since seeds and environments vary, it is advisable to experiment, using a good sprouting book as a guide.

Refrigerated sprouts last up to a week. But since they are growing in your kitchen, the "farm" couldn't be any closer. It is best to harvest as needed to optimize their nutrient value. (Harvesting sprouts simply involves taking them from the jar.) Sprouts are so inexpensive that we discard rather than save any surplus.

If your baby has not arrived on the scene yet, use your leisure time now to practice sprouting. Learn to make sprout omelets, add the sprouts to sandwich fillings, use them as snacks, simmer them with fish, or drop them into soups (just before serving).

The process of germination induces an increase in nutrient content. Anything that can grow into a plant or an animal must obviously have a select store of power. Sprouting leads to the manufacture of new protein, sugars, and fats within the growing seed. Using a variety of sprouts can supply *complete* protein, to say nothing of vitamins and minerals. We sincerely hope you'll take the time to learn to sprout. Once you know what you're doing, the involvement is no more than ten minutes in the morning and ten minutes at night. Not enough to be a burden; just enough to give you pleasure and provide your breast milk with very special quality nutrients. When your child is about six years old, the responsibility can be handed down.

Consuming primal foods boils down to shopping the perimeter of the supermarket and staying away from the center aisles, where the canned, packaged, and frozen products are displayed — they look good on the outside (the photography is great), but their contents do not measure up to the quality of the graphics. *Our goal is excellence.*

CHAPTER

~ 11 ~

The Best of Breast-Feeding Hints

IN WHICH WE TELL YOU

what worked best for women who have successfully breast-fed

The best of breast-feeding hints do not come from physicians (most of whom are men who have never had the experience), or from researchers who study demographics, or from those who test animal responses. They come from women who have breast-fed.

Hang in there. That's the best philosophy for successful breast-feeding.

— KATHI KAMEN GOLDMARK

The following breast-feeding hints have been contributed by Kathi Kamen Goldmark, Nancy Dyer, Catherine Hayden, Alice Cutler, Angela Milner, Angie Jones, Amanda Metcalf-Welch, Sandra Bryson, Marion Sakow, Julia Romero, and Lorraine Killian.

MISCELLANY

· Don't deliver your baby in a teaching hospital. You don't want thirty people in the room watching your performance.
· If you had drugs during labor or delivery, don't expect your baby to be an enthusiastic sucker right away. It takes a while for the baby to respond. The longer the delivery, the longer it takes for your baby to wake up.
· Even if you haven't had drugs, your baby may not be interested in sucking right away. There are so many other things for a new infant to observe. You'll notice that if anyone speaks to the baby, he or she will turn toward the voice.
· Don't wait if you need professional help if you're having trouble

breast-feeding. Many problems do go away by themselves, but others may get worse.

· Drink lots of water. It makes a great difference in your physical well-being.
· When you are breast-feeding in a public area, remember that nursing is less conspicuous than a crying baby.
· Always keep a spare blanket in your car or carriage in the event you have to nurse in public.
· Wear easy-access clothing, with buttons down the front or blouses that raise easily from the waist.
· Weight loss is easy even when you eat a lot. Don't feel guilty about consuming more calories.
· The second time around, everything works like a charm.

NURSING POSITIONS

· Sit on a straight-backed chair with your knee and leg propped up on a stool on the breast-feeding side.
· Lie on your side with your arm up. You can rest while the baby sucks. Later on, the baby gets into its own favorite position.
· Place a pillow under your arm on a rocking chair.
· Try the "football hold." Hold your baby under your arm with its head near your breast and its feet below your armpit.
· If you have had stitches, try lying on your side.
· Try a pillow under the baby.

LET-DOWN REFLEX HINTS

· Take a warm shower and massage your breasts.
· Be prepared for the sexual arousal that occurs during the breast-feeding process.
· Always listen to music when you feed. Music will relax you and help with the let-down reflex.
· To encourage let-down reflex, use visualization techniques. Think of a warm fire, or even visualize a diagram of the breast and the let-down reflex procedure.
· To encourage let-down reflex, visualize babies playing in pools of milk, or think of little babies sucking and sucking and sucking — milk flowing, flowing, flowing.

· If you have not been able to give up smoking, light up *after* your baby starts sucking. Smoking usually inhibits let-down. Better still, wait until your baby has finished feeding and is in another room.

THE FEEDING PROCESS

· Pull your nipple outward with your fingers to stimulate erection.
· Get the nipple deep into the baby's mouth and up against the upper palate. Support the breast and position it to make it easy for the baby to suck.
· Form a V with your fingers above and below the nipple when presenting the breast to your baby; this keeps the breast from the baby's nose so that he or she can breathe easily and grasp the nipple easily.
· If things don't feel quite right, place your finger in the baby's mouth to stop the suction. The baby should have most of the areola as well as the nipple itself in its mouth.
· The baby's mouth has to be directly in line with the nipple. Not halfway, not crooked, but directly in line.
· Put some breast milk on your nipple if the baby seems reluctant to start nursing.
· You may find you have a preference for holding your baby to your left breast (regardless of whether you are right- or left-handed). This may be because the baby is more relaxed — the sound of your heart has a soothing effect.
· Be sure your clothing is not in the way.
· Don't wear a bra for a half hour after nursing. Breasts like a lot of air.
· Start each feeding on opposite breasts because there will be more milk in the breast used last in the previous session. This balances the milk production in both breasts.
· Since it is suggested that you alternate breasts with each feeding, wear a ribbon or bracelet on the side you are to start with at the next feeding.
· Place your nipple next to the baby's cheek to encourage the baby to turn to the breast. This also stimulates nipple erection.
· If you or your baby is not feeling well, get into a tub of warm water with your baby. You will be amazed at how this facilitates the nursing process.

COPING

· Get out of the hospital as soon as possible after your baby is born.
· All the nice things you expect might not happen the first few days. Be patient.
· Be sure to have a handy support system if you've never breast-fed before. Have the telephone numbers of several experienced mothers on hand.
· Have someone give you massages as often as possible.
· Use nursing time to read to your other children or to play word games with them.
· Live with your baby for the first six weeks. Let anyone else handle shopping and cooking.
· Whenever you feel frustrated, remember that your baby is getting the best food possible.
· Don't be in a hurry to get your life back to the way it was before the baby.
· Don't worry about your appearance or how the house looks when guests arrive. Your baby is more important.
· Remember the Lamaze training slogan: "There's no such thing as not enough milk."
· Don't get out of your bathrobe for at least a month.
· If you don't rest the first six weeks, it will take six months to get back to normal.
· Don't "go crazy" when you have to be away. An occasional bottle of expressed milk or formula should not provoke guilt.
· If you are a highly structured person who needs to have the next twenty-four hours planned, you'd better get some counseling. Nursing has to be "loose." You sleep when your baby sleeps.
· Get an answering machine so you won't be tense about missing a call.
· When your baby is a little older, you can nurse and talk to friends on the phone at the same time.

EXPRESSING MILK

· Drink a glass of water each time before starting.
· Before your first attempt, try a glass of dark beer.
· The best time to express milk is at the time of a missed feeding.

- A warm, wet washcloth applied to the breast is helpful until you experience the let-down reflex.
- A warm shower before expressing milk is helpful.
- As soon as you become tense, milk flow stops. So do whatever you can to relax.
- Watch television while pumping milk. This takes your mind off the pumping process and helps relaxation.
- Invite an experienced breast-feeder to stay with you the first few times. Otherwise, the process can be frustrating.
- To pump milk, you have to apply pressure to the areola, either by hand or with a pump. A mechanical pump may be a more difficult technique to learn at first, but once mastered, it is easier than pumping by hand.
- When you are away from your baby, it is helpful to look at photos of your child to stimulate the reflex action.
- Don't thaw frozen milk in boiling water. It may curdle.

BREAST PROBLEMS

- Do not stop breast-feeding if you have mastitis.
- Change positions at each feeding to alleviate soreness.
- Nipple soreness goes away.
- If your nipples are inverted, try using shields. Shields are available in any drugstore. The shield forms a plastic tent over the areola and is very effective in pushing the nipple out, giving the baby a chance to grasp at it.
- If you apply lanolin *before* nipple problems develop, or when you feel a twinge of irritation, you'll never have serious difficulties.
- Ideally, your breast should not fill until your baby is feeding. A problem with engorgement may be a reflection of how you are relating to your baby at the beginning. The process works perfectly as soon as there is *interrelationship*.
- Air dry your nipples whenever possible.
- If breasts are engorged, always express a little milk before feeding. It's more difficult for the baby to feed if the breast is hard.
- Use breast milk to clear baby's stuffy nose (especially before feeding), to cure watery eyes, or to soothe sore nipples.

WEANING

· Don't rush the weaning process. There are more visits to the pediatrician and more aches and pains after weaning than before.
· Take your time weaning. Anthropologists who studied traditional tribes report that where weaning was delayed there were peaceful tribes. Abrupt weaning at six months occurred in those groups whose behavior was very structured, and these tribes were warlike.
· We are always rushing, and maybe that's why we are also in a hurry to give the baby solid foods. Take it from mothers who have done it both ways, it's much easier to feed breast milk exclusively — until your baby discovers the crumbs on the kitchen table.

Ultimately, the responsibility for producing quality milk and having a successful breast-feeding experience is yours. And so are the rewards. Good luck!

Epilogue

IN WHICH WE BID YOU FAREWELL

while reminding you of the important responsibilities you have to yourself, to the next generation, and perhaps to the world in general as you help to change the history of your time

One of the great medical advances of the past decade has been the scientific validation of the importance of species-specific milk. The next advance, in its infancy of world acceptance at this time, is understanding that if a new mother is to be able to nurture her child, she herself needs to be nurtured.

Although most professionals cite the time-honored cliché "breast is best," little instruction is provided to assist mothers in mastering the technique or in learning just how to make breast *best*.

The World Health Organization, in its recent progress reports, agrees that mothers must be in good health before they can breast-feed their children. Children in developing countries cannot get enough milk from their mothers after feeding for three months. Indigenous weaning foods may not sustain normal development. It is the responsibility of governments to ensure the health and adequate nutrition of mothers and infants — to put an end to the tragedies of early death for the children of third world countries, as well as to the subtle (and sometimes not so subtle) behavioral and physical defects of many American children.

It is the exclusive right of every child in the world to start life with mother's milk. But for lifetime benefits — for optimal physical and emotional development — the milk must be of high quality.

If we have appeared to be hard-hitting or exaggerated in our reporting, it is because the time has come to stop perpetuating myths. We cannot have a life of quality on fast foods.

Nourish the mother, thereby the infant.

APPENDIX

❦ A ❦

Breast Pumps

Breast pumps were evaluated in the January 1983 issue of *Clinical Pediatrics.* The researchers state:

> A good pump must completely evacuate the milk from the breast at each use, stimulate further secretion, and do this rapidly enough to allow frequent evacuation. In addition, it must be clean and safe even when used by a mother under physical and emotional stress. . . . The important place of psychosocial factors in reflex function is shown by the fact that some women have been successful collecting milk by hand expression or with poor-performance pumps, while others have been unsuccessful even with the best pumps. The best chance of stimulating and maintaining an abundant milk supply in problem cases is with the use of a good pump.

Recommended pumps are: Comfort Plus (by Kaneson), Egnell, Le Pump, and Gentle Expression. Hand pumps like Comfort Plus work fine once you learn the technique. They are also portable and inexpensive. Gentle Expression is battery-operated. Electric pumps are costly but efficient and are available for rental.

APPENDIX

B

Resources

Food and Supplements

For additional information on any products mentioned, send self-addressed, stamped envelope to:
Nutrition Encounter
Box 689
Larkspur, CA 94939

For information on prenatal and postnatal products, equipment, and care, write to:
Babyco
Box 2791
Eugene, OR 97402

For organically grown food not available at your local natural food store, contact:
Walnut Acres
Penns Creek, PA 17862

For organically grown apples, contact:
Kaste's Morningside
Galesville, WI 54630

For organic nuts in the shell and sprouting seeds, contact:
Jaffe Bros.
Box 636
Valley Center, CA 92082

For information on children's vitamins cited, contact:
Freeda Vitamins
36 East 41st Street
New York, NY 10017
Telephone: 212–685–4980
Freeda Vitamins products are sold via mail order.

For information on vitamin and mineral preparations for lactation,
contact:
Natrol
Box 5000
20371 Prairie Street
Chatsworth, CA 91311
Telephone: 818-701-9966
Natrol products are sold in health food stores.

Eclectic Institute, Inc.
11231 S.E. Market Street
Portland, OR 97216
Telephone: 503-256-4330
Eclectic Institute products are sold through doctors.

For information on Protein-Aide sesame seeds, contact:
International Protein Industries, Inc.
Box 871
Smithtown, NY 11787
Telephone: 516-231-7940
Protein-Aide sesame seeds are sold in health food stores.

For information on chlorella, contact:
Sun Chlorella California, Inc.
2641 Manhattan Beach Boulevard
Redondo Beach, CA 90278
Telephone: 213-536-0088
Sun Chlorella products are sold in health food stores.

Organizations

Information and assistance in breast-feeding:
La Leche League International
9616 Minneapolis Avenue
Franklin Park, IL 60131

Excellent health-freedom organization, monthly journal, and area conventions:
National Health Federation
212 West Foothill Boulevard
Monrovia, CA 91016
Telephone: 818-359-8334

Relaxation Aids

For information on relaxation music tapes, contact:
Halpern Sounds
1775 Old County Road #9
Belmont, CA 94002
Two applicable tapes are *Relaxation* (*Soundwave 2000 Series*) and *Lullabies and Sweet Dreams*.

Books

Ford, Marjorie Winn, et al. *The Deaf Smith Country Cookbook* (New York: Collier Books, 1973).

Kalokerinos, Archie. *Every Second Child* (New Canaan, CT: Keats Publishing, Inc., 1981).

Kamen, Betty, and Kamen, Si. *Kids Are What They Eat: What Every Parent Needs to Know about Nutrition* (New York: Arco Publishing, Inc., 1983).

Kamen, Betty, and Kamen, Si. *Total Nutrition during Pregnancy: How to Be Sure You and Your Baby Are Eating the Right Stuff* (New Canaan, CT: Keats Publishing, Inc., 1986).

La Leche League Publications

Magazines

Health Freedom News, monthly magazine of the National Health Federation, 212 West Foothill Boulevard, Monrovia, CA 91016

Health News and Review, published bimonthly by Keats Publishing, Inc., 27 Pine Street, New Canaan, CT 06840

Let's Live, monthly magazine published by Oxford Industries, Inc., 444 North Larchmont Boulevard, Los Angeles, CA 90004

Mothering, quarterly published by Mothering Publications, Inc., Box 8410, Santa Fe, NM 87504

APPENDIX

 C

Glossary

ABC. Alternative birthing center; a home away from home; a warm and cozy hospital room in which to give birth.

Acidophilus. See Carrot-grown acidophilus.

Amino acids. The building blocks of protein; twenty different amino acids are commonly found in protein.

Antibody. A molecule designed to destroy toxins in your body.

Antigen. Any substance (toxin, bacteria, or foreign matter) that stimulates the immune response, thereby inducing the formation of antibodies.

Apgar test. A method for determining an infant's condition at birth by scoring the heart rate, respiratory effort, muscle tone, reflex irritability, and color.

Areola. The brown area surrounding the nipples; its function is to protect the nipples during nursing.

Bioavailability. A measure of how easily a substance is assimilated by the body; high bioavailability means the body can use all or most of the offering.

Brewer's yeast. An extremely healthful dietary product rich in B vitamins; grown especially as a nutritional supplement.

Carrot-grown acidophilus. "Good-guy" bacteria grown on carrot juice that prevent invasion of harmful bacteria in the gut.

Casein. The fraction of cow's milk protein that forms the tough curd.

Celiac disease. Faulty absorption of food caused by sensitivity to gluten, found largely in wheat.

Chlorella. A one-celled organism resplendent with chlorophyll and other nutrients that enhance the immune system; a beneficial supplement.

Colic. An attack of abdominal pain caused by spasmatic contractions of the intestine, most common during the first three months of life.

Colitis. Inflammation of the colon.

Colostrum. The first mother's milk, which flows for a few days after delivery and is fully charged with protective qualities; "antiseptic paint" for baby's digestive tract.

Demand feeding. Feeding the baby at its request rather than according to a fixed schedule.

Desiccated liver. Dried liver; usually extracted from organically fed animals; a beneficial nutritional supplement.

Detoxify. To get rid of substances in the body that are unusable or even dangerous.

Dextrose. A form of sugar; often dissolved in water and given to babies to keep them quiet, a practice we do not recommend.

DHA. Docosahexaenoic acid, a fraction of body oil found in cold-water fish; the most abundant fatty acid utilized in brain development; found with EPA (*see* EPA).

DNA. Deoxyribonucleic acid, a nucleic acid of complex molecular structure occurring in cell nuclei as the basic structure of the genes; found in every living cell and responsible for cell replication.

Engorgement. Congestion of the breasts, which can be painful and which interferes with baby's ability to suck; caused by vascular dilation as well as arrival of milk.

Enzymes. A protein capable of accelerating or producing a specific reaction in the body — for example, digestive enzymes are responsible for functions of digestion, and so on.

EPA. Eicosapentaenoic acid, a fraction of body oil found in cold-water fish; required for the substances that control blood clotting; improves blood viscosity and lowers cholesterol and triglycerides; found with DHA (*see* DHA).

Episiotomy. A cut made to facilitate delivery when the doctor thinks your baby is too big and you are too small.

Essential fatty acids. A component of dietary fat; essential because you don't make them yourself and because they are needed for health and brain function.

Expression. The process of extracting milk from the breast for later use in feeding the baby or to relieve engorgement.

Fat-soluble vitamins. Substances found in the fat portion of foods that are needed in small quantities for healthy growth and for the preservation of life itself; absence or poor absorption can cause deficiency disease; stored by the body; specifically, vitamins A, D, E, and K.

Fatty acid. An overall term that describes body fat; made up of compounds necessary to promote optimal brain growth.

Foremilk. The breast milk released at the beginning of a feeding.

Formula. Mixtures of liquid or powdered food substances produced by food processing companies as a substitute for breast-feeding.

GLA. Gamma-linolenic acid; a useful form of oil converted by the body; found in mother's milk and in only a few botanical sources.

Hindmilk. The breast milk released in the latter part of a feeding; has higher fat content.

Jaundice. A depositing of bile pigments in the skin and mucous membranes with resulting yellow appearance.

Lactase. An enzyme that helps to digest lactose.

Lactation. A term referring to both milk production and breast-feeding.

Lactobacillus bifidus. "Good-guy" organisms in the intestinal tracts of breast-fed infants.

Lactose. The sugar in milk; it facilitates calcium and iron absorption.

Let-down reflex. Natural reflex caused by infant's sucking, which sets off release of oxytocin hormone, causing milk to flow toward nipples.

Mastitis. Inflammation of the breast; may be accompanied by abscess formation.

Mature milk. Milk produced by a mother nursing an older baby.

Meconium. The first stool passed by the newborn infant; dark green in color and mucilaginous in texture.

Milk-ejection reflex. *See* Let-down reflex.

Nipple-erection reflex. A reflex action causing the nipples to harden in anticipation of breast-feeding.

Oxytocin. A hormone stimulated by sucking; releases milk from milk sacs into ducts; a vital component of the let-down reflex.

Primal food. A whole or real food; one that has not been mushed, mashed, or mangled in any way.

Prolactin. A hormone that stimulates and sustains the formation of milk.

Protein complementarity. The combining of different food products to supply the best possible amino acid profile for conversion to human protein.

RNA. Ribonucleic acid; a nucleic acid that carries the genetic codes that control cellular protein synthesis.

Tamari. A Japanese soy sauce.

Tempeh. A food product made from soybeans by means of fermentation; meaty in texture and flavor; contains significant amount of vitamin B_{12}.

Tofu. Soaked, cooked, and curdled soybeans used in Asian cooking; high in quality protein, low in fat.

Trans fats. An unhealthful form of fat caused by oxidation, rancidity, overheating, and reheating of oils.

Transitional milk. Breast milk produced between first milk (colostrum) and mature milk; appears during first few weeks of feeding.

Water-soluble vitamins. Substances found in the water portion of foods that are needed in small quantities for health, growth, and the preservation of life itself; absence or poor absorption can cause deficiency disease; not usually stored in the body; specifically, the B-complex vitamins and vitamin C.

Weaning. The *gradual* introduction of solid food into your baby's diet.

APPENDIX

 D

References

Prologue

1. F. R. Sinatra, "Food Faddism in Pediatrics," *Journal of the American College of Nutrition* 3 (1984):169.

2. D. B. Jelliffe and E. P. Jelliffe, "Current Concepts in Nutrition: 'Breast Is Best': Modern Meanings," *New England Journal of Medicine* 297 (1977):912.

3. D. J. Ellis, "Secondary School Students' Attitudes and Beliefs about Breast Feeding," *Journal of School Health* 53 (1983):600.

4. E. Ludescher et al., "A Survey of Infant Feeding during the First Six Months of Life," *Pediatrics Padol* 16 (1981):51.

5. M. J. Houston, "Breast Feeding: Success or Failure," *Journal of Advanced Nursing* 6 (1981):447.

6. Ellis, "Secondary School Students' Attitudes."

7. J. D. Leeper, T. Milo, and T. R. Collins, "Infant Feeding and Maternal Attitudes among Mothers of Low Income," *Psychological Reports* 53 (1983):259.

8. E. E. Ekwo, L. B. Dusdieker, and B. M. Booth, "Factors Influencing Initiation of Breast Feeding," *American Journal of Diseases of Children* 137 (1983):375.

9. P. G. Wolman, "Feeding Practices in Infancy and Prevalence of Obe-

sity in Preschool Children," *Journal of the American Dietetics Association* 84 (1984):436.

10. M. Gueri, P. Jutsum, and R. Hoyte, "Breast Feeding Practices in Trinidad," *Bulletin of the Pan American Health Organization* 12 (1978):316.

11. A. W. Myeres, "A Retrospective Look at Infant Feeding Practices in Canada," *Journal of the Canadian Dietetic Association* 40 (1979):200.

12. S. R. Kemberling, "Supporting Breast Feeding," *Pediatrics* 63 (1979):60.

Chapter 1   Breast Milk: The Mystery of Its Mastery

1. H. Hopkins, "Next to Mother's Milk, There's Infant Formula," *FDA Consumer* 81-2139 (1980):14.

2. R. G. Whitehead, "Nutrition: The Changing Scene, Nutritional Aspects of Human Lactation," *Lancet* 1 (1983):167.

3. A. R. Vet, "Implantation and Development of the Gut Flora in the Newborn Animal," *Laboratoire d'Ecologie Microbienne* 14 (1983):354.

4. J. F. Soothill, "Immunological Aspects of Infant Feeding," in *Pediatric Immunology*, eds. J. F. Soothill, A. R. Hayward, and C. B. S. Wood (Oxford, England: Blackwell, 1983), p. 110.

5. K. Campbell, "Feeding the Newborn Infant," *Medical Journal of Australia* 1 (1978):274.

6. Lester A. Luz, M.D., pediatrician, personal communication, March 1985.

7. W. B. Pittard, III, "Breast Milk Immunology," *American Journal of Diseases of Children* 133 (1979):83.

8. A. S. Goldman and C. W. Smith, "Host Resistance Factors in Human Milk," *Journal of Pediatrics* 192 (1973):1082.

9. L. A. Hanson et al., "Protective Factors in Milk and the Development of the Immune System," *Pediatrics* 75, suppl. (1985):172.

10. Fr. Gillin and D. Reiner, "Human Breast Milk: A Broad Range of Anti-Parasite Activity," *Science* 221 (1983):1290.

11. P. D. Buisseret, "Allergy," *Scientific American* 247 (1982):86.

12. N. Kretchmer, "Summary: Gastrointestinal and Immunologic Development," *Pediatrics* 75, suppl. (1985):167.

13. W. A. Walker, "Absorption of Protein and Protein Fragments in the Developing Intestine: Role in Immunologic/Allergic Reactions," *Pediatrics* 75, suppl. (1985):167.

14. J. Riordan and B. A. Countryman, "Principles and Practice: Basics of Breastfeeding — Part III: The Biological Specificity of Breast Milk,"

Journal of Obstetric and Gynecologic and Neonatal Nursing 9 (1980):273.

15. L. S. Hurley, *Developmental Nutrition* (Englewood Cliffs, New Jersey: Prentice-Hall, Inc., 1980), p. 275.

16. K. M. Shahani, A. J. Kwan, and B. A. Friend, "Role and Significance of Enzymes in Human Milk," *American Journal of Clinical Nutrition* 33 (1980):1861.

17. S. Auricchio, "Does Breast Feeding Protect against the Development of Clinical Symptoms of Celiac Disease in Children?" *Journal of Pediatrics, Gastroenterology, and Nutrition* 2 (1983):428.

18. F. Bronner and J. W. Coburn, *Disorders of Mineral Metabolism* (New York: Academic Press, 1981), p. 99.

19. L. D. MacDonald, R. S. Gibson, and J. E. Miles, "Changes in Hair Zinc and Copper Concentrations of Breast Fed and Bottle Fed Infants during the First Six Months," *Acta Pediatrica Scandinavica* 71 (1982):785.

20. J. F. de Wijn, "Obesity in Children, III: Feeding Pattern in Relation to the Possible Development of Obesity," *Tijd Kindergeneeskd* 49 (1981):214.

21. J. D. Kark et al., "Validity of Maternal Reporting of Breast Feeding History and the Association with Blood Lipids in Seventeen-Year-Olds in Jerusalem," *Journal of Epidemiology and Community Health* 38 (1984):218.

22. Y. K. Wong and B. S. Wood, "Breast Milk Jaundice and Oral Contraceptives," *British Medical Journal* 4 (1971):403.

23. R. G. Carpenter, "Prevention of Unexpected Infant Death," *Lancet* 1 (1983):723.

24. D. B. Jelliffe and E. F. P. Jelliffe, *Human Milk in the Modern World* (New York: Oxford University Press, 1978), p. 89.

25. R. S. Cron, H. W. Shutter, and A. H. Lahmann, "Epidemic Infectious Diarrhea of the Newborn," *American Journal of Obstetrics and Gynecology* 40 (1940):88.

26. J. C. Hanna, "Breast Feeding versus Bottle Feeding in Relation to Oral Habits," *Journal of Dentistry for Children* 34 (1967):243.

27. G. Tank and C. A. Storvick, "Caries Experience of Children of One to Six Years Old in Two Oregon Communities," *Journal of the American Dental Association* 70 (1965):100.

28. A. Lucas et al., "Metabolic and Endocrine Responses to a Milk Feed in Six-Day-Old Term Infants: Differences between Breast and Cow's Milk Formula Feeding," *Acta Pediatrica Scandinavica* 70 (1981):195.

29. R. A. Lawrence, *Breast Feeding: A Guide for the Medical Profession* (St. Louis: C. V. Mosby Company, 1980), p. 68.

30. R. Ing, J. H. C. Ho, and N. L. Petrakis, "Unilateral Breast Feeding and Breast Cancer," *Lancet* 2 (1977):8029.

31. G. Dick, "The Etiology of Multiple Sclerosis," *Proceedings of the Royal Society of Medicine* 69 (1976):611.

32. G. R. Osborn, "Relationship of Hypotension and Infant Feeding to Etiology of Coronary Disease," *Collections of the International Research of Science* 169 (1968):193.

33. G. T. Lealman et al., "Calcium, Phosphorus, and Magnesium Concentrations in Plasma during First Week of Life and Their Relation to Type of Milk Feed," *Archives of Diseases of Childhood* 51 (1976):377.

34. Lawrence, *Breast Feeding: A Guide*, p. 78.

35. J. W. B. Douglas, "Extent of Breast Feeding in Great Britain in 1946 with Special Reference to Health and Survival of Children," *Journal of Obstetrics and Gynecology* 57 (1950):335.

36. A. Menendez-Patterson et al., "Effect of Early Pre- and Postnatal Acquired Malnutrition on Development and Sexual Behavior in the Rat," *Pharmacology, Biochemistry, and Behavior* 17 (1982):659.

37. J. C. Pearce, "The Art of Mothering," *Mothering* 35 (1985):17.

38. D. M. Fergusson, A. L. Beautrals, and P. A. Silva, "Breast Feeding and Cognitive Development in the First Seven Years of Life," *Social Science and Medicine* 16 (1982):1705.

39. B. Rodgers, "Feeding in Infancy and Later Ability and Attainment: A Longitudinal Study," *Developmental Medicine and Child Neurology* 20 (1978):421.

40. N. Newton, "Battle between Breast and Bottle," *Psychology Today* 49 (1972):68.

41. M. Hanafy, "Maternal Nutrition and Lactation Performance in Egypt," in *Maternal Nutrition during Pregnancy and Lactation: A Nestle Foundation Workshop*, eds. H. Aebi and R. Whitehead (Nestle Foundation Publication Series No. 1, 1979), p. 222.

42. W. G. Whittlestone, "Breast Feeding: A Foundation of Preventive Medicine," *Nutrition and Health* 1 (1983):133.

43. R. H. Hall, "Infant Formula," *En-Trophy* 3 (1980):10.

44. C. Hoeffer and M. C. Hardy, "Later Development of Breast Fed and Artificially Fed Infants," *Journal of the American Medical Association* 92 (1929):615.

45. F. Oski, "Is Bovine Milk a Health Hazard?" *Pediatrics* 75, suppl. (1985):182.

46. "Control of Nutritional Anemia with Special Reference to Iron Deficiency," World Health Organization Technical Report, Series No. 580, Geneva, 1975.

47. J. W. Gerrard, "Allergy in Infancy," *Allergy Pediatrics Annals* 3 (1974):9.

48. M. Delire, C. L. Cambiaso, and P. L. Masson, "Circulating Immune Complexes in Infants Fed on Cow's Milk," *Nature* 272 (1978):632.

49. Summary, "The Early Feeds: Human Milk versus Formula and Bovine Milk," *Pediatrics* 75, suppl. (1985):157.

50. Buisseret, "Allergy."

51. Kretchmer, "Summary."

52. C. Woodruff, "Iron Nutrition in the Breast-Fed Infant," *Journal of Pediatrics* 90 (1977):36.

53. R. Jenness, "The Composition of Milk," in *Lactation: A Comprehensive Treatise*, vol. 3, eds. B. Larson and V. R. Smith (New York: Academic Press, 1974).

54. L. Hambraeus, "Proprietary Milk versus Human Breast Milk in Infant Feeding," *The Pediatric Clinics of North America* 24 (1977):19.

55. Riordan and Countryman, "Principles and Practice."

56. Oski, "Bovine Milk."

57. D. B. Jelliffe, "World Trends in Infant Feeding," *American Journal of Clinical Nutrition* 29 (1976):1227.

58. Jelliffe and Jelliffe, *Human Milk*, p. 26.

59. M. Bateman, "Baby Big and the Magic Milkmen," *Sunday Times* (London), March 16, 1975.

60. R. Shane, "Perspectives on Adverse Effects of Milks and Infant Formulas Used in Infant Feeding," *Journal of the American Dietetic Association* 82 (1983):373.

61. S. Arnon, "Breast Feeding and Toxigenic Intestinal Infections: Missing Links in Crib Death?" *Reviews of Infectious Diseases* 6, suppl. (1984):193.

62. "Episodes of Illness in Breast-Fed and Bottle-Fed Infants in Jerusalem," *Israeli Journal of Medical Science* 20 (1984):395.

63. J. Ek and E. Magnus, "Plasma and Red Cell Folate Values and Folate Requirements in Formula-Fed Term Infants," *Journal of Pediatrics* 100 (1982):738.

64. A. P. Simopoulos, "Growth Characteristics in Patients with Bartter's Syndrome," *Nephron* 23 (1979):130.

65. H. I. Goldman and F. Deposito, "Hypoprothrombinemic Bleeding in Young Infants: Association with Diarrhea, Antibiotics, and Milk Substitutes," *American Journal of Diseases of Children* 111 (1966):430.

66. W. F. J. Cuthbertson, "Essential Fatty Acid Requirements in Infancy," *American Journal of Clinical Nutrition* 29 (1976):559.

67. C. E. Healy, "Acidosis and Failure to Thrive in Infants Fed Nutramigen," *Pediatrics* 49 (1972):910.

68. "Firm Recalls Baby Formula," *Oakland Tribune*, April 15, 1985.

69. M. Freundlich et al., "Infant Formula as a Cause of Aluminum Toxicity in Neonatal Uremia," *Lancet* 2 (1985):527.

70. Y. Bergevin, C. Dougherty, and M. S. Kramer, "Do Infant Formula Samples Shorten the Duration of Breast Feeding?" *Lancet* 1 (1983):1148.

71. Hall, *En-Trophy*, pp. 1-16.

72. J. Riordan and B. A. Countryman, "Principles and Practice: Basics of Breast Feeding — Part I: Infant Feeding Patterns Past and Present," *Journal of Obstetric and Gynecologic and Neonatal Nursing* 9 (1980):207.

Chapter 2   Breast-Feeding: The Expectations

1. M. Gunther, "Instinct and the Nursing Couple," *Lancet* 1 (1955):575.

2. D. B. Jelliffe and E. F. P. Jelliffe, *Human Milk in the Modern World* (New York: Oxford University Press, 1978), p. 2.

3. V. Elwin, "Man In India," *Notes on the Juangs* 28 (1948):1.

4. R. A. Lawrence, *Breast Feeding: A Guide for the Medical Profession* (St. Louis: C. V. Mosby Company, 1980), p. 116.

5. "Good News for 'Innies': Up Front Facts about Inverted Nipples," editorial, *Keeping Abreast Journal* 1 (1976):46.

6. R. V. Short, in *Breast Feeding and the Mother*, Ciba Foundation Symposium 45 (Amsterdam: Elsevier Scientific Publication Co., 1976), p. 73.

7. "Lactation, Maternal Nutrition, and Fertility," *Nutrition Reviews* 40 (1982):268.

8. B. Kamen and S. Kamen, *In Pursuit of Youth: Everyday Nutrition for Everyone Over 35* (New York: Dodd, Mead & Co., 1984), p. 42.

9. R. M. Feeley, "Copper, Iron, and Zinc Contents of Human Milk at Early Stages of Lactation," *American Journal of Clinical Nutrition* 37 (1983):443.

10. K. Campbell, "Feeding the Newborn Infant," *Medical Journal of Australia* 1(1978):274.

11. S. R. Kemberling, "Supporting Breast Feeding," *Pediatrics* 63 (1979):60.

12. E. Pollitt, B. Consolazio, and F. Goodkin, "Changes in Nutritive Sucking during a Feed in Two-Day- and Thirty-Day-Old Infants," *Early Human Development* 5 (1981):201.

13. A. Lucas, P. J. Lucas, and J. D. Baum, "Pattern of Milk Flow in Breast-Fed Infants," *Lancet* 2 (1979):58.

14. Lucas, Lucas, and Baum, "Pattern."

15. N. Newton and M. Newton, "Relationship of Ability to Breast Feed and Maternal Attitudes toward Breast Feeding," *Pediatrics* 5 (1950):869.

16. J. Jeffs, "Why Do Mothers Breast Feed?" *Nursing Times* 73 (1977):911.

Chapter 3   Breast-Feeding: The Reality

1. R. Sosa et al., "The Effect of Early Mother-Infant Contact on Breast Feeding, Infection, and Growth," in *Breast Feeding and the Mother, Ciba Foundation Symposium* 45 (Amsterdam: Elsevier Scientific Publication Co., 1976), p. 179.

2. U. Goteberg, "Long Term Effects of Early Mother/Infant Contact," *Journal of Family Practice* 8 (1979):511.

3. J. Riordan and B. A. Countryman, "Principles and Practice: Basics of Breast Feeding — Part IV: Preparation for Breast Feeding and Early Optimal Functioning," *Journal of Obstetric and Gynecologic and Neonatal Nursing* 9 (1980):277.

4. B. Wharton, "A Quinquennium in Infant Feeding," *Archives of Diseases of Childhood* 57 (1982):895.

5. M. R. Hally, "A Study of Infant Feeding: Factors Influencing Choice of Method," *University of Newcastle Upon Tyne Health Care Research Unit* (1982):111.

6. P. de Chateau, "A Study of Factors Promoting and Inhibiting Lactation," *Developmental Medicine and Child Neurology* 19 (1977):575.

7. M. J. Houston, "Breast Feeding: Success or Failure," *Journal of Advanced Nursing* 6 (1981):447.

8. R. A. Lawrence, *Breast Feeding: A Guide for the Medical Profession* (St. Louis: C. V. Mosby Company, 1980), p. 176.

9. B. Hochstrasser and J. C. Vuille, "Nutrition and Somatic Development of Infants in the Canton of Berne," *Society of Preventive Medicine* 25 (1980):177.

10. B. Kamen and S. Kamen, *In Pursuit of Youth: Everyday Nutrition for Everyone Over 35* (New York: Dodd, Mead & Co., 1984), p. 61.

11. G. Gerstner, W. Grunberger, and S. Leodolter, "Causes of Lactation Inhibition in the Early Puerperium," *Journal of Geburtshife Perinatology* 186 (1982):97.

12. Lawrence, *Breast Feeding: A Guide*, p. 124.

13. J. Riordan and B. A. Countryman, "Principles and Practice: Basics of Breastfeeding — Part III: The Biological Specificity of Breast Milk,"

Journal of Obstetric and Gynecologic and Neonatal Nursing 9 (1980):273.

14. D. Raphael, *The Tender Gift: Breast Feeding* (New York: Schocken Books, Inc., 1976).

15. P. E. Hartman and C. G. Prosser, "Physiological Basis of Longitudinal Changes in Human Milk Yield and Composition," *Federal Proceedings* 43 (1984):2448.

16. L. R. Waletzky and E. C. Herman, "Relactation," *American Family Physician* 14 (1976):69.

17. R. G. Whitehead, "Nutrition: The Changing Scene, Nutritional Aspects of Human Lactation," *Lancet* 1 (1983):167.

18. E. M. E. Poskitt, "Infant Feeding: A Review," *Human Nutrition: Applied Nutrition* 37A (1983):271.

19. J. C. Pearce, "Nurturing Intelligence: The Other Side of Nutrition," *Nutrition and Health* 1 (1983):143.

20. J. W. Reynolds, "Water," *Developmental Nutrition* 10, Ross Laboratories (1974).

21. S. G. Almroth, "Water Requirements of Breast-Fed Infants in a Hot Climate," *American Journal of Clinical Nutrition* 31 (1978):1154.

22. D. F. Horrobin et al., "Action of Prolactin on Human Renal Function," *Lancet* 2 (1971):352.

23. C. J. Bacon and J. M. Wylie, "Mothers' Attitudes to Infant Feeding at Newcastle General Hospital in Summer 1975," *British Medical Journal* 1 (1976):308.

Chapter 4   Breast Milk and the Primal Diet

1. L. S. Hurley, *Developmental Nutrition* (Englewood Cliffs, New Jersey: Prentice-Hall, Inc., 1980), p. 271.

2. R. M. Pitkin, "Nutritional Support in Obstetrics and Gynecology," *Clinical Obstetrics and Gynecology* 19 (1976):489.

3. J. C. Edozien, M. A. R. Khan, and C. I. Waslien, "Protein Deficiency in Man: Results of a Nigerian Village Study," *Journal of Nutrition* 106 (1976):312.

4. B. Kamen and S. Kamen, *Total Nutrition during Pregnancy: How to Be Sure You and Your Baby Are Eating the Right Stuff* (New Canaan, Connecticut: Keats Publishing, Inc., 1986), p. 148.

5. A. F. Anglemier and M. W. Montgomery, "Amino Acids, Peptides, and Proteins," in *Principles of Food Science: Food Chemistry*, Part I, ed. O. R. Fennema (New York: Marcel Dekker, 1976), p. 231.

6. M. A. Crawford, P. M. Msuya, and A. Munhambo, "Structural Lipids and Their Polyenoic Constituents in Human Milk," in *Dietary*

Lipids and Postnatal Development, eds. G. Calli, J. Jacini, and A. Pecile (New York: Raven Press, 1973), p. 41.

7. A. J. Sinclair and M. A. Crawford, "The Effect of a Low-Fat Maternal Diet on Neonatal Rats," *British Journal of Nutrition* 29 (1973):127.

8. L. Hambraeus, "Maternal Diet and Human Milk Composition," in *Maternal Nutrition during Pregnancy and Lactation: A Nestle Foundation Workshop*, eds. H. Aebi and R. Whitehead (Nestle Foundation Publication Series No. 1, 1979):237.

9. T. C. Byerley, "Effects of Agricultural Practices on Foods of Animal Origin," in *Nutritional Evaluation of Food Processing*, 2nd ed., eds. R. S. Harris and E. Karmas (Westport, Connecticut: Avi, 1975), pp. 58–97.

10. E. M. E. Poskitt, "Infant Feeding: A Review," *Human Nutrition: Applied Nutrition* 37A (1983):271.

11. W. S. Harris, W. E. Connor, and S. Lindsey, "Will Dietary Omega-3 Fatty Acids Change the Composition of Human Milk?" *American Journal of Clinical Nutrition* 40 (1984):780.

12. M. A. Crawford, M. M. Gale, and M. H. Woodford, "Linoleic Acid and Linolenic Acid Elongation Products in Muscle Tissue of Syncerus Caffer and Other Ruminant Species," *Biochemical Journal* 115 (1969):25.

13. C. J. Lammi-Keefe and R. G. Jensen, "Fat Soluble Vitamins in Human Milk," *Nutrition Reviews* 42 (1984):365.

14. N. F. Butte and D. H. Calloway, "Evaluation of Lactational Performance of Navajo Women," *American Journal of Clinical Nutrition* 34 (1981):2210.

15. M. Hanafy, "Maternal Nutrition and Lactation Performance in Egypt," in *Maternal Nutrition during Pregnancy and Lactation: A Nestle Foundation Workshop*, eds. H. Aebi and R. Whitehead (Nestle Foundation Publication Series No. 1, 1979):225.

16. T. Tamura, Y. Yoshimura, and T. Arakawa, "Milk Folate: Folate Status in Lactating Mothers and Infants," *Federal Proceedings* 38 (1979):393.

17. Health Promotion: Improved Nutrition, Public Health Report, suppl. (1983):132.

18. D. B. Jelliffe, "Breast Milk and the World Protein Gap," *Clinical Pediatrics* 7 (1968):96.

19. Hurley, *Developmental Nutrition*, p. 265.

20. F. L. Cerklewski, "Effect of Suboptimal Zinc Nutrition during Gestation and Lactation on Rat Molar Tooth Composition and Dental Caries," *Journal of Nutrition* 111 (1981):1780.

21. P. B. Moser and R. D. Reynolds, "Dietary Zinc Intake and Zinc Concentrations of Plasma, Erythrocytes, and Breast Milk in Antepartum

and Postpartum Lactating and Nonlactating Women: A Longitudinal Study," *American Journal of Clinical Nutrition* 38 (1983):101.

22. R. S. Beach, M. E. Gershwin, and L. S. Hurley, "Zinc, Copper, and Manganese in Immune Function and Experimental Oncogenesis," *Nutrition and Cancer* 3 (1982):172.

23. J. C. Smith, Jr., E. R. Morris, and R. Ellis, "Zinc: Requirements, Bioavailabilities, and Recommended Dietary Allowances," *Progress in Clinical Biology Research* 129 (1983):147.

24. A. A. Albanese, *Current Topics in Nutrition and Disease.* Vol. 3, *Nutrition for the Elderly* (New York: Alan R. Liss, 1980), p. 208.

25. B. Kamen and S. Kamen, *Osteoporosis: What It Is, How to Prevent It, How to Stop It* (New York: Pinnacle Books, 1984), p. 20.

26. P. J. Atkinson and R. R. West, "Loss of Skeletal Calcium in Lactating Women," *Journal of Obstetrics and Gynecology* 77 (1970):555.

27. Hurley, *Developmental Nutrition,* p. 264.

28. Kamen and Kamen, *Osteoporosis,* p. 34.

29. S. H. Bassett et al., "Metabolism in Idiopathic Steatorrhea. I. The Influence of Dietary and Other Factors on Lipid and Mineral Balance," *Journal of Clinical Investigation* 18 (1939):101.

30. Kamen and Kamen, *Total Nutrition during Pregnancy,* p. 33.

31. Kamen and Kamen, *Osteoporosis,* p. 156.

32. Pitkin, "Nutritional Support," p. 501.

33. R. Reiser and Z. Sidelman, "Control of Serum Cholesterol Homeostasis by Cholesterol in the Suckling Rat," *Journal of Nutrition* 102 (1972):1009.

34. C. J. Glueck and R. C. Tsang, "Pediatric Nutrition: Potential Relationship to the Development of Atherosclerosis," in *Human Nutrition: A Comprehensive Treatise, I, Nutrition: Pre- and Postnatal Development,* ed. M. Winick (New York: Plenum Press, 1979), pp. 368–69.

35. P. M. Kris-Etherton et al., "The Influence of Early Nutrition on the Serum Cholesterol of the Adult Rat," *Journal of Nutrition* 109 (1979):1244.

36. M. J. Whichelow, "Calorie Requirements for Successful Breast Feeding," *Archives of Diseases of Childhood* 50 (1975):669.

37. Hurley, *Developmental Nutrition,* p. 267.

38. J. E. Chappell, "Trans Fatty Acids in Human Milk Lipids: Influence of Maternal Diet and Weight Loss," *American Journal of Clinical Nutrition* 42 (1985):49.

39. J. Dwyer, "Nutritional Support during Pregnancy and Lactation," *Primary Care* 9 (1982):475.

40. R. H. Hall, "The Brain and Fatty Acids," *En-Trophy* 3 (1980):8.

41. Kamen and Kamen, *Total Nutrition during Pregnancy*, p. 147.

42. Kamen and Kamen, *Total Nutrition during Pregnancy*, p. 36.

43. C. A. Gushurst et al., "Breast Milk Iodide: Reassessment in the 1980s," *Pediatrics* 73 (1984):354.

44. R. A. Lawrence, *Breast Feeding: A Guide for the Medical Profession* (St. Louis: C. V. Mosby Company, 1980), p. 181.

45. M. M. Hanafy et al., "Maternal Nutrition and Lactation Performance," *Journal of Tropical Pediatrics* 18 (1972):187.

46. S. Rattigan, A. V. Ghisalberti, and P. E. Hartmann, "Breast Milk Production in Australian Women," *British Journal of Nutrition* 45 (1981):243.

47. C. Gopalan and A. N. Naidu, "Nutrition and Fertility," *Lancet* 2 (1972):1077.

48. S. J. Foman, *Infant Nutrition*, 2nd ed. (Philadelphia: W. B. Saunders, 1974).

49. R. Whitehead, "Concluding Remarks," *Maternal Nutrition during Pregnancy and Lactation: A Nestle Foundation Workshop*, eds. H. Aebi and R. Whitehead (Nestle Foundation Publication Series No. 1, 1979):238.

50. P. G. Lunn et al., "Influence of Maternal Diet on Plasma-Prolactin Levels during Lactation," *Lancet* 1 (1980):623.

51. R. Sosa, M. Klaus, and J. J. Urrutia, "Feed the Mother, Thereby the Infant," *Journal of Pediatrics* 88 (1976):668.

Chapter 5   All about Nutrient Supplementation

1. T. W. Rowland et al., "Malnutrition and Hypernaturemic Dehydration in Breast-Fed Infants," *Journal of the American Medical Association* 247 (1982):247.

2. L. Salmenpera, "Vitamin C Nutrition during Prolonged Lactation: Optimal in Infants While Marginal in Some Mothers," *American Journal of Clinical Nutrition* 40 (1984):1050.

3. E. Vuori, "Intake of Copper, Iron, Manganese, and Zinc by Healthy, Exclusively Breast-Fed Infants during the First Three Months of Life," *British Journal of Nutrition* 42 (1979):407.

4. C. J. Lammi-Keefe and R. G. Jensen, "Fat Soluble Vitamins in Human Milk," *Nutrition Reviews* 42 (1984):365.

5. A. D. Deodhar, R. Rajalakshmi, and C. V. Ramakrishnan, "Effect of Dietary Supplementation on Vitamin Contents of Breast Milk," *Acta Pediatrica Scandinavica* 53 (1964):42.

6. H. L. Greene, "Water-Soluble Vitamins," in *Textbook of Gastroen-*

terology and Nutrition in Infancy. Vol. 1, *Gastrointestinal Development and Perinatal Nutrition,* ed. E. Lebenthal (New York: Raven Press, 1981), p. 586.

7. S. M. Sneed, C. Zane, and M. R. Thomas, "The Effects of Ascorbic Acid, Vitamin B_6, Vitamin B_{12}, and Folic Acid Supplementation on the Breast Milk and Maternal Nutritional Status of Low Socioeconomic Lactating Women," *American Journal of Clinical Nutrition* 34 (1981):34.

8. K. D. West and A. Kirksey, "Influence of Vitamin B_6 Intake on the Content of the Vitamin in Human Milk," *American Journal of Clinical Nutrition* 29 (1976):961.

9. Sneed, *Supplementation,* p. 34.

10. Salmenpera, "Vitamin C," p. 1050.

11. A. Kalokerinos, *Every Second Child* (New Canaan, Connecticut: Keats Publishing, Inc., 1981), pp. 97–98.

12. L. O. Byerley and A. Kirksey, "Effects of Different Levels of Vitamin C Intake on the Vitamin C Concentration in Human Milk and the Vitamin C Intakes of Breast-Fed Infants," *American Journal of Clinical Nutrition* 41 (1985):665.

13. C. J. Bates et al., "Seasonal Variations in Ascorbic Acid Status and Breast Milk Ascorbic Acid Levels in Rural Gambian Women in Relation to Dietary Intake," *Transactions of the Royal Society of Tropical Medical Hygiene* 76 (1982):341.

14. D. B. Jelliffe and E. F. P. Jelliffe, *Human Milk in the Modern World* (New York: Oxford University Press, 1978), p. 74.

15. R. W. Chesney, "Human Milk: A Heterogeneous Living Fluid," Mead-Johnson, Nutritional Directive (no date).

16. L. Reeve, R. W. Chesney, and H. F. DeLuca, "Vitamin D of Human Milk: Identification of Biologically Active Forms," *American Journal of Clinical Nutrition* 36 (1982):122.

17. R. Brommage and H. F. DeLuca, "Vitamin D–Deficient Rats Produce Reduced Quantities of a Nutritionally Adequate Milk," *American Journal of Physiology* 246 (1984):221.

18. K. Kuratani, "Vitamin E Content of Milk and Serum in Children," *Acta Pediatrica Japonica* 8 (1966):55.

19. Lloyd J. Filler, Jr., et al., "Vitamin K Supplementation for Infants Receiving Milk Substitute Infant Formulas and for Those with Fat Malabsorption," in American Academy of Pediatrics, Committee on Nutrition, *Pediatrics* 48 (1971):483.

20. J. M. Sutherland, H. I. Glueck, and G. Glaser, "Hemorrhagic Disease of the Newborn," *American Journal of Diseases of Children* 113 (1967):524.

21. M. Seelig, *Magnesium Deficiency in the Pathogenesis of Disease* (New York: Plenum Book Co., 1980), p. 67.

22. A. Higashi et al., "Zinc and Copper Contents in Breast Milk of Japanese Women," *Tohoku Journal of Experimental Medicine* 137 (1982):41.

23. N. Krebs et al., "The Effects of a Dietary Zinc Supplement during Lactation on Longitudinal Changes in Maternal Zinc Status and Milk Zinc Concentrations," *American Journal of Clinical Nutrition* 41 (1985):560.

24. R. M. Feeley et al., "Copper, Iron, and Zinc Contents of Human Milk at Early Stages of Lactation," *American Journal of Clinical Nutrition* 37 (1983):443.

25. Martin Milner, N.D., personal communication, March 1985.

26. A. Kirksey et al., "Influence of Mineral Intake and Use of Oral Contraceptives before Pregnancy on the Mineral Content of Human Colostrum and of More Mature Milk," *American Journal of Clinical Nutrition* 32 (1979):32.

27. G. B. Fransson, M. Gebre-Medhin, and L. Hambraeus, "The Human Milk Contents of Iron, Copper, Zinc, Calcium, and Magnesium in a Population with a Habitually High Intake of Iron," *Acta Pediatrica Scandinavica* 73 (1984):471.

28. Seelig, *Magnesium*, pp. 13–14.

29. L. S. Hurley, *Developmental Nutrition* (Englewood Cliffs, New Jersey: Prentice-Hall, Inc., 1980), p. 295.

30. F. L. Wang et al., "Magnesium Depletion during Gestation and Lactation in Rats," *Journal of Nutrition* 101 (1971):1201.

31. E. B. Flink, "Magnesium Deficiency: Etiology and Clinical Spectrum," *Acta Medica Scandinavica* 209 (1981):125.

32. W. G. Whittlestone, "Breast Feeding: A Foundation of Preventive Medicine," *Nutrition and Health* 1 (1983):133.

33. R. A. Lawrence, *Breast Feeding: A Guide for the Medical Profession* (St. Louis: C. V. Mosby Company, 1980), p. 85.

34. B. Kamen and S. Kamen, *Total Nutrition during Pregnancy: How to Be Sure You and Your Baby Are Eating the Right Stuff* (New Canaan, Connecticut: Keats Publishing, Inc., 1986), p. 150.

35. P. J. Green, "Iron Supplements in Pregnancy," *Lancet* 2 (1980):87.

36. G. M. Owen, P. J. Garry, and E. M. Hooper, "Iron Nutrition of Infants Exclusively Breast Fed the First Five Months," *Journal of Pediatrics* 99 (1981):237.

37. Horace, *Epistles*, in *Bartlett's Familiar Quotations*, centennial edition, ed. John Bartlett (Boston: Little, Brown, 1955), p. 109.

38. M. Nath and P. Geervani, "Diet and Nutrition of Pregnant and

Lactating Women and Infants of Urban Slums of Hyderabad," *Indian Journal of Nutrition and Dietetics* 15 (1978):422.

39. Nath and Geervani, "Diet and Nutrition."

40. Lawrence, *Breast Feeding: A Guide*, p. 181.

41. J. Bland, "Assessing and Managing Biochemical Individuality," lecture, San Francisco, January 1985.

42. W. S. Harris, W. E. Connor, and S. Lindsey, "Will Dietary Omega-3 Fatty Acids Change the Composition of Human Milk?" *American Journal of Clinical Nutrition* 40 (1984):780.

43. J. C. Putnam et al., "The Effect of Variations in Dietary Fatty Acids on the Fatty Acid Composition of Erythrocyte Phosphatidylcholine and Phosphatidylethanolamine in Human Infants," *American Journal of Clinical Nutrition* 36 (1982):106.

44. D. O. Rudin, "The Major Psychoses and Neuroses as Omega-3 Essential Fatty Acid Deficiency Syndrome: Substrate Pellagra," *Biological Psychiatry* 16 (1981):837.

45. I. Colquhoun and S. Bunday, "A Lack of Essential Fatty Acids as a Possible Cause of Hyperactivity in Children," *Medical Hypotheses* 7 (1981):673.

46. R. Cook, "Infant Feeding and Vitamin D," *British Medical Journal* 280 (1980):1319.

47. R. Cathcart, lecture, Orthomolecular Society of San Francisco, July 1985.

48. M. Hamada et al., "The Host-Mediated Anti-Tumor Effect of Various Preparations Made of Chlorella Pyrenoidosa," *21st Japan Bacteriology Convention*, November 1984, Kanazawa Medical University, Kanazawa, Japan.

49. L. Wang, "Effect of Chlorella on the Levels of Glycogen, Triglyceride and Cholesterol in Ethionine Treated Rats," *Journal of the Formosan Medical Association* 79 (1980):1.

50. Martin Milner, N.D., personal communication, March 1985.

51. Jelliffe and Jelliffe, *Human Milk*, p. 41.

52. R. H. Hall, "Malnutrition and the Rat Brain," *En-Trophy* 3 (1980):2.

Chapter 6   Keeping Contaminants at Bay

1. J. W. A. Findlay et al., "Analgesic Drugs in Breast Milk and Plasma," *Clinical Pharmacological Therapeutics* 4 (1981):625.

2. R. A. Lawrence, *Breast Feeding: A Guide for the Medical Profession* (St. Louis: C. V. Mosby Company, 1980), p. 167.

3. S. J. Szefler and D. D. Shen, "Drug Excretion in Breast Milk," in *Textbook of Gastroenterology and Nutrition in Infancy.* Vol. 1, *Gastrointestinal Development and Perinatal Nutrition,* ed. E. Lebenthal (New York: Raven Press, 1981), p. 334.

4. Szefler and Shen, "Drug Excretion," p. 334.

5. Szefler and Shen, "Drug Excretion," p. 336.

6. Lawrence, *Breast Feeding: A Guide,* p. 324.

7. E. M. Curtis, "Oral-Contraceptive Feminization of a Normal Male Infant," *Obstetrics and Gynecology* 23 (1964):295.

8. G. H. Miller and L. R. Hughes, "Lactation and Genital Involution Effects of a New Low Dose Oral Contraceptive on Breast Feeding Mothers and Their Infants," *Obstetrics and Gynecology* 35 (1970):44.

9. A. Hecht, "Advice on Breast Feeding and Drugs," *FDA Consumer Report* 80-3098 (1979).

10. Szefler and Shen, "Drug Excretion," p. 337.

11. B. Kamen and S. Kamen, *Total Nutrition during Pregnancy: How to Be Sure You and Your Baby Are Eating the Right Stuff* (New Canaan, Connecticut: Keats Publishing, Inc., 1986), p. 179.

12. I. Sherman, *Natural Remedies for Better Health* (Healdsburg, California: Naturegraph Publishers, 1970), p. 83.

13. B. Kamen and S. Kamen, *In Pursuit of Youth: Everyday Nutrition for Everyone Over 35* (New York: Dodd, Mead & Co., 1984), p. 70.

14. W. J. Darby, P. Ghalioungui, and L. Grivetti, *Food: The Gift of Osiris,* vol. 2 (New York: Academic Press, 1977), p. 771.

15. A. M. Yurchak and W. J. Jusko, "Theophylline Secretion into Breast Milk," *Pediatrics* 57 (1976):518.

16. Lawrence, *Breast Feeding: A Guide,* p. 328.

17. M. Dunlop, J. M. Court, and R. G. Larkins, "The Effects of Maternal Carbohydrate (Sucrose) Supplementation on the Growth of Offspring of Pregnancies with Habitual Caffeine Consumption," *Biology of the Neonate* 40 (1981):196.

18. H. Vorherr, "Excretion of Certain Drugs into Milk," *Postgraduate Medicine* 56 (1974):97.

19. G. G. Nahas et al., "Inhibition of Cellular Mediated Immunity in Marijuana Smokers," *Science* 183 (1974):419.

20. E. Cobo, "The Effect of Different Doses of Ethanol on the Milk-Ejecting Reflex in Lactating Women," *American Journal of Obstetrics and Gynecology* 115 (1973):817.

21. A. W. Pruitt et al., "The Transfer of Drugs and Other Chemicals into Human Breast Milk," *Pediatrics* 72 (1983):375.

22. E. L. Abel, "Emotionality in Offspring of Rats Fed Alcohol While Nursing," *Journal of Studies on Alcohol* 36 (1975):654.

23. Kamen and Kamen, *Total Nutrition during Pregnancy*, p. 163.

24. R. E. Kron et al., "Neonatal Narcotics Abstinence," *Journal of Pediatrics* 88 (1976):637.

25. G. P. Biacoia, C. Catz, and S. J. Yaffe, "Environmental Hazards in Milk and Infant Nutrition," *Clinical Obstetrics and Gynecology* 26 (1983):458.

26. Lester A. Luz, M.D., pediatrician, personal communication, March 1985.

27. "Partially Hydrogenated Fats in the Diets of Nursing Mothers: Effect on Contents of Trans Fatty Acids and Prostaglandins in Milk," *Nutrition Reviews* 42 (1984):311.

28. C. A. Gushurst et al., "Breast Milk Iodide: Reassessment in the 1980s," *Pediatrics* 73 (1984):354.

29. A. G. Schauss, "Nutrition and Behavior: Complex Interdisciplinary Research," *Nutrition and Health* 3 (1984):9.

30. B. Kamen and S. Kamen, *Kids Are What They Eat: What Every Parent Needs to Know about Nutrition* (New York: Arco Publishing, 1983), p. 90.

31. Lawrence, *Breast Feeding: A Guide*, p. 325.

32. T. Honda, "A Study of Aurantiasis in Japanese Children," *Proceedings of the Xth International Congress of Nutrition*, Kyoto, Japan, 1975.

33. S. L. Hatcher, "The Psychological Experience of Nursing Mothers upon Learning of a Toxic Substance in Their Breast Milk," *Psychiatry* 45 (1982):172.

Chapter 7   Problem Solving: The Preemie, the Colicky, the Non-Sleepy

1. E. E. Ziegler, "Infants of Low Birth Weight: Special Needs and Problems," *American Journal of Clinical Nutrition* 41 (1985):440.

2. K. Schultz, G. Soltesz, and J. Mestyan, "The Metabolic Consequences of Human Milk and Formula Feeding in Premature Infants," *Acta Pediatrica Scandinavica* 69 (1980):647.

3. S. Gross, "Growth and Biochemical Response of Preterm Infants Fed Human Milk or Modified Infant Formula," *New England Journal of Medicine* 308 (1983):237.

4. A. Lucas, S. Suzuki, and R. R. A. Coombs, "IgA and Preterm Milk," *Lancet* 1 (1982):1241.

5. W. A. Walker, "Absorption of Protein and Protein Fragments in the Developing Intestine: Role in Immunologic/Allergic Reactions," *Pediatrics* 75, suppl. (1985):167.

6. "Medical News," *Journal of the American Medical Association* 244 (1980): 1887.

7. C. Simonin, M. Ruegg, and D. Sidiropoulos, "Comparison of the Fat Content and Fat Globule Size Distribution of Breast Milk from Mothers Delivering Term and Preterm," *American Journal of Clinical Nutrition* 40 (1984):820.

8. P. Guerrini et al., "Human Milk: Relationship of Fat Content with Gestational Age," *Early Human Development* 5 (1981):187.

9. O. G. Brooke, "Nutrition and Malnutrition in Neonates and Immature Infants," *Nutrition and Health* 1 (1983):213.

10. S. Atkinson, "Calcium and Phosphorus Requirements of Low Birth Weight Infants: A Nutritional and Endocrinological Perspective," *Nutrition Reviews* 41 (1983):69.

11. B. Kamen and S. Kamen, *In Pursuit of Youth: Everyday Nutrition for Everyone Over 35* (New York: Dodd, Mead & Co., 1984), p. 68.

12. L. Mervyn, *Minerals and Your Health* (New Canaan, Connecticut: Keats Publishing Co., 1980), p. 93.

13. R. S. Shah and R. Rajalakshmi, "Vitamin A Status of the Newborn in Relation to Gestational Age, Body Weight, and Maternal Nutritional Status," *American Journal of Clinical Nutrition* 40 (1984):794.

14. P. B. Kulkarni et al., "Rickets in Very Low Birth Weight Infants," *Journal of Pediatrics* 96 (1980):249.

15. J. R. Moran et al., "Concentrations and Total Daily Output of Micronutrients in Breast Milk of Mothers Delivering Preterm: A Longitudinal Study," *Journal of Pediatrics and Gastroenterology and Nutrition* 2 (1983):629.

16. I. Blom et al., "Zinc Deficiency with Transitory Acrodermatitis Enteropathica in a Boy of Low Birth Weight," *British Journal of Dermatology* 104 (1981):459.

17. Zeigler, "Low Birth Weight," p. 441.

18. S. J. Gross, S. A. Landaw, and F. A. Oski, "Vitamin E and Neonatal Hemolysis," *Pediatrics* 59 (1977):995.

19. "Preterm Milk Is at Least as Nutritious as Formula," *Nutrition Reviews* 42 (1984):281.

20. M. Rowland, A. A. Paul, and R. G. Whitehead, "Lactation and Infant Nutrition," *British Medical Bulletin* 37 (1981):77.

21. S. Sepkowitz, "Low Birth Weight Infants," *New England Journal of Medicine* 312 (1985):1387.

22. Walker, "Protein Fragments."

23. D. B. Thomas, "Infantile Colic," *Medical Journal of Australia* 16 (1981):542.

24. D. B. Thomas, letter, "Infant Colic and Drugs in Labor," *Lancet* 1 (1981):493.

25. Thomas, "Infant Colic."

26. J. O. Warner, "Food Allergy in Fully Breast-Fed Infants," *Clinical Allergy* 10 (1980):133.

27. B. Kamen and S. Kamen, *Osteoporosis: What It Is, How to Prevent It, How to Stop It* (New York: Pinnacle Books, 1984), p. 85.

28. G. H. C. Jenkins, "Milk-Drinking Mothers with Colicky Babies," *Lancet* 2 (1981):261.

29. I. Jakobsson and T. Lindberg, "Cow's Milk Proteins Cause Infantile Colic in Breast-Fed Infants: A Double-Blind Crossover Study," *Pediatrics* 71 (1983):268.

30. B. Kamen and S. Kamen, *Kids Are What They Eat: What Every Parent Needs to Know about Nutrition* (New York: Arco Publishing, 1983), p. 161.

31. Jakobsson and Lindberg, "Cow's Milk Proteins."

32. R. A. Lawrence, *Breast Feeding: A Guide for the Medical Profession* (St. Louis: C. V. Mosby Company, 1980), p. 150.

33. I. G. Wickes, "A History of Infant Feeding," *Archives of Diseases of Childhood* 128 (1953):151.

34. M. Weissbluth, "Dicyclomine in Infantile Colic," *Journal of Pediatrics* 105 (1984):503.

35. M. C. O. Bax, "Sleep Disturbance in the Young Child," *British Medical Journal* (1980):1177.

36. Lawrence, *Breast Feeding: A Guide*, p. 128.

37. P. Wright, H. A. Macleod, and M. J. Cooper, "Waking at Night: The Effect of Early Feeding Experience," *Child Care, Health, and Development* 9 (1983):309.

38. J. Carter, "The Ecology of the Urban Adaptation Syndrome: The Decline of Breast Feeding," *Journal of Holistic Medicine* 6 (1984):64.

39. M. Weissbluth, A. T. Davis, and J. Poncher, "Night Waking in Four- to Eight-Month-Old Infants," *Journal of Pediatrics* 104 (1984):477.

40. S. L. Huffman, "Maternal and Child Nutritional Status: Its Association with the Risk of Pregnancy," *Social Science and Medicine* 17 (1983):1529.

41. Lester Luz, M.D., pediatrician, personal communication, September 1985.

42. The Nutrition Report, "What If You Want More Sleep," *American Health*, June 1985, p. 102.

43. Michael Gerber, M.D., personal communication, April 1985.

44. A. P. Lange et al., "Neonatal Jaundice after Labor Induced or Stimulated by Prostaglandin E2 or Oxytocin," *Lancet* 1 (1982):991.

45. E. M. E. Poskitt, "Infant Feeding: A Review," *Human Nutrition: Applied Nutrition* 37A (1983):271.

46. "Hospital Policies, Breast Feeding, and Neonatal Jaundice," *Breast-Feeding Abstracts* 2 (1983):1.

47. Lawrence, *Breast Feeding: A Guide*, p. 179.

48. "Milk Hypersensitivity," *Nutrition and the M.D.* 11 (1985):2.

Chapter 8   Breast-Feeding in the Late Twentieth Century: Milk, Emotions, and Emancipation

1. J. Carter, "The Ecology of the Urban Adaptation Syndrome: The Decline of Breast Feeding," *Journal of Holistic Medicine* 6 (1984):64.

2. M. Liebhaber et al., "Alterations of Lymphocytes and of Antibody Content of Human Milk after Processing," *Journal of Pediatrics* 91 (1977):897.

3. W. B. Pittard, "Breast Milk Immunology: A Frontier in Infant Nutrition," *American Journal of Diseases of Children* 133 (1979):83.

4. C. Garza and B. L. Nichols, "Studies of Human Milk Relevant to Milk Banking," *Journal of the American College of Nutrition* 3 (1984):123.

5. O. G. Brooke, "Nutrition and Malnutrition in Neonates and Immature Infants," *Nutrition and Health* 1 (1983):213.

6. J. M. Wardell, C. M. Hill, and S. W. D'Souza, "Effect of Pasteurization and of Freezing and Thawing Human Milk on Its Triglyceride Content," *Acta Pediatrica Scandinavica* 70 (1981):467.

7. A. Lucas, P. J. Lucas, and J. D. Baum, "Pattern of Milk Flow in Breast-Fed Infants," *Lancet* 2 (1979):57.

8. J. Aernandez et al., "Effect of Storage Processes on the Bacterial Growth–Inhibiting Activity of Human Breast Milk," *Pediatrics* 63 (1979):597.

9. N. Newton, "Trebly Sensuous Women," *Psychology Today* 5 (1971):68.

10. M. P. M. Richards, "Breast Feeding and the Mother-Infant Relationship," *Acta Pediatrica Scandinavica* 299, suppl. (1982):33.

11. L. T. Switzky, P. M. Vietze, and H. N. Switzky, "Attitudinal and Demographic Predictors of Breast-Feeding and Bottle-Feeding Behavior by Mothers of Six-Week-Old Infants," *Psychological Reports* 45 (1979):3.

12. K. Pryor, *Nursing Your Baby* (New York: Pocket Books, 1983), p. 143.

13. L. Waletzky, "Husbands' Problems with Breast Feeding," *American Journal of Orthopsychiatry* 49 (1979):349.

14. K. M. Robson, H. A. Brant, and R. Kumar, "Maternal Sexuality during First Pregnancy and after Childbirth," *British Journal of Obstetrics and Gynecology* 88 (1981):882.

15. Serafina Corsello, M.D., personal communication, May 1985.

Chapter 9   Getting from Breast Milk to Table Food

1. V. Fildes, "Weaning the Elizabethan Child — 2," *Nursing Times* 76 (1980):1402.

2. N. Kretchmer, "Weaning: Enzymatic Adaptation," *American Journal of Clinical Nutrition* 41 (1985):391.

3. D. M. Fergusson, L. J. Horwood, and F. T. Shannon, "Risk Factors in Childhood Eczema," *Journal of Epidemiology and Community Health* 36 (1982):118.

4. L. Ross, "Weaning Practices," *Journal of Nurse-Midwifery* 26 (1981):9.

5. L. A. Hanson et al., "Protective Factors in Milk and the Development of the Immune System," *Pediatrics* 75 (1985):172.

6. P. Juto and B. Bjorksten, "Serum IgE in Infants and Influence of Type of Feeding," *Clinical Allergy* 10 (1980):593.

7. R. A. Lawrence, *Breast Feeding: A Guide for the Medical Profession* (St. Louis: C. V. Mosby Company, 1980), pp. 153–54.

8. L. A. Barness, "Introduction of Supplemental Foods to Infants," in *Textbook of Gastroenterology and Nutrition in Infancy.* Vol. 1, *Gastrointestinal Development and Perinatal Nutrition,* ed. E. Lebenthal (New York: Raven Press, 1981), pp. 287–91.

9. B. Kamen and S. Kamen, *Kids Are What They Eat: What Every Parent Needs to Know about Nutrition* (New York: Arco Publishing, 1983), p. 111.

10. A. N. Eden, *Positive Parenting* (New York: Bobbs-Merrill, 1980), p. 125.

11. L. Smith, *Feed Your Kids Right* (New York: McGraw-Hill, 1979), p. 223.

12. D. B. Jelliffe and E. F. P. Jelliffe, *Human Milk in the Modern World* (New York: Oxford University Press, 1978), p. 406.

13. S. R. Kemberling, "Supporting Breast Feeding," *Pediatrics* 63 (1979):60.

14. J. A. McMillan, S. A. Landaw, and F. A. Oski, "Iron Sufficiency in Breast-Fed Infants and the Availability of Iron from Human Milk," *Pediatrics* 58 (1976):686.

15. Kamen and Kamen, *Kids*, p. 111.

16. Barness, "Introduction," p. 290.

17. F. A. Oski, "Is Bovine Milk a Health Hazard?" *Pediatrics* 75, suppl. (1985):182.

18. A. G. Schauss, "Nutrition and Behavior: Complex Interdisciplinary Research," *Nutrition and Health* 3 (1984):9.

19. S. J. Foman and E. E. Ziegler, "Skim Milk in Infant Feeding," Department of Health, Education, and Welfare, publ. no. (HSA) 77-5102. (Washington, D.C.: U.S. Government Printing Office, 1977.)

20. R. G. Barr, M. D. Levine, and J. B. Watkins, "Recurrent Abdominal Pain of Childhood Due to Lactose Intolerance: A Prospective Study," *New England Journal of Medicine* 300 (1979):1449.

21. W. M. Liebman, "Recurrent Abdominal Pain in Children: Lactose and Sucrose Intolerance: A Prospective Study," *Pediatrics* 64 (1979):43.

22. E. Lebenthal et al., "Recurrent Abdominal Pain and Lactose Absorption in Children," *Pediatrics* 67 (1981):828.

23. A. Wald et al., "Lactose Malabsorption in Recurrent Abdominal Pain of Childhood," *Journal of Pediatrics* 100 (1982):65.

24. E. Rinaldi et al., "High Frequency of Lactose Absorbers among Adults with Idiopathic Senile and Presenile Cataract in a Population with a High Prevalence of Primary Lactose Malabsorption," *Lancet* 1 (1984):355.

25. F. J. Simoons, "A Geographic Approach to Senile Cataracts: Possible Links with Milk Consumption, Lactase Activity and Galactose Metabolism," *Digest of Diseases in Science* 27 (1982):257.

26. H. R. Jenkins, "Food Allergy: The Major Cause of Infantile Colitis," *Archives of Diseases of Childhood* 59 (1984):326.

27. P. S. Harland and V. Lizaraga, "Breast Feeding and Atopic Disease," *Lancet* 2 (1979):898.

28. E. Lebenthal, "Impact of Digestion and Absorption in the Weaning Period on Infant Feeding Practices," *Pediatrics* 75, suppl. (1985):207.

29. E. Rossi and H. Moser, "Genetic Abnormalities of Pancreatic and Intestinal Function," in *Textbook of Gastroenterology and Nutrition in Infancy.* Vol. 2, *Gastrointestinal Development and Perinatal Nutrition,* ed. E. Lebenthal (New York: Raven Press, 1981), p. 876.

30. B. S. Lindblad and J. J. Rafter, "Increased Excretion of a Brain Depressor Amine in Infantile Celiac Disease and in Healthy Infants on a High Protein Milk Diet," *Acta Pediatrica Scandinavica* 69 (1980):643.

31. J. A. Birkbeck, "The Age of Weaning: A Statement of the Infant Nutrition Subcommittee of the Pediatric Society of New Zealand," *New Zealand Medical Journal* 95 (1982):584.

32. A. S. Levine, T. P. Labuza, and J. E. Morley, "Food Technology: A

Primer for Physicians," *New England Journal of Medicine* 312 (1985):628.

33. V. Asperen, A. S. Kemp, and C. M. Mellis, "A Prospective Study of the Clinical Manifestations of Atopic Disease in Infancy," *Acta Pediatrica Scandinavica* 73 (1984):80.

34. C. F. Adams, *Nutritive Value of American Foods in Common Units*, Agriculture Handbook No. 456 (Washington, D.C.: Superintendent of Documents, 1975), p. 284.

35. T. Monte, "Warning: Honey May Be Hazardous to Your Infant," *Nutrition Action* (1979):10.

36. R. H. Hall, "Phasing In Solid Food," *En-Trophy* 17 3 (1981):11.

37. J. E. Morley et al., "Effect of Exorphins on Gastrointestinal Function, Hormonal Release, and Appetite," *Gastroenterology* 84 (1983):1517.

38. J. E. Morley, "Food Peptides: A New Class of Hormones?" *Journal of the American Medical Association* 247 (1982):2379.

39. M. Giovannini et al., "Protein Content of Homogenized Meat Products," *Minerva Pediatrica* 31 (1979):477.

40. R. C. Wunderlich and D. K. Kalita, *Nourishing Your Child* (New Canaan, Connecticut: Keats Publishing, Inc., 1984), pp. 78–79.

INDEX

Comfort Plus breast pump, 223
Commercial baby foods, 185–86
Complementarity, protein, 60–61
Complex carbohydrates, 63
Concentrated food supplements,
99–103, 107–8
Conjunctivitis, 42
Constipation
home remedies for, 134–35, 145
laxatives for, 132
Contaminants
additives, 140–41
alternatives to, 133–37
in breast milk, 127–48
detoxifying, 142–43
drugs, 129–33
recreational drugs, 137–39
single-food overdose, 141–42
toxic transfer of, 139–42
Contraceptives
breast-feeding as, 26–27
oral, 96, 132, 148
Convenience foods, healthful, 200–
201
Cooking
microwave, 185
modifying, 196, 197–98
Copper
drugs and, 148
lactation nutrient chart for, 119
Corsello, Dr. Serafina, 173–74
Cortisone, nutrients affected by, 147
Cow's milk. See Milk, cow's
Cream of Carrot Soup, 203

Dairy products. See also Milk, cow's
intolerance to, 182–83
Delicious Millet, 198
Delivery. See Childbirth
Demand feeding, 10, 36, 45
in the hospital, 38
prolactin and, 27
sore nipples and, 41
Desiccated liver, 98, 100, 107–8
Detoxifying foods, 142–43, 145
Dextrose, 38. See also Sugar water
DHA, 100–101, 108
Diarrhea
home remedies for, 135–36
infectious, 9
Diet
baby's behavior and, 44–45

milk supply and, 44–45
rules for, 23
Dieting, while lactating, 70–71
Digitalis, nutrients affected by, 148
Dilantin, nutrients affected by, 148
Diuretics
effects of, 132
nutrients affected by, 148
Division of Nephrology, Bone and
Mineral Metabolism, University
of Kentucky, 14
Docosahexaenoic acid (DHA), 62
Doctor
selection of, 49
support of breast-feeding by, 22–24,
30
Dried baby foods, 186
Drugs
alternatives to, 133–37
breast milk, 129–33, 143
during childbirth, 156–57
during labor, 37–38
over-the-counter, 129–33
prescribed, 129–33
reactions with nutrients, 147–48
recreational, 137–39, 144

Earache, breast milk and, 7
Easy Fish Salad, 199
Easy Turkey Lunch, 199
Eczema, cow's milk and, 183
Eden, Dr. Alvin, 180–81
Egg and Tofu Salad, 203
Eggs
allergy to, 184
nutritional value of, 61, 76, 78
Egnell breast pump, 223
Eicosapentaenoic acid (EPA), 62
Emergency formulas, 190–93
Emotions. See also Stress
calcium absorption and, 68
effect on milk production, 6, 26
Engorgement
breast texture and, 24
relieving, 40–41, 52, 217
Environmental contaminants, 139–43,
145
Enzymes
in breast milk, 8
in expressed milk, 169
infant's development of, 181
EPA, 62